Math Expressions

Homework and Remembering
Blackline Masters

Developed by
The Children's Math Worlds Research Project

PROJECT DIRECTOR AND AUTHOR
Dr. Karen C. Fuson

D1278086

This material is based upon work supported by the
National Science Foundation
under Grant Numbers
ESI-9816320, REC-9806020, and RED-935373.

Any opinions, findings, and conclusions, or recommendations expressed in this material
are those of the author and do not necessarily reflect the views of the National Science Foundation.

HOUGHTON MIFFLIN HARCOURT

Teacher Reviewers

Kindergarten
Patricia Stroh Sugiyama
Wilmette, Illinois

Barbara Wahle
Evanston, Illinois

Grade 1
Sandra Budson
Newton, Massachusetts

Janet Pecci
Chicago, Illinois

Megan Rees
Chicago, Illinois

Grade 2
Molly Dunn
Danvers, Massachusetts

Agnes Lesnick
Hillside, Illinois

Rita Soto
Chicago, Illinois

Grade 3
Jane Curran
Honesdale, Pennsylvania

Sandra Tucker
Chicago, Illinois

Grade 4
Sara Stoneberg Llibre
Chicago, Illinois

Sheri Roedel
Chicago, Illinois

Grade 5
Todd Atler
Chicago, Illinois

Leah Barry
Norfolk, Massachusetts

Credits

Cover art: © Arco Images GmbH/Alamy
Illustrative art: Dave Klug
Technical art: Morgan-Cain & Associates

Printed in the U.S.A.

ISBN: 978-0-547-47952-1

1 2 3 4 5 6 7 8 9 10 1413 19 18 17 16 15 14 13 12 11 10

4500230077   X B C D E

Name _____   Date _____

Homework

Solve for the unknown number.

1. $3 \times 7 =$ _____

2. $32 / 4 =$ _____

3. $7 \times 5 =$ _____

4. $6 \times$ _____ $= 24$

5. $5 \times$ _____ $= 30$

6. $3 \times$ _____ $= 24$

7. $15 / 3 =$ _____

8. $20 / 5 =$ _____

9. $18 / 6 =$ _____

10. $9 \cdot 2 =$ _____

11. $3 \cdot 9 =$ _____

12. $4 \cdot 4 =$ _____

Write an equation for each word problem and then solve the problem.

Show your work.

13. There are 4 measuring cups in a set. Mr. Merton's science class has 7 sets of measuring cups. How many cups are there altogether? _____

14. A carousel has 40 horses. There are 4 horses in each row. How many rows are there on the carousel? _____

15. Morgan has 24 dollars. She wants to buy party hats that cost 3 dollars each. How many party hats can Morgan buy? _____

16. The Garcias have a grandfather clock that needs to be wound once a week. How many times will they need to wind it during the month of February, which has 28 days? _____

17. There are 8 cars in a repair shop. All 8 cars need 4 new tires. How many tires will be needed in all? _____

18. Write a multiplication or division word problem of your own. Then write an equation and solve the problem.

_____

_____

_____

Multiplication as Equal Groups **1**

Remembering

Complete.

1. $2 \times \underline{\hspace{1cm}} = 6$

2. $10 / 5 = \underline{\hspace{1cm}}$

3. $\underline{\hspace{1cm}} \times 3 = 12$

4. $\underline{\hspace{1cm}} \times 5 = 25$

5. $6 \cdot \underline{\hspace{1cm}} = 24$

6. $7 \times 2 = \underline{\hspace{1cm}}$

7. $16 / 8 = \underline{\hspace{1cm}}$

8. $\underline{\hspace{1cm}} \times 1 = 9$

9. $\underline{\hspace{1cm}} \cdot 4 = 20$

10. $3 \times \underline{\hspace{1cm}} = 18$

11. $\underline{\hspace{1cm}} \times 7 = 28$

12. $9 / 3 = \underline{\hspace{1cm}}$

13. $4 \times 10 = \underline{\hspace{1cm}}$

14. $2 \cdot \underline{\hspace{1cm}} = 4$

15. $\underline{\hspace{1cm}} \times 6 = 6$

Write an equation. Then solve the problem.

16. Tanya plans to read 2 books each month. If she achieves her goal, how many books will she read in one year?

_____

_____

17. To prepare for a math test, Elena studied for one and one-half hours. For how many minutes did Elena study?

_____

_____

18. Anthony wants to distribute 15 toys equally to each of his 5 friends. How many toys should each friend receive?

_____

_____

19. Kelvin's birthday is 14 days from today. How many weeks will it be until Kelvin celebrates his birthday?

_____

_____

20. A kennel is caring for 5 pets. Last week, the kennel cared for 3 times as many pets. How many pets did the kennel care for last week?

_____

_____

21. An egg carton has spaces for one dozen eggs. If there are 2 rows of 4 eggs in the carton, how many spaces in the carton are empty?

_____

_____

Multiplication as Equal Groups

Homework

Name the kind of situation shown, and write an equation.
Then solve each problem.

1. A large box of crayons holds
60 crayons. There are 10 crayons in
each row. How many rows are there?

Situation: _____

Equation: _____

_____

2. A poster is 4 feet long by 3 feet
wide. How many square feet of
wall space will it cover?

Situation: _____

Equation: _____

_____

3. A bingo card has 5 rows and
5 columns of squares. Jasmine and
her friend need every square covered
to win. How many squares must be
covered to win the game?

Situation: _____

Equation: _____

_____

4. There are 28 students in
Mrs. Fletcher's class. She has
divided them into 7 groups for a
science project. How many students
are there in each group?

Situation: _____

Equation: _____

_____

Find the unknown length (_l_), width (_w_), or area (_A_). Remember: $A = l \times w$.

5. $6 \times 3 = A$

$A =$ _____

6. $8 \times w = 32$

$w =$ _____

7. $A = 7 \cdot 5$

$A =$ _____

8. $45 / 5 = l$

$l =$ _____

9.
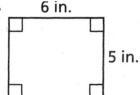

6 in.

5 in.

Area = _____ sq in.

10.
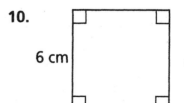

6 cm   Area = 36 sq cm

length = _____ cm

11. A rectangle has an area of 18 square meters. The length and
width are whole numbers. Write all the possible lengths and
widths for this rectangle.

_____

_____

Name _____   **Date** _____

Remembering

Complete.

1. 3 × 3 = _____

2. 10 × _____ = 20

3. _____ × 5 = 30

4. _____ × 7 = 21

5. 24 / 6 = _____

6. 1 × _____ = 11

7. 4 × 8 = _____

8. 9 × _____ = 36

9. _____ × 8 = 72

Find the unknown Length.

10. $7 \cdot w = 42$

    $w =$ _____

11. $A = 6 \cdot 8$

    $A =$ _____

12. $l \cdot 6 = 18$

    $l =$ _____

13. $9 \times 9 = A$

    $A =$ _____

14. $27 = 3 \cdot w$

    $w =$ _____

15. $l \times 4 = 24$

    $l =$ _____

16. $2 \times w = 14$

    $w =$ _____

17. $63 = l \cdot 9$

    $l =$ _____

18. $40 = 4 \cdot w$

    $w =$ _____

Write the missing measurement.

19.

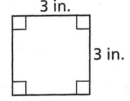

3 in.

3 in.

Area = _____ sq in.

20.

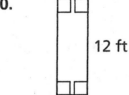

12 ft

Area = 24 sq ft

width = _____ ft

Write an equation. Then solve the problem.

21. On its keypad, a portable phone has 21 buttons, and there are 3 buttons in each row. How many rows of buttons are on the keypad?

    Equation _____

    _____

22. Twenty people at Jeff's school are going on a field trip. If 5 people can ride in each car, how many cars are needed for the field trip?

    Equation _____

    _____

Name _____ **Date** _____

Homework

Write the situation: equal groups, array, or area. Then write an equation and solve the problem.

1. In the Cozy Cafe there are 6 chairs at each table. Altogether, there are 42 chairs. How many tables are there at the Cozy Cafe?

Situation: _____

Equation: _____

_____

2. Hester measured the patio in her backyard. It is 10 feet long and 9 feet wide. How many square feet of ground does it cover?

Situation: _____

Equation: _____

_____

3. Miguel visited an apple orchard. He saw 8 rows and 6 columns of trees. How many apple trees are there in all?

Situation: _____

Equation: _____

_____

4. The movie theater in Cloverville has 72 seats arranged in 9 rows. How many seats are in each row?

Situation: _____

Equation: _____

_____

Find the unknown area (*A*), length (*l*), or width (*w*) in each equation.

5. $9 \times 7 = A$

$A =$ _____

6. $l = 81 \div 9$

$l =$ _____

7. $6 \cdot 7 = A$

$A =$ _____

8. $64 \div 8 = w$

$w =$ _____

9. $5 \times l = 35$

$l =$ _____

10. $27 / 9 = w$

$w =$ _____

11. $40 = 5 \times l$

$l =$ _____

12. $4 \times l = 36$

$l =$ _____

13. $56 \div w = 8$

$w =$ _____

14. $A = 8 \times 6$

$A =$ _____

15. $45 = l \times 5$

$l =$ _____

16. $25 \cdot w = 100$

$w =$ _____

Answer each question.

17. If $8 \times 12 = 96$, then what is 12×8? _____

18. If $144 \div 9 = 16$, then what is 16×9? _____

Remembering

Multiply or divide.

1. 8 • 9 = _____   2. 7 • 7 = _____   3. 4 • 2 = _____

4. 99 ÷ 9 = _____   5. 16 / 4 = _____   6. 56 ÷ 8 = _____

7. 9 × 9 = _____   8. 63 ÷ 7 = _____   9. 3 × 7 = _____

10. 20 / 4 = _____   11. 5 × 5 = _____   12. 13 × _____ = 13

13. 9 • 5 = _____   14. 27 ÷ 9 = _____   15. 10 • 10 = _____

16. 8 / 8 = _____   17. $\frac{18}{9}$ = _____   18. $\frac{80}{8}$ = _____

Write each quotient.

19. $2\overline{)20}$ 20. $6\overline{)30}$ 21. $7\overline{)63}$ 22. $8\overline{)24}$ 23. $5\overline{)0}$

24. $5\overline{)15}$ 25. $4\overline{)24}$ 26. $9\overline{)36}$ 27. $3\overline{)9}$ 28. $4\overline{)28}$

Solve.

29. Aimee invited 5 friends to her birthday party. If Aimee and her friends will sit in equal numbers at 2 tables, how many people will be seated at each table?

_____

30. A quilt is made of 8 rows of squares, and there are 6 squares in each row. Each square measures 1 foot on a side. Explain how to find the area of the quilt in square feet. Then write the area.

_____

_____

_____

_____

Explore the Multiplication Table

Homework

Complete.

1. $9 \times$ _____ $= 36$

2. $81 \div 9 =$ _____

3. $1 \cdot$ _____ $= 26$

4. _____ $\times 5 = 25$

5. $32 \div 4 =$ _____

6. $0 \times 9 =$ _____

7. $0 \div 16 =$ _____

8. $14 \cdot$ _____ $= 0$

9. _____ $\times 10 = 10$

10. $49 \div 7 =$ _____

11. $4 \cdot$ _____ $= 28$

12. $40 \div 8 =$ _____

For each problem, tell what kind of situation is described. Then write an equation and solve.

13. A marching band volunteers to paint a mural. The mural covers an area of 15 square feet. If the mural is 5 feet wide, what is its length?

    Situation: _____

    Equation: _____

    _____

14. The marching-band director orders 10 packages of music books. Each package has 8 music books. How many music books will she receive?

    Situation: _____

    Equation: _____

    _____

15. Each drummer has 4 drumsticks, making a total of 36 drumsticks. How many drummers are in the band?

    Situation: _____

    Equation: _____

    _____

16. The band has 48 people. There are 6 people in each row. How many rows are there in the marching band?

    Situation: _____

    Equation: _____

    _____

Which of these answers cannot be right? How do you know?

17. $32 \times 14 = 448$ $\qquad$ $53 \times 17 = 906$ $\qquad$ $46 \times 18 = 828$

_____

_____

_____

_____

Remembering

Solve for the unknown.

1. $72 \div \underline{\hspace{1cm}} = 8$

2. $\frac{32}{8} = \underline{\hspace{1cm}}$

3. $\underline{\hspace{1cm}} \div 8 = 6$

4. $5 \times \underline{\hspace{1cm}} = 30$

5. $7 = \underline{\hspace{1cm}} \div 6$

6. $\underline{\hspace{1cm}} = 8 \times 8$

7. $\underline{\hspace{1cm}} = 35 \div 5$

8. $7 \times \underline{\hspace{1cm}} = 56$

9. $\underline{\hspace{1cm}} \times 10 = 100$

10. $\underline{\hspace{1cm}} = 24 \div 6$

11. $3 \times \underline{\hspace{1cm}} = 0$

12. $20 \div \underline{\hspace{1cm}} = 5$

13. $27 = 9 \times \underline{\hspace{1cm}}$

14. $\underline{\hspace{1cm}} = 2 \times 8$

15. $6 = \underline{\hspace{1cm}} \div 2$

16. $\underline{\hspace{1cm}} \times 4 = 40$

17. $3 = 6 \div \underline{\hspace{1cm}}$

18. $\underline{\hspace{1cm}} \times 8 = 0$

19. $9 \times \underline{\hspace{1cm}} = 45$

20. $\underline{\hspace{1cm}} = 36 \div 6$

21. $54 = \underline{\hspace{1cm}} \times 6$

22. $15 - 6 = \underline{\hspace{1cm}}$

23. $12 - 12 = 1 \times \underline{\hspace{1cm}}$

24. $7 \times \underline{\hspace{1cm}} = 8 + 6$

Solve.

25. The attendance for 2 performances of a school play was 361 people in total. If 193 people attended the first performance, how many attended the second?

_____

26. The school purchased 63 new computers. An equal number of these new computers were given to 9 classes. How many new computers did each class receive?

_____

27. A classroom contains 4 rows of desks. There are 7 desks in each row. How many desks does the classroom contain?

_____

28. A bulletin board has a length of 7 feet. The width is 3 feet. What is the area of the wall covered by the bulletin board?

_____

29. During the first lunch period of the day, 48 students sit in equal groups at each of 8 cafeteria tables. What number of students sit at each table?

_____

30. The students sit in 5 rows in the auditorium. If 40 students are equally seated in the rows, how many students sit in each row?

_____

Solve each word problem. Label your answer.

1. Maria created artwork by placing all of her seashells in 4 rows on a wall. In each row, she arranged 8 seashells. How many seashells did Maria collect in all?

   _____

2. Arturo collected 18 seashells. He wants to divide the seashells evenly among his 3 best friends. How many seashells will each friend receive?

   _____

Use the pictograph and key to solve.

Katie planted pumpkins in the spring. Now she is selling them This pictograph shows how many pumpkins she sold this weekend.

Friday	🎃 🎃 🎃 🎃
Saturday	🎃 🎃 🎃 🎃 🎃 🎃 🎃
Sunday	🎃 🎃 🎃

Key: 🎃 = 6 pumpkins

3. How many pumpkins did Katie sell this weekend?

   _____

4. How many more pumpkins did she sell on Saturday than on Friday?

   _____

5. On Sunday Katie sold the pumpkins for $3.00 each or 2 for $5.00. What is the least amount of money she could have taken in?

   _____

6. On Friday Katie sold half the pumpkins for $3.00 each and the rest at 2 for $5.00. How much money did she take in on Friday?

   _____

Remembering

Dear Math Student,

I am giving a party tomorrow, and I invited 10 people to come. I bought 10 party bags and planned to put 8 marbles in each bag. Now I hear that my two cousins will be in town, so there will be 12 people altogether.

How many marbles will I need to buy? I don't know how to multiply 12 × 8. It is not part of my multiplication table.

Please send me a letter explaining how to figure this out. Thank you.

Sincerely,

Puzzled Penguin

_____

_____

_____

_____

_____

_____

_____

_____

_____

Will the following products be even or odd? How do you know?

1. 57 × 57 _____ **2.** 82 × 96 _____

3. 91 × 23 _____ **4.** 76 × 75 _____

5. 27 × 81 _____ **6.** 92 × 20 _____

7. 45 × 55 _____ **8.** 31 × 31 _____

9. 73 × 84 _____ **10.** 52 × 32 _____

Homework

Complete.

1. $6 \times 3 =$ _____

2. $7 \times 9 =$ _____

3. $4 \times 0 =$ _____

4. $30 \div 5$ _____

5. $18 \div 2 =$ _____

6. $70 \div 7 =$ _____

7. $36 \div$ _____ $= 9$

8. $3 \times$ _____ $= 24$

9. _____ $\div 8 = 0$

10. _____ $\times 7 = 35$

11. $60 =$ _____ $\times 6$

12. $4 = 28 \div$ _____

13. $72 = 8 \times$ _____

14. $2 =$ _____ $\div 10$

15. _____ $= 45 \div 9$

16. $21 =$ _____ $\times 7$

17. $8 = 64 \div$ _____

18. _____ $\times 374 = 0$

Solve.

19. Using only whole numbers, Nikki wrote as many multiplication equations as she could with 12 as the product. What were her equations?

_____

_____

20. Pablo wrote four division equations with 6 as the quotient. What could have been the four division equations that he wrote?

_____

_____

For each problem, tell what kind of situation is described. Then write an equation and solve.

21. Each student gathered 10 leaves for the group art project. The group collected a total of 80 leaves. How many students are in the group?

Situation: _____

Equation: _____

_____

22. The display had storage boxes in stacked rows. Each row had 7 boxes. If a total of 42 boxes were used, how many rows were in the display?

Situation: _____

Equation: _____

_____

Remembering

Complete.

1. $5 \times$ _____ $= 0$

2. $1 \times$ _____ $= 28$

3. $6 \times$ _____ $= 36$

4. $63 \div 9 =$ _____

5. _____ $\times 7 = 56$

6. $8 \times$ _____ $= 24$

7. $50 \div$ _____ $= 10$

8. $6 \times$ _____ $= 12$

9. $\frac{54}{9} =$ _____

10. $24 \div$ _____ $= 6$

11. _____ $\div 8 = 9$

12. _____ $\times 4 = 16$

13. $5 \times$ _____ $= 40$

14. $35 \div 7 =$ _____

15. _____ $\div 6 = 8$

16. $9 \times 7 =$ _____

17. _____ $\div 11 = 1$

18. _____ $= 64 \div 8$

22. _____ $\div 15 = 0$

23. $16 \times$ _____ $= 0$

24. $12 \times$ _____ $= 24$

Complete.

25. If $10 \times 25 = 250$, then what is $250 \div 10$? _____

26. If $144 \div 24 = 6$, then what is 6×24? _____

27. If $15 \times 15 = 225$, then what is $225 \div 15$? _____

28. If $156 \div 13 = 12$, then what is $156 \div 12$? _____

29. If $288 \div 18 = 16$, then what is 18×16? _____

30. If $9 \times 45 = 405$, then what is $405 \div 45$? _____

Solve.

31. Tom found that the product of 14×3 is 12. Is this product correct? If not, explain how to find the correct product.

_____

_____

32. Katrina has 20 photographs to arrange in an array in the school's yearbook. How many different ways can she arrange the photographs? Explain how you found your answers.

_____

_____

_____

Homework

Write the situation: equal groups, array, area, or combination.
Then write an equation and solve the problem.

1. A chessboard has 8 rows of squares. There are 64 squares total. How many columns are on a chessboard?

   Situation: _____

   Equation: _____

   _____

2. A sandbox is 9 feet long and 6 feet wide. How many square feet of ground does the sandbox cover?

   Situation: _____

   Equation: _____

   _____

3. The Ferris wheel in Paradise Park has 10 seats. Each seat can hold 3 people. How many people can ride the Ferris wheel at the same time?

   Situation: _____

   Equation: _____

   _____

4. Dan makes invitations out of red, white, and blue paper. Each has a star or a flag pattern. How many kinds of invitations can he make?

   Situation: _____

   Equation: _____

   _____

5. Mr. Caruso is a builder who always builds the same kind of house. Only the materials are different. How many different houses can Mr. Caruso build?

   Situation: _____

   Equation: _____

   _____

Red Brick	Tile Roof
Brown Brick	Slate Roof
Yellow Brick	Cedar Roof

Find the unknown number in each equation.

6. $a = 6 \times 7$

   $a = $ _____

7. $b = 81 \div 9$

   $b = $ _____

8. $5 \cdot 8 = c$

   $c = $ _____

9. $7e = 21$

   $e = $ _____

10. $10f = 50$

    $f = $ _____

11. $42 \div 6 = g$

    $g = $ _____

12. $72 = 9k$

    $k = $ _____

13. $54 = 9p$

    $p = $ _____

Practice multiplications and divisions with your Target.

Remembering

Complete.

1. $11 \times$ _____ $= 88$

2. _____ $\div 12 = 1$

3. $6 \times 8 =$ _____

4. _____ $\div 2 = 5$

5. $5 \times$ _____ $= 45$

6. _____ $\div 6 = 9$

7. $2 \times 3 =$ _____

8. _____ $\times 5 = 35$

9. $4 \times$ _____ $= 16$

10. _____ $\div 7 = 7$

11. $20 \div 4 =$ _____

12. $35 \div 7 =$ _____

13. $2 \times$ _____ $= 16$

14. _____ $\div 3 = 9$

15. _____ $\times 4 = 36$

16. _____ $\times 6 = 36$

17. $4 \times$ _____ $= 0$

18. $63 \div 7 =$ _____

Write each quotient.

19. $8\overline{)32}$

20. $7\overline{)14}$

21. $3\overline{)30}$

22. $5\overline{)25}$

23. $9\overline{)81}$

Solve for the unknown.

24. $18 \div l = 6$

$l =$ _____

25. $8w = 72$

$w =$ _____

26. $1 \cdot 10 = A$

$A =$ _____

27. $\frac{12}{w} = 6$

$w =$ _____

28. $9 * 3 = A$

$A =$ _____

29. $\frac{l}{7} = 3$

$l =$ _____

Write an equation and use it to solve the problem.

30. A café lunch menu offers a choice of a sandwich or salad, and four types of soup. Find the number of different combinations of a sandwich or salad, and a soup. Explain your answer.

_____

_____

_____

_____

_____

Make Combinations

Homework

The graph below shows the number of planes arriving in River City today.

Number of Planes Arriving in River City

Time	Number of Planes
Morning	✈ ✈ ✈ ✈ ✈ ✈ ✈ ✈ ✈ ✈
Afternoon	✈ ✈

Key: ✈ = 1 Plane

1. There were _____ times as many planes in the morning as in the afternoon.

2. There were _____ as many planes in the afternoon as in the morning.

Tell what situation is shown, write an equation, and solve the problem.

3. Amanda has 63 bracelets. She decides to divide the bracelets equally among 7 friends. How many bracelets does she give each friend?

   Situation: _____

   Equation: _____

   _____

4. Mr. Gordon is planting a garden. He plans to make his garden 12 feet by 3 feet. How many square feet will his garden be?

   Situation: _____

   Equation: _____

   _____

Find the unknown number in each equation.

5. $8a = 56$

   $a =$ _____

6. $b = 63 \div 9$

   $b =$ _____

7. $5 \cdot 6 = c$

   $c =$ _____

8. $6d = 54$

   $d =$ _____

9. $49 \div 7 = e$

   $e =$ _____

10. $7f = 63$

    $f =$ _____

11. $5g = 45$

    $g =$ _____

12. $64 = 8h$

    $h =$ _____

13. $36 / 6 = j$

    $j =$ _____

Use your Target to practice multiplications and divisions.

Remembering

Solve for the unknown.

1. $7 = 56 \div k$

   $k =$ _____

2. $4 = 28 / y$

   $y =$ _____

3. $10 \times c = 50$

   $c =$ _____

4. $24 = 3r$

   $r =$ _____

5. $6q = 54$

   $q =$ _____

6. $m / 8 = 6$

   $m =$ _____

7. $5 = s \div 9$

   $s =$ _____

8. $6 \times 6 = b$

   $b =$ _____

9. $40 \div g = 5$

   $g =$ _____

Write an equation and use it to solve the problem.

10. This summer, it has rained only $\frac{1}{4}$ as much as last summer. Last summer, 12 inches of rain fell. What amount of rain has fallen this summer?

    Equation: _____

    _____

11. Clarice is $\frac{1}{5}$ as old as her mother, and twice as old as her brother Jason. Clarice's mother is 30 years old. How old is Jason?

    Equation: _____

    _____

The graph below shows the number of books that a student in Mrs. Jacobsen's class read during April and May.

April	📖 📖 📖 📖
May	📖 📖 📖 📖 📖 📖 📖 📖

Key: 📖 = 2

Complete each statement.

12. There were _____ times as many books read during May as during April.

13. There were _____ as many books read during April as during May.

Understand Comparisons

Homework

Solve for the unknown.

1. $5 \cdot 6 = a$

$a =$ _____

2. $b = 64 \div 8$

$b =$ _____

3. $c = 7 \times 8$

$c =$ _____

4. $40 \div 5 = d$

$d =$ _____

5. $7e = 49$

$e =$ _____

6. $50 \cdot f = 100$

$f =$ _____

7. $54 \div 9 = g$

$g =$ _____

8. $4h = 28$

$h =$ _____

9. $45 = 5k$

$k =$ _____

10. $6l = 36$

$l =$ _____

11. $9n = 0$

$n =$ _____

12. $72 = 8p$

$p =$ _____

Identify the kind of situation and write an equation. Then solve the problem.

13. Isabel earned 42 dollars mowing lawns last month. Her sister earned only $\frac{1}{6}$ as much. How much money did Isabel's sister earn?

Situation: _____

Equation: _____

_____

14. Daniel packed black, tan, and blue shorts in his suitcase. He also packed 6 different T-shirts. How many different outfits will Daniel have?

Situation: _____

Equation: _____

_____

15. A large muffin tray holds 5 muffins across and 7 muffins down. How many muffins can the tray hold?

Situation: _____

Equation: _____

_____

16. The Richardson family has a tent that covers 54 square feet of ground. It is 9 feet long. How wide is the tent?

Situation: _____

Equation: _____

_____

17. Farmer O'Malley bought new horseshoes for all of his horses today. He bought 36 horseshoes. How many horses does Farmer O'Malley have?

Situation: _____

Equation: _____

_____

18. Mrs. Pinckett planted 8 rose bushes in her garden. She planted 3 times as many azalea bushes. How many azalea bushes did she plant?

Situation: _____

Equation: _____

_____

Practice multiplications and divisions with your Target.

Name _____ Date _____

Remembering

Solve for the unknown.

1. $x = 42 \div 7$

   $x =$ _____

2. $10 \times y = 50$

   $y =$ _____

3. $5c = 45$

   $c =$ _____

4. $t \times 2 = 0$

   $t =$ _____

5. $n \div 8 = 9$

   $n =$ _____

6. $7 \times 8 = q$

   $q =$ _____

7. $\frac{r}{9} = 7$

   $r =$ _____

8. $\frac{48}{6} = w$

   $w =$ _____

9. $\frac{36}{f} = 4$

   $f =$ _____

10. $4h = 31 - 3$

    $h =$ _____

11. $k = 27 \div 3$

    $k =$ _____

12. $16 - 9 = z$

    $z =$ _____

13. $s \div 6 = 8$

    $s =$ _____

14. $45 \div b = 5$

    $b =$ _____

15. $e = 32 \div 8$

    $e =$ _____

Write an equation. Then use the equation to solve the problem.

16. When deciding what to wear, a student must choose from 2 pairs of jeans and 5 T-shirts. How many different combinations of one pair of jeans and one T-shirt can be made?

    _____

17. One section of a theater contains 6 rows of seats. Each row has the same number of seats. Altogether, 54 people can sit in the seats. How many seats are in each row in that section of the theater?

    _____

18. The number of basketball coaches in a league is $\frac{1}{7}$ the number of players. How many coaches are at the school if 63 players are in the league?

    _____

19. At a figure skating performance, $\frac{1}{3}$ of the skaters completed a triple jump. If 18 skaters performed, how many skaters did not complete a triple jump?

    _____

Practice with Multiplication Problems

Homework

Name _____ **Date** _____

1. Write the next two numbers in this sequence:

   9 18 27 36 45 _____ _____

2. If you multiply 67 × 67, will your answer be even or odd?
   _____ How do you know? _____

3. If 35 × 25 is 875, then what is 875 ÷ 25? _____

4. What is n in this equation: 18 × 3 = 9 × n?_____

5. What is n in this equation: 7 × 6 = 5 × 6 + n × 6?_____

6. If one person counts by 3 to 60 and another person counts
   by 6 to 60, will any of those numbers be the same? Explain.

   _____

   _____

   _____

7. Complete the Scrambled Multiplication Table.

×										
20					70					
14			63	21	49		28		35	
		80				64		48		
			81	27				54		
8				12	28				20	
	1		9							
				9			12	18		
		60		18	42			36		
	5		45			40				
		20	18				8		10	

Solve.

8. At the dog show there are 56 retrievers.
   There are only $\frac{1}{8}$ as many collies. How
   many collies are at the show?

   _____

9. A small track has 9 rows of bleachers.
   Each row holds 8 people. How many
   people can sit in the bleachers?

   _____

Name _____ Date _____

Remembering

Complete the Scrambled Multiplication Table.

1.

×										
	12					36				
			56							64
		36					30			
	6			20				4		
		30				45				
			21	30			15			
	27				36					72
		10			40			20		
				10				2		
	21	7								

Write an equation and solve the problem.

2. Zachary's birthday is 9 weeks from today. In how many days will Zachary be celebrating his birthday?

_____

3. A school bus can carry 40 passengers seated in rows of 4. How many rows of seats are in the bus?

_____

4. A board game is shaped like a square array and is made up of 36 squares. How many rows and how many columns are in the array?

_____

5. In a middle school fifth-grade class, there are 5 girls for every 4 boys. Altogether, the class has 27 students. How many boys are in the class?

_____

6. On a separate sheet of paper, write an equal-groups problem and an area problem. Make one be a division problem.

Write Word Problems

Name _____   **Date** _____

Homework

For each table, write the rule and complete the table. Then write an equation.

1.

Rule:	
Input	**Output**
0	
4	2
8	
12	6
16	

Equation: _____

2.

Rule:	
Input	**Output**
6	1
9	
11	
14	9
8	

Equation: _____

For each table, write a rule using words and an equation with two variables. Then complete the table.

3.

Rule in Words					
Equation					
Hours (h)	1		3		5
Distance in miles (d)	4	8		16	20

4.

Rule in Words					
Equation					
Number of insects (i)		2	3	4	5
Number of legs (l)	6	12	18		

5.

Rule in Words							
Equation							
Number of trees (t)	1	2	3	5	8	9	10
Number of shrubs (s)	4	8	12	20	32	36	

6.

Rule in Words						
Equation						
Sue's age (s)	5	10	14	17		27
Ted's age (t)	3	8			17	25

Name _____ **Date** _____

Remembering

Solve for the unknown.

1. $q = \frac{56}{8}$

$q =$ _____

2. $5 = \frac{20}{r}$

$r =$ _____

3. $\frac{v}{9} = 8$

$v =$ _____

4. $6c = 36$

$c =$ _____

5. $9s = 63$

$s =$ _____

6. $45 = a \times 5$

$a =$ _____

7. $2g = 8$

$g =$ _____

8. $n = 49 \div 7$

$n =$ _____

9. $9 \times 8 = u$

$u =$ _____

Solve.

10. $8 \times 0 =$ _____

11. $1 \times 12 =$ _____

12. $9 \times 1 =$ _____

13. $0 \div 6 =$ _____

14. $1 \times 19 =$ _____

15. $0 \div 45 =$ _____

16. $64 \times 1 =$ _____

17. $0 \times 82 =$ _____

18. $0 \div 27 =$ _____

Identify the type of situation and write an equation. Then solve the problem.

19. Each row of a display contains 4 vases. The display contains 24 vases altogether. How many rows of vases are in the display?

Situation: _____

Equation: _____

_____

20. Marco has 8 red T-shirts and $\frac{1}{4}$ as many blue T-shirts as red T-shirts. How many blue T-shirts does Marco have?

Situation: _____

Equation: _____

_____

Solve.

21. This winter, 36 inches of snow fell. Last winter, only $\frac{1}{3}$ as much snow fell. How many more inches of snow fell this winter compared to last winter?

_____

22. In a class of 18 students at Woodworth School, there are $\frac{1}{2}$ as many girls as boys. How many girls are in the class? How many boys?

_____

Functions

Homework

Find the unknown number in each equation.

1. $p = 3 + (4 \times 5)$ _____

2. $4t + 1 = 25$ _____

3. $5 \times (6 + 3) = m$ _____

4. $6r - 3 = 15$ _____

5. $(12 - 8) \times 7 = b$ _____

6. $n = 16 - (3 \times 4)$ _____

7. $9s = 17 + 1$ _____

8. $5 + (8 \times 6) = c$ _____

9. $7d + 5 = 26$ _____

10. $(6 \times 5) - (4 \times 5) = h$ _____

Write an equation. Then solve the problem.   *Show your work.*

1. Mr. Corelli made a tray of cookies that held 5 across and
   7 down. There are 38 students in Mr. Corelli's class. How
   many more cookies does he need if each student is to
   get one cookie?

   Equation: _____

   _____

2. Leah bought 2 boxes of cookies. She ate 3 cookies and
   found that she had 21 left. How many cookies were in
   each box?

   Equation: _____

   _____

3. Arturo built 3 sandcastles with 6 towers each. Paco built
   5 sandcastles with 4 towers each. Who built more
   towers? How many more?

   Equation: _____

   _____

4. Ashley has 35 dollars. She wants to buy 4 bags of
   peanuts at 2 dollars each. How much money will she
   have left?

   Equation: _____

   _____

Name _____   Date _____

Remembering

Write an equation. Then solve the problem.   *Show your work.*

1. The Parkers' lawn is 10 yards long by 9 yards wide. They want to build a patio that is 4 yards by 5 yards. How many square yards of lawn will the Parkers have left when the patio is done?

   Equation: _____

   _____

2. Sarah sleeps 10 hours each night. Julio sleeps only 8 hours each night. How much more sleep does Sarah get in a week than Julio?

   Equation: _____

   _____

Complete the Scrambled Multiplication Table below.

×										
	49	7	70	14	28		56	21	35	
	70	10		20	40	60	80		50	90
		1	10	2	4	6	8	3		9
		6	60		24	36	48	18	30	54
	14	2	20	4		12	16	6	10	18
	56		80	16	32	48		24	40	72
	21	3	30		12	18	24	9		27
	28		40	8	16	24	32		20	36
	63	9		18		54		27	45	81
		5	50	10	20	30	40	15	25	

Equations with Parentheses

Homework

Name _____ **Date** _____

Solve each problem. *Show your work.*

1. Michael has 21 T-shirts. One third of them are blue. How many of Michael's T-shirts are blue?

    _____

2. A gift-wrapping department has 4 colors of ribbon, 2 kinds of bows, and 7 kinds of wrapping paper. How many different gift-wrap styles are possible?

    _____

3. Anne-Marie has saved 9 dollars for a new coat. That is $\frac{1}{6}$ as much money as she needs. How much does the coat cost?

    _____

4. Last year it rained on 63 days in Mudville. There were 7 times as many days of rain in Mudville as in Desert Hills. How many days did it rain in Desert Hills last year?

    _____

5. Mrs. Ricardo makes toy cars to sell at craft fairs. She has 8 colors of paint, 5 body styles, and 2 kinds of wheels. How many different kinds of cars can she make?

    _____

6. At a country-music concert, 48 people played guitars. That number is 6 times as many as the number of people who played banjos. How many people at the concert played banjos?

    _____

7. There are 8 apples left on the table. There are $\frac{1}{4}$ as many apples as bananas left on the table. How many bananas are there?

    _____

Remembering

Use the pictograph and key to solve.

Bob, Reza, and Yoshi run laps around the track every day after school. This pictograph shows how many laps they ran last week.

Bob	👟 👟 👟 👟 👟 👟
Reza	👟 👟 👟 👟 👟 👟 👟 👟
Yoshi	👟 👟 👟 👟 👟

Key: 👟 = 8 laps

1. How many laps did Reza run last week? _____

2. How many more laps did Bob run than Yoshi? _____

3. How many more or fewer laps did Bob and Yoshi together run than Reza?

   _____

4. Yoshi ran the same number of laps every day except Friday, when he ran 12 laps. How many laps did he run on Wednesday?

   _____

Complete the Scrambled Multiplication Table.

5.

×									
	18				21				
		30					90		
				20		2			
					56			28	
			20			4			
		16			64		72		
			30		42				
		3					4		
		18			63				
	30			50					

Combinations and Comparisons

Homework

Solve each problem. Label your answer.

1. Rachel has 4 times as many markers as Polly has. Rachel has 36 markers. How many markers does Polly have?

   _____

2. Sean sold 63 balloons at the fair. That is 7 times as many as Oscar sold. How many balloons did Oscar sell?

   _____

3. Ramon scored 72 points in basketball games this year. His friend Paco scored $\frac{1}{8}$ as many points as Ramon. How many points did Paco score?

   _____

4. Chris has 6 different cookie cutters, 4 kinds of frosting, and 2 kinds of sprinkles. How many different kinds of cookies can she make?

   _____

5. Meg and Kurt are building a tree house. They have 3 kinds of roofing material, 4 colors of paint, and 2 doors to choose from. How many different ways could they build the tree house?

   _____

6. Mrs. Grant's garden is a square that is 5 yards on each side. Mrs. Diego's garden is a square that is 10 yards on each side. The area of Mrs. Diego's garden is how many times as large as the area of Mrs. Grant's garden?

   _____

Solve each Factor Puzzle.

7.

8.
	27
35	45

9.
	7
25	35

10.
27	24
	40

11.
6	9
8	

12.
15	
9	6

13.
12	
24	32

14.
25	50
	30

15. On a separate sheet of paper, write a Factor Puzzle for your classmates to solve. You may use a Multiplication Table.

Remembering

Complete.

1. Write the next two numbers: 9, 18, 27, _____, _____

2. If you multiply 51×51, will your answer be even or odd?
_____ How do you know? _____

3. If $52 \times 38 = 1,976$, then what is $1,976 \div 38$? _____

4. What is b in this equation: $15 \times 7 = 21 \times b$? _____

5. What is b in this equation: $5 \times 6 = 5 \times 4 + 5 \times b$? _____

6. If one person counts by 4s to 80 and another person counts
by 8s to 80, will any of those numbers be the same? Explain
which ones.

_____

_____

_____

7. Which two of these answers cannot be right? How do you know?

a. $18 \times 17 = 305$ **b.** $21 \times 21 = 441$ **c.** $32 \times 48 = 1,535$

_____

_____

_____

_____

_____

Find the unknown number in each equation.

8. $8a = 48$

$a =$ _____

9. $5b + 1 = 46$

$b =$ _____

10. $3 \times (6 + 2) = d$

$d =$ _____

11. $7e - 2 = 47$

$e =$ _____

12. $\frac{1}{3}g = 8$

$g =$ _____

13. $16 + h = 24$

$h =$ _____

Practice with Factors

Homework

Name _____ **Date** _____

Solve.

Show your work.

1. A fruit company makes two gift boxes of oranges—the Ruby Box and the Emerald Box. The Ruby Box has 8 rows and 6 columns of oranges. The Emerald Box has 7 rows and 7 columns of oranges. Which box has more oranges? How many more?

   _____

2. On his camping trip, Gus saw 18 hawks. He saw 6 times as many hawks as owls. How many owls did Gus see?

   _____

3. Melissa collected three kinds of autumn leaves when she was out walking today—elm, maple, and oak. She has 2 times as many maple leaves as elm leaves and 5 times as many oak leaves as elm leaves. Altogether, she has 32 leaves. How many of each kind does she have?

   _____

4. Everyone at Luke's party has 2 balloons except Ashley, because one of her balloons popped. There are 17 balloons at the party. How many people are at the party?

   _____

5. Patty bought 5 harmonicas for 3 dollars each and 4 whistles for 3 dollars each. How much money did Patty spend?

   _____

Find the unknown number in each equation. Write a 1 in front of an unknown that is alone if it will help you.

6. $c + 3c = 32$ _____

7. $6d - 3d + 2d = 35$ _____

8. $5a - a - 2a = 18$ _____

Remembering

Find the unknown number in each equation below.

1. $6h + 3h = 63$

    $h =$ _____

2. $5(4 \times 2) = g$

    $g =$ _____

3. $l = (2 \times 8) - (3 \times 2)$

    $l =$ _____

4. $m + 3m = 28$

    $m =$ _____

5. $56 \div r = 8$

    $r =$ _____

6. $\frac{1}{8}b = 6$

    $b =$ _____

7. $s = 9(7 - 2)$

    $s =$ _____

8. $4d + d = 45$

    $d =$ _____

9. $8w - 4w = 20$

    $w =$ _____

Write *odd* or *even*.

10. The product of two even numbers is an _____ number.

11. The product of an odd number and an even number is an _____ number.

12. The product of two odd numbers is an _____ number.

Write an equation and use it to solve the problem.

13. A rectangle has an area of 48 sq cm and a length of 16 cm. What is the width of the rectangle?

    _____

14. A rectangle has a width of 10 inches and an area of 5 square inches. What is the length of the rectangle?

    _____

Solve. Explain your answer.

15. A stamp collector is arranging 100 stamps in rows with the same number of stamps in each row. How many different ways could she arrange the stamps if she would like more than 2 rows but fewer than 10 rows?

    _____

    _____

    _____

    _____

Homework

Use the Commutative Property to solve for *n* in these equations.

1. $45 \times 7 = 7 \times n$

$n =$ _____

2. $n \times 8 = 8 \times 29$

$n =$ _____

3. $36 \times n = 9 \times 36$

$n =$ _____

Use the Associative Property to solve each problem.

4. $(9 \times 3) \times 3 =$ _____

5. $2 \times (5 \times 7) =$ _____

6. $(8 \times 4) \times 2 =$ _____

Use the Distributive Property to write each problem with only two factors. Then solve the problems.

7. $(7 \times 3) + (7 \times 5) =$ _____

8. $(3 \times 9) + (4 \times 9) =$ _____

9. $(8 \times 5) + (8 \times 4) =$ _____

10. $(2 \times 6) + (8 \times 6) =$ _____

Solve.

11. For Fall Festival, Mrs. Marco bought 6 bags of Golden Delicious apples. She handed out 43 apples and had 5 left over. How many apples were in each bag?

_____

12. Juice boxes are sold in packs of 6. Tony brought 5 packs of juice boxes to a party, and Victor brought 4 packs. How many juice boxes are there at the party altogether?

_____

13. Everyone in Mrs. Bowman's art class has 8 jars of paint except Jerome, who has 10. There are 74 jars of paint in the room. How many students are there in Mrs. Bowman's art class?

_____

_____

14. Lisa needs to make 2 times as many tuna as cheese sandwiches and 4 times as many ham as cheese sandwiches. If Lisa makes 56 sandwiches, how many of each of the 3 kinds will she make?

_____

_____

Name _____ **Date** _____

Remembering

Find the unknown number in each equation.

1. $4h + 5h = 63$

    $h =$ _____

2. $4(2 \times 5) = g$

    $g =$ _____

3. $4 \times (5 + 1) = i$

    $i =$ _____

4. $l = (2 \times 6) - (4 \times 2)$

    $l =$ _____

5. $m + 4m = 25$

    $m =$ _____

6. $(48 \div 8) - 3 = p$

    $p =$ _____

7. $72 \div r = 8$

    $r =$ _____

8. $\frac{1}{8}b = 5$

    $b =$ _____

9. $k = (3 \times 9) - (5 \times 0)$

    $k =$ _____

10. $s = 8(9 - 2)$

    $s =$ _____

11. $6d + d = 42$

    $d =$ _____

12. $r = 17 + (6 \times 5)$

    $r =$ _____

Complete each Factor Puzzle.

13.

	6
8	16

14.

4	
5	15

For each function table, write the rule in words and as an equation.
Then complete the table.

15.

Rule in Words							
Equation							
Number of people (*p*)	1	2		4		6	7
Number of feet (*f*)	2		6	8	10	12	

16.

Rule in Words							
Equation							
Number of eyes (*e*)	0		3	5	6		10
Number of legs (*l*)		6	9	15		24	30

Properties of Multiplication

Homework

1. Connections

Jill has four of her five game scores:

8, 6, 6, 3

Her average score for the five games is 6 points. What is the fifth game score? Write an equation to help solve the problem.

_____

_____

_____

2. Representation

Tyler is looking at a map. He wants to stop at three towns on Highway 57. Town A is 15 miles from Town B. Town A is 26 miles from Town C. Town B is between Towns A and C. How many miles are between Towns B and C? Draw a picture to support your answer.

_____

3. Communication

The students are selling tickets to the School Fair. All tickets cost the same amount. Carly sold 3 tickets for a total of $9. Karen sold 6 tickets for a total of $18. Brendan sold 4 tickets for a total of $12. Use a function table to find the price per ticket and the total cost of 9 tickets. Show the rule and the equation you used to find the costs.

_____

_____

_____

4. Reasoning and Proof

Lilly wrote the equation below to demonstrate the Commutative Property.

$(2 + 3) + (3 + 4) = (3 + 4) + (2 + 3)$

Does her equation demonstrate the Commutative Property? Explain why or why not.

_____

_____

_____

Name _____ Date _____

Remembering

Find the unknown number in each equation.

1. $25 - (3 + 6) + (2 \times 4) = c$

$c =$ _____

2. $5a - 3a = 18$

$a =$ _____

3. $g = 7(10 - 3)$

$g =$ _____

4. $63 \div (26 - 19) = w$

$w =$ _____

5. $6 + y = 17$

$y =$ _____

6. $4 = \frac{1}{2}v$

$v =$ _____

7. $27 = 8k + k$

$k =$ _____

8. $9(4 + 5) = e$

$e =$ _____

9. $5q = 35$

$q =$ _____

10. $m = 11 + (3 \times 8) - (4 \times 6)$

$m =$ _____

11. $12r - 4r = 48$

$r =$ _____

12. $\frac{1}{6} h = 9$

$h =$ _____

Solve. Show your work.

13. You know that $8 \times 9 = 72$. How can you use this to find the product of 8×8? _____

14. On Monday, Hugo read 4 pages. On Tuesday, he read three times as many pages as on Monday. On Wednesday, he read twice as many pages as on Monday. How many pages did Hugo read in all during the three days?

_____

15. Carmen bought 3 boxes of pencils. Each box has the same number of pencils. She used 5 pencils and had 7 pencils left over. How many pencils were in each box?

_____

16. Belle bought packages of beads for her project. Ben bought twice as many packages as Belle. Micalla bought three times as many packages as Belle. Altogether, they bought 24 packages of beads. How many packages did each person buy?

_____

_____

17. Kari is 10 years old. Her sister is half her age. Explain why $10 \times \frac{1}{2}$ can be used to find her sister's age.

_____

_____

Use Mathematical Processes

Homework

1. How many decimeters make 1 meter? _____

2. How many square decimeters make 1 square meter? _____

3. How many centimeters make 1 meter? _____

4. How many square centimeters make 1 square meter? _____

5. How many millimeters make 1 meter? _____

6. How many square millimeters make 1 square meter? _____

Find the area of each rectangle. Show your work.

7.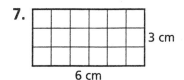
3 cm
6 cm

8. 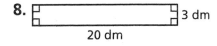 3 dm
20 dm

9. 2 m 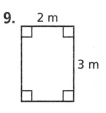 3 m

_____   _____   _____

_____   _____   _____

10. Jason is tiling a patio. The tiles are each 1 square decimeter. The patio is 6 meters long and 4 meters wide. How many tiles will Jason need?

_____

What metric unit would you use to find each?

11. the area of a gymnasium _____

12. the length of a pencil _____

13. the area of a door _____

14. the length of an eyelash _____

15. the area of a book cover _____

16. the area of a driveway _____

Remembering

Marville and Geotown had a new voter registration contest. The pictograph shows the results by day.

Marville on Friday	🗒🗒🗒🗒🗒
Geotown on Friday	🗒🗒🗒🗒🗒🗒🗒🗒🗒🗒
Marville on Saturday	🗒🗒🗒🗒🗒🗒🗒🗒🗒
Geotown on Saturday	🗒🗒🗒🗒🗒🗒
Marville on Sunday	🗒🗒🗒🗒🗒🗒🗒🗒
Geotown on Sunday	🗒🗒

Key: 🗒 = 8 new voters

Use the pictograph and key to solve.

1. Which town was in the lead on Friday?

   _____

2. By how many new voters was that town ahead on Friday?

   _____

3. How many more new voters were registered on Sunday in Marville than in Geotown?

   _____

Solve the problems below. Make a drawing if it helps.   *Show your work.*

4. Ramon planted 3 rows of seeds. He put 8 seeds in each row. Each row of seeds was 42 inches long. How far apart did Ramon plant the seeds?

   _____

5. Bunches of 6 roses were selling for $8. Anita paid $40 for roses. How many roses did she buy?

   _____

6. Ms. Goldfarb has 12 turquoise beads and 3 times as many amber beads. She is making 8 pins with the same number of beads on each pin. How many beads will be on a pin?

   _____

Name _____ **Date** _____

Homework

Find the perimeter and area of each rectangle.

1.

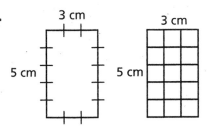

P = _____

A = _____

2.

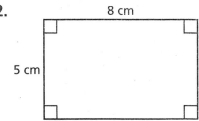

P = _____

A = _____

3.

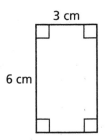

P = _____

A = _____

4.

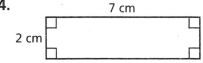

P = _____

A = _____

5.

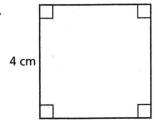

P = _____

A = _____

Solve the word problem.

6. Kaya is wallpapering one wall of her room. The wall is 10 feet long and 8 feet tall. How many square feet of wallpaper will Kaya need? _____

7. Kaya's room is 12 feet long and 10 feet wide. She wants to put a border at the top of the walls. How many feet of border does she need? _____

Remembering

Solve.

1. $18 \times 0 =$ _____
2. $98 \times 1 =$ _____
3. $0 \div 85 =$ _____
4. $54 \div 1 =$ _____

5. $0 \div 22 =$ _____
6. $98 \div 1 =$ _____
7. $0 \times 14 =$ _____
8. $54 \times 1 =$ _____

9. $y = 5$. Find $30 \div y$. _____
10. $z = 7$. Find $3 \times z$. _____

11. $t = 2$. Find $10 \div t$. _____
12. $x = 6$. Find $18 \div x$. _____

13. $s = 11$. Find $5 \times s$. _____
14. $u = 8$. Find $6 \times u$. _____

15. If $h = 12$ and $t = 36$, what is $t \div h$? _____

16. If $a = 4$ and $s = 10$, what is $a \times s$? _____

17. If $v = 9$ and $m = 8$, what is $v \times m$? _____

18. If $u = 77$ and $d = 7$, what is $u \div d$? _____

19. If $s = 4$ and $t = 20$, what is $s \div t$? _____

20. If $m = 12$ and $p = 5$, what is $m \times p$? _____

Solve the problems below.   *Show your work.*

21. Simon bought 4 packages of holiday greeting cards.
    Each package was $6. How much did he spend?

    _____

22. Simon's packages contained 36 cards altogether.
    How many cards were in each package?

    _____

23. Each package contained 3 different designs of cards.
    How many cards of each design did Simon buy?

    _____

    _____

Remember to use your Target and Division Cards to practice.

Homework

1. Look at the parallelograms. Which two parallelograms have the same area? Show your work.

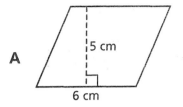

A   5 cm   6 cm

B   4 cm   6 cm

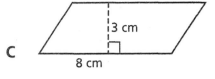

C   3 cm   8 cm

2. Look at the right triangles. Which two triangles have the same area? Show your work.

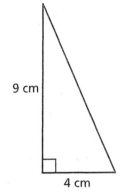

E   9 cm   4 cm

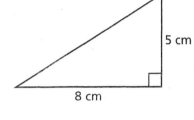

F   5 cm   8 cm

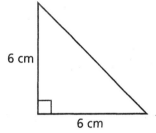

G   6 cm   6 cm

3. For each right triangle, draw the rectangle made by drawing sides opposite the two shorter sides in the triangle. Find the area of each rectangle.

4. How does the area of each rectangle relate to the area of either right triangle inside it?

_____

Remembering

There are 36 buttons in a jar. There are 3 times as many red buttons as white buttons.

1. How many white buttons are there? _____

2. How many red buttons are there? _____

Hint: Let w = the number of white buttons
    and $3w$ = the number of red buttons.

There are 40 yellow and blue marbles in a bag. There are 4 times as many blue marbles as yellow marbles.

3. How many yellow marbles are there? _____

4. How many blue marbles are there? _____

A board game comes with 9 white and green number cubes. There are twice as many white cubes as green cubes.

5. How many green number cubes are there? _____

6. How many white number cubes are there? _____

There are 30 bows in a bag. There are 5 times as many small bows as large bows.

7. How many large bows are there? _____

8. How many small bows are there? _____

There are 20 red and blue pens in a box. There are 3 times as many blue pens as red pens.

9. How many red pens are there? _____

10. How many blue pens are there? _____

Area of Right Triangles and Parallelograms

Homework

Find the area of each triangle.

1.

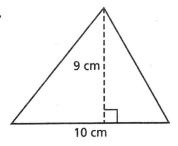

9 cm

10 cm

_____

2.

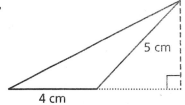

5 cm

4 cm

_____

3.

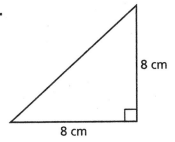

8 cm

8 cm

_____

4.

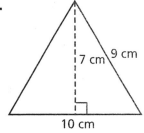

7 cm   9 cm

10 cm

_____

5.

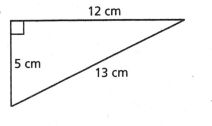

12 cm

5 cm

13 cm

_____

6.

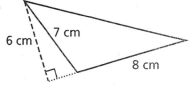

6 cm   7 cm

8 cm

_____

Remembering

Find the unknown number.

1. $k \div 7 = 8$

$k =$ _____

2. $63 \div s = 7$

$s =$ _____

3. $21 = 3d$

$d =$ _____

4. $32 + p = 40$

$p =$ _____

5. $z = (8 \times 8) + (2 \times 5)$

$z =$ _____

6. $4c + 2 = 18$

$c =$ _____

7. $t = 7 \times (6 + 3)$

$t =$ _____

8. $12 - (10 - 3) = w$

$w =$ _____

Solve the problems below.   *Show your work.*

9. Julie walked 6 times as far as Sylvia. If Sylvia walked 5 km, then how far did Julie walk?

_____

10. Andrew spent half as much money as Justin. If Justin spent $16, then how much money did Andrew spend?

_____

11. Brian owns 3 times as many puzzles as Jenna. If Jenna has 4 puzzles, then how many puzzles does Brian own?

_____

12. Emilio has 3 times as many coins as Anna. If Emilio has 27 coins, then how many coins does Anna have?

_____

Find the perimeter and area.

1.

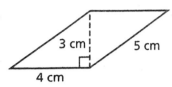

3 cm 5 cm
4 cm

P = _____

A = _____

2.

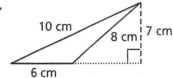

10 cm 8 cm 7 cm
6 cm

P = _____

A = _____

3.

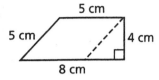

5 cm
5 cm 4 cm
8 cm

P = _____

A = _____

4.

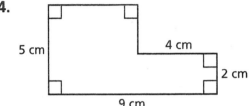

5 cm 4 cm
2 cm
9 cm

P = _____

A = _____

5.

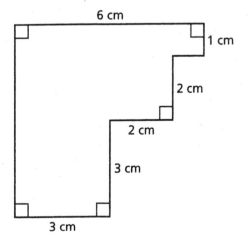

6 cm
1 cm
2 cm
2 cm
3 cm
3 cm

P = _____

A = _____

6.

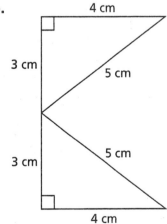

4 cm
3 cm 5 cm
3 cm 5 cm
4 cm

P = _____

A = _____

Name _____   **Date** _____

Remembering

Find the perimeter and area.

1.

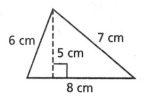

P = _____

A = _____

2.

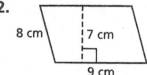

P = _____

A = _____

3.

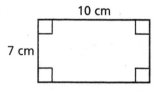

P = _____

A = _____

4.

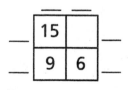

P = _____

A = _____

Solve the Factor Puzzles.

5.

15	
9	6

6.

25	50
	30

7.

12	32
27	

8.

49	28
63	

9.

56	
49	63

10.

	72
28	32

Consolidate Perimeter and Area

Complete.

1. 36 in. = _____ ft

2. 12 ft = _____ yd

3. 36 in. = _____ yd

4. _____ in. = 4 ft

5. _____ ft = 2 yd

6. _____ in. = 3 yd

Find the perimeter and area of each figure in feet.

7.
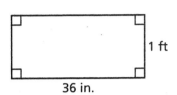
36 in. 1 ft

P = _____

A = _____

8.
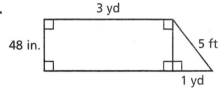
3 yd 48 in. 5 ft 1 yd

P = _____

A = _____

Find the perimeter and area of each figure in yards.

9.
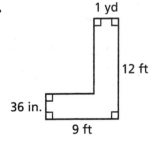
1 yd 12 ft 36 in. 9 ft

P = _____

A = _____

10.
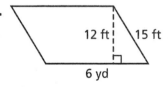
12 ft 15 ft 6 yd

P = _____

A = _____

Remembering

Solve the Factor Puzzles.

1.

4	
20	45

2.

	7
24	12

3.

	9
48	54

4.

16	18
	81

Which one of the equations is not true? _____
Explain your answer.

5. $9 \times 3 = 3 \times 9$ 6. $9 + 3 = 3 + 9$ 7. $9 \div 3 = 3 \div 9$

_____

_____

Solve the word problems.   *Show your work.*

8. Mrs. Armstrong's class made a paper chain that is 15 feet
long. They want to put it around the bulletin board. The
bulletin board is 4 feet long and 3 feet wide. Is the
chain long enough to go all the way around? How do
you know?

_____

_____

_____

9. The Sanchez family is building a sandbox 6 feet long
and 4 feet wide. How many square feet will the sandbox
cover?

_____

Customary Units of Length

Name _____ **Date** _____

Homework

The following shows how place value and money are related.

ones	.	tenths	hundredths	thousandths
($1.00)		(dimes)	(pennies)	(tenths of a penny)

Write each fraction as a decimal and then say it.

1. $\frac{349}{1,000}$ _____   2. $\frac{6}{10}$ _____   3. $\frac{58}{100}$ _____   4. $\frac{27}{1,000}$ _____

5. $\frac{2}{10}$ _____   6. $\frac{9}{100}$ _____   7. $\frac{6}{1,000}$ _____   8. $\frac{71}{100}$ _____

9. $\frac{90}{100}$ _____   10. $\frac{843}{1,000}$ _____   11. $\frac{5}{10}$ _____   12. $\frac{4}{100}$ _____

13. $\frac{1}{1,000}$ _____   14. $\frac{45}{100}$ _____   15. $\frac{896}{1,000}$ _____   16. $\frac{58}{1,000}$ _____

Solve.

17. A large building has 1,000 windows, and 5 of the windows need to be replaced. What decimal represents the number of windows that need to be replaced?

_____

18. At a reception, 23 of 100 pieces of wedding cake have been eaten. What decimal number represents the number of pieces of cake that have been eaten?

_____

19. Jody made 10 party invitations. Yesterday she mailed 4 of them. What decimal represents the number of invitations that have been mailed?

_____

20. There are 1,000 vehicles in a stadium parking lot; 422 of the vehicles are trucks. What decimal represents the number of vehicles that are trucks?

_____

Name _____ **Date** _____

Remembering

Solve for each unknown.

1. $9 \times w = 63$

  $w =$ _____

2. $42 \div 7 = c$

  $c =$ _____

3. $q \times 8 = 40$

  $q =$ _____

4. $k \div 6 = 9$

  $k =$ _____

5. $7d = 56$

  $d =$ _____

6. $28 \div 4 = x$

  $x =$ _____

7. $6 \cdot 8 = h$

  $h =$ _____

8. $36 \div z = 9$

  $z =$ _____

9. $8 \cdot g = 72$

  $g =$ _____

In each table, write a multiplication rule. Include two variables in each rule you write. Then complete the table.

10.

Rule:					
Number of packages (p)	3	5	8		11
Number of erasers (e)	27		72	90	

11.

Rule:					
Number of rows (r)	2	4	6		
Number of seats (s)	16	32		64	88

Solve.

12. Lyle found the area of the figure on the right to be 34 in.² and the perimeter to be 40 in. Is he correct? If not, explain how to find each correct answer.

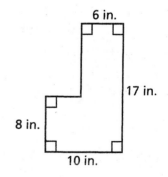

_____

_____

13. Julio earned $\frac{1}{4}$ the number of points as Paulos. If Julio earned 8 points, how many points did Paulos earn?

_____

Decimals as Equal Divisions

Homework

Write each amount as a decimal number.

1. 9 tenths _____

2. 52 thousandths _____

3. 8 hundredths _____

4. 3 cents _____

5. $\frac{65}{100}$ _____

6. $\frac{548}{1,000}$ _____

7. $\frac{12}{1,000}$ _____

8. $\frac{7}{100}$ _____

9. 4 thousandths _____

Circle the value that is *not* equivalent to the other values.

10. 0.47   0.470   0.407   0.4700

11. 0.5   0.50 $\frac{5}{10}$ 0.05

12. 0.801   0.810   0.81   0.8100

13. 0.700   0.70   0.07   0.7

14. 0.39   0.390 $\frac{39}{100}$ $\frac{39}{1,000}$

15. 0.04   0.40   0.040   0.0400

Compare. Write > (greater than) or < (less than).

16. 0.36 $\bigcirc$ 0.8

17. 0.405 $\bigcirc$ 0.62

18. 0.91 $\bigcirc$ 0.95

19. 0.45 $\bigcirc$ 0.4

20. 0.836 $\bigcirc$ 0.83

21. 0.299 $\bigcirc$ 0.3

22. 0.621 $\bigcirc$ 0.612

23. 0.7 $\bigcirc$ 0.07

24. 0.504 $\bigcirc$ 0.54

A store had the same amount of five fabrics. The chart shows the how much of each fabric is left. Use the data to answer each question.

25. The store sold the most of which fabric? Explain.

_____

26. The store sold the least of which fabric? Explain.

_____

27. The same amount of which fabrics is left? Explain.

_____

Red fabric	0.510 yd
Blue fabric	0.492 yd
Yellow fabric	0.6 yd
White fabric	0.51 yd
Black fabric	0.48 yd

Name _____ **Date** _____

Remembering

Solve for each unknown.

1. $h \times 7 = 49$

   $h =$ _____

2. $s \div 8 = 7$

   $s =$ _____

3. $8 \times b = 32$

   $b =$ _____

4. $48 \div 6 = x$

   $x =$ _____

5. $10 \cdot a = 0$

   $a =$ _____

6. $54 \div 9 = y$

   $y =$ _____

7. $5 \cdot 4 = d$

   $d =$ _____

8. $63 \div n = 9$

   $n =$ _____

9. $6 \cdot t = 36$

   $t =$ _____

10. $72 \div r = 9$

    $r =$ _____

11. $5 \times 9 = v$

    $v =$ _____

12. $\frac{27}{3} = m$

    $m =$ _____

Solve the Factor Puzzles.

13.

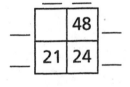

14.

21	
63	54

15.

21	63
	36

Solve.

16. Franco is ordering lunch with a drink, sandwich, and a salad. He has a choice of 3 drinks, 2 sandwiches, and 4 salads. How many possible lunches are there?

    _____

17. Tamara has 4 times as many pages to read for her book report as Maria. Tamara has 20 pages left to read. How many pages does Maria have left to read?

    _____

18. Dae Youn wants to place new carpet in his room. The floor in his room has a width of 6 feet and a length of 10 feet. How much carpet does he need?

    _____

Equate and Compare

Homework

Write a decimal number for each word name.

1. nine thousand, six hundred five and nine tenths

_____

2. two hundred ten thousand, fifty and nineteen hundredths

_____

3. three tenths

_____

4. seven thousandths

_____

5. eight hundredths

_____

Write each amount as a decimal number.

6. $\frac{602}{1,000}$ _____

7. $\frac{21}{100}$ _____

8. $4\frac{9}{10}$ _____

9. $14\frac{27}{100}$ _____

10. $35\frac{712}{1,000}$ _____

11. $9\frac{5}{100}$ _____

12. $24\frac{13}{1,000}$ _____

13. $3\frac{68}{100}$ _____

14. $2\frac{1}{1,000}$ _____

15. $63\frac{7}{10}$ _____

16. $\frac{84}{1,000}$ _____

17. $29\frac{4}{1,000}$ _____

18. $8\frac{17}{1,000}$ _____

19. $\frac{6}{100}$ _____

20. $5\frac{106}{1,000}$ _____

21. $37\frac{3}{100}$ _____

Circle the value that is not equivalent to the other values.

22. 2.6   2.60   2.06   2.600

23. 4.07   4.070   4.70   4.0700

24. 65.800   65.8   65.08   65.80

25. 37.6   37.060   37.0600   37.06

Compare. Write > (greater than) or < (less than).

26. 14.08 ◯ 14.80

27. 789.152 ◯ 789.15

28. 3.071 ◯ 3.007

Order the decimal numbers from least to greatest.

29. 943.18, 94.18, 943.179, 94.183,

_____

Remembering

1. $6 \times a = 24$

$a =$ _____

2. $28 \div 7 = x$

$x =$ _____

3. $j \times 7 = 42$

$j =$ _____

4. $y \times 9 = 54$

$y =$ _____

5. $k \cdot 9 = 81$

$k =$ _____

6. $56 \div 8 = s$

$s =$ _____

7. $8 \cdot 5 = z$

$z =$ _____

8. $63 \div u = 9$

$u =$ _____

9. $6 \cdot n = 48$

$n =$ _____

Describe the angles that appear to be formed by the intersection of the lines as acute, obtuse or right.

10.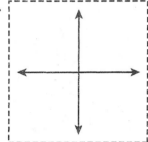

_____

11.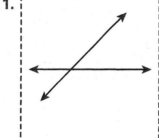

_____

12. Erika drew a triangle having a base of 6 inches and a height of 8 inches. Trevor drew a square having a side measure of 5 inches. Rena drew a parallelogram having a base of 12 inches and a height of 2 inches.

Of the figures that were drawn, which has the greatest area? On the lines below, explain your answer.

> area of a parallelogram = base × height
>
> area of a square = side × side
>
> area of a triangle = $\dfrac{\text{base} \times \text{height}}{2}$

Show your work.

_____

_____

_____

Thousands to Thousandths

Homework

The chart at the right shows the average speed of four horses during a race. Use the data to answer each question.

Fast Jack	47.510 mph
Gold Dust	47.492 mph
Fire Brand	47.6 mph
Relentless	47.51 mph

1. Which horse had the greatest speed?

_____

2. Which horse had the slowest speed?

_____

3. Which horses had identical speeds?

_____

Copy each exercise. Then add or subtract.

4. $0.9 + 0.06 =$ _____   5. $0.47 + 0.258 =$ _____   6. $0.56 + 0.913 =$ _____

7. $1.4 - 0.9 =$ _____   8. $5 - 1.5 =$ _____   9. $3.7 - 2.49 =$ _____

10. $0.008 + 0.6 =$ _____   11. $0.482 + 0.309 =$ _____   12. $19 + 1.044 =$ _____

13. $3 - 0.005 =$ _____   14. $0.409 - 0.20 =$ _____   15. $6.07 - 4 =$ _____

Name _____ **Date** _____

Remembering

Solve for each unknown.

1. $a \div 4 = 10$

$a =$ _____

2. $3 \cdot c = 27$

$c =$ _____

3. $24 \div d = 6$

$d =$ _____

4. $e \times 9 = 36$

$e =$ _____

5. $64 \div 8 = j$

$j =$ _____

6. $8b = 16$

$b =$ _____

7. $g = 5 \times 7$

$g =$ _____

8. $7 = h \div 3$

$h =$ _____

9. $30 = 6 \cdot r$

$r =$ _____

10. $(16 - 7) \times 2 = m$

$m =$ _____

11. $p = 16 - (7 \times 2)$

$p =$ _____

12. $(2 \times 3) - (1 \times 5) = v$

$v =$ _____

13. $2 \times (3 - 1) \times 5 = s$

$s =$ _____

14. $w = (24 \div 3) + 9$

$w =$ _____

15. $5 + 7 + (6 \div 3) = q$

$q =$ _____

Solve.

16. Yoshi is making cards. He can choose from 4 colors of markers and 5 colors of paper. How many different ways can he create a card?

_____

17. On the front of each card, Yoshi centers 3 rows with 6 stickers in each row. How many stickers does he use on the front of each card?

_____

18. To make cards, Yoshi bought new markers. Each package he bought had 8 markers. He used 7 markers and had 25 markers left. How many package of markers did he buy?

_____

19. Yoshi figured out that it costs him $2 for the supplies to make one card. So, he decided to sell each card for $5. If he sells 6 cards, how much does Yoshi earn in profit?

_____

Adding and Subtracting Decimals

Homework

Compare. Write > (greater than) or < (less than).

1. 0.15 ◯ 0.9

2. 0.52 ◯ 0.307

3. 0.48 ◯ 0.6

4. 0.283 ◯ 0.238

5. 0.75 ◯ 1.4

6. 0.5 ◯ 0.05

7. 2 ◯ 0.2

8. 3.088 ◯ 3.1

9. 7.40 ◯ 4.7

Write each whole number.

10. 80 thousand = _____

11. nine million = _____

12. seven billion = _____

13. 42 million, 120 = _____

Copy each exercise. Then add.

14. 0.7 + 0.05 = _____

15. 0.48 + 0.159 = _____

16. 0.25 + 0.618 = _____

Copy each exercise. Then subtract.

17. 10 − 0.35 = _____

18. 0.7 − 0.19 = _____

19. 3.6 − 2 = _____

Write these related pairs.

20. 1 million _____

21. 1 millionth _____

22. 6 billion _____

23. 6 billionth _____

24. Write 2 ways in which whole numbers and decimal numbers are different.

_____

_____

_____

_____

_____

Remembering

Solve for each unknown.

1. $s \times 4 = 16$

$s =$ _____

2. $d \div 2 = 10$

$d =$ _____

3. $7 \times e = 49$

$e =$ _____

4. $72 \div 9 = x$

$x =$ _____

5. $6 \cdot c = 42$

$c =$ _____

6. $54 \div 9 = r$

$r =$ _____

7. $8 \cdot 6 = v$

$v =$ _____

8. $32 \div g = 8$

$g =$ _____

9. $7 \cdot t = 63$

$t =$ _____

Write acute, right, or obtuse for each triangle.

10.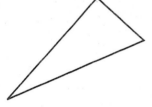

_____

11.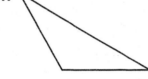

_____

12.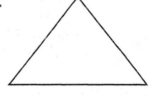

_____

In each table, write a multiplication rule in words and as an equation with two variables. Then complete the table.

13.

Rule in words:					
Equation					
Hours (*h*)	1	2	3		6
Distance in miles (*m*)	10	20		50	60

14.

Rule in words:					
Equation					
Distance in feet (*f*)		1	4	2	5
Seconds (*s*)	0	2		4	10

       Billions to Billionths

Homework

Write the word name for each decimal number.

1. 0.06 _____

2. 24.7 _____

3. 1.308 _____

Follow the directions to change the number in the box.

764,259.03

4. Increase the number by 100,000. _____

5. Decrease the number by 1 hundredth. _____

6. Increase the number by 5 tenths. _____

7. Write a number with 2 more in the ten thousands place. _____

8. Rearrange the digits to make the greatest possible decimal number with two decimal places. _____

Write each number.

9. five hundred thousand = _____

10. 4 thousand and 6 tenths = _____

11. 10 and 8 hundredths = _____

12. 390 and 7 thousandths = _____

Compare. Write > (greater than) or < (less than).

13. 657,894 ◯ 657,994

14. 120,705 ◯ 1,207,051

15. 3,246,000,800 ◯ 3,246,001,800

16. 4,900,754,001 ◯ 490,075,400

17. 7,504,180 ◯ 7,503,190

18. 27,546,709 ◯ 27,543,893

19. 91,257,306 ◯ 991,257,375

20. 638,697,345 ◯ 638,687,345

21. 1,753,682 ◯ 1,753,692

22. 8,004,752,390 ◯ 8,004,752,490

Remembering

Copy each exercise. Then add or subtract.

1. 23 + 1.75 = _____

2. 0.9 − 0.62 = _____

3. 0.41 + 0.007 = _____

4. 6.12 − 3.1 = _____

5. 5 + 2.01 = _____

6. 5 − 4.106 = _____

Use these numbers for exercises 7 and 8:   3.7   0.196   3.07   0.02   0.5

7. Order the numbers from least to greatest. _____

8. Order the numbers from greatest to least. _____

Choose the correct number from the box at the right.

918	300.15	87.8
88.7	176.9	40.287
40,287	91.8	30,015

9. three hundred and fifteen hundredths _____

10. eighty-eight and seven tenths _____

11. forty and two hundred eighty-seven thousandths _____

12. ninety-one and eight tenths _____

Solve.

13. What is the perimeter, in centimeters, of the figure below?

Perimeter = _____

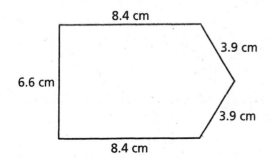

8.4 cm

3.9 cm

6.6 cm

3.9 cm

8.4 cm

Use Place Value

Homework

Use the number 724,062.581 for each exercise.

1. Increase the number by 0.007. _____

2. Decrease the number by 100,000. _____

3. Add 8 in the hundreds place. _____

4. Subtract 2 from the hundredths place. _____

Copy each exercise. Then add or subtract.

5. $37 + 45¢ = _____   6. $82.06 + 25¢ = _____   7. 59¢ + $4.23 = _____

8. 9 m + 0.05 m = _____ 9. 6.4 m + 0.07 m = _____ 10. 5 m + 0.08 m = _____

11. 231 + 0.26 = _____   12. 46.08 + 0.97 = _____   13. 92.24 + 3.6 = _____

Solve.   *Show your work.*

14. Olivia is buying a jacket that costs $84. The sales tax
    that will be added to the cost of the jacket is $4.65.
    What is the total cost of the jacket?

    _____

Remembering

Compare. Write = (is equal to) or ≠ (is not equal to).

1. 6.003 ◯ 6.03

2. 106.72 ◯ 106.9

3. 98.07 ◯ 98.070

4. 5 ◯ 5.000

5. 0.14 ◯ 0.104

6. 0.1 ◯ 0.100

7. 0.000 ◯ 0

8. 11.0 ◯ 11

9. 5.020 ◯ 5.002

10. 18.6 ◯ 18.60

11. 0.2 ◯ 2.0

12. 7.04 ◯ 7.40

Use the number 427,389.106 for exercises 13–20.

13. The digit 7 is in the _____ place.

14. The digit 1 is in the _____ place.

15. What digit is in the hundreds place? _____

16. What digit is in the thousandths place? _____

17. The digit 9 is in the _____ place.

18. What digit is in the ten thousands place? _____

19. The digit 4 is in the _____ place.

20. Write the number using words.

_____

_____

_____

Use the digits 6, 9, and 1 for exercises 21–24. Use each digit once.

21. Write the greatest three-digit whole number. _____

22. Write the smallest three-digit whole number. _____

23. Write the greatest three-digit decimal number in hundredths. _____

24. Write the smallest three-digit decimal number in tenths. _____

Add Whole Numbers and Decimals

Name _____   Date _____

Homework

Add each pair of numbers.

1. 80,615.405 + 3,468.27

2. 512,019 + 6,478.084

3. 2.765 + 19.6529

4. 0.825 + 647.52

5. 10,856.29 + 9,753.779

6. 901,728.6 + 7,286.903

Use the number $4,697,385.65 for exercises 7–12.

7. Add 3 million dollars. _____

8. Subtract 5 thousand dollars. _____

9. Add 20 dollars. _____

10. Take $10,000 away. _____

11. Add 2 dimes. _____

12. Subtract 1 penny. _____

Name _____ **Date** _____

Remembering

Solve for each unknown.

1. $(5 \cdot 8) \div 4 = c$ **2.** $d = 72 \div (9 - 1)$ **3.** $a = (5 \times 6) - 17$

     $c =$ _____ $d =$ _____ $a =$ _____

4. $(35 + 7) \div 7 = r$ **5.** $21 \cdot s = 0$ **6.** $3t = (4 + 5) \times 3$

     $r =$ _____ $s =$ _____ $t =$ _____

Solve.

Emilio is planting a garden, but he has mixed up the seeds. The seeds now need to be sorted. He has a book that tells him the lengths of different seeds. The lengths are shown below.

Emilio doesn't completely understand decimal numbers. You can help him by listing the seeds from longest to shortest. Then Emilio will be able to identify and sort his seeds.

Sizes of Seeds   **Seeds in Order of Size**

Tomato 0.3 cm   Longest   **7.** _____

Pumpkin 1.25 cm   **8.** _____

Watermelon 0.9 cm   **9.** _____

Carrot 0.15 cm   **10.** _____

Corn 0.75 cm   **11.** _____

Eggplant 0.25 cm   Shortest   **12.** _____

Write the perimeter and the area of the figure below.

13. Perimeter = _____

14. Area = _____

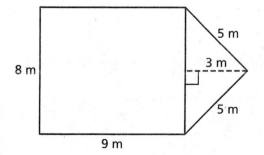

Homework

Copy each exercise. Then subtract.

1. 6,000 − 348 = _____   2. 7,364 − 937 = _____   3. 50,821 − 3,617 = _____

4. 720.95 − 286.4 = _____   5. 18,652 − 4.31 = _____   6. 350.6 − 176.54 = _____

Solve.   *Show your work.*

7. Ahmad had a piece of rope that was 7.14 meters long. He cut off 0.095 meters to practice making knots. What was the length of the rope after the cut?

   _____

8. Natasha has a large collection of books. The thickest book measures 4.9 centimeters. The thinnest book measures 1.8 centimeters. What is the difference in thicknesses of those two books?

   _____

9. Yoshi saved $1,238.46 for a vacation in Mexico. While in Mexico, she spent $975. What amount of money did Yoshi not spend?

   _____

10. Tarantulas are one of the largest spiders on Earth. A tarantula can grow to be about 6.8 centimeters long. A spitting spider can grow to be about 0.9 centimeters long. About how much longer are the largest tarantulas than the largest spitting spiders?

   _____

Remembering

Circle the value in each group that is not equivalent to the other values.

1. 9.050   9.05   09.050   0.950   09.05

2. 1.410   1.041   01.41   1.4100   01.410

3. 2.650   02.65   2.605   2.65   02.650

Write each decimal number.

4. 2 thousand and 8 tenths _____

5. 31 thousand and 57 hundredths _____

6. 94 thousand, 631 and 7 thousandths _____

7. six million and five hundredths _____

Write each amount as a decimal number.

8. 6 tenths _____   9. 4 thousandths _____   10. 2 hundredths _____

11. $\frac{18}{100}$ _____   12. $9\frac{3}{10}$ _____   13. $\frac{26}{1,000}$ _____

14. 73 hundredths _____   15. 1 tenth _____   16. 8 thousandths _____

Calculate the perimeter (P) of each figure in *feet*.

17.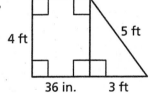

$P =$ _____

18.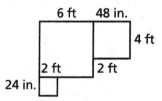

$P =$ _____

19.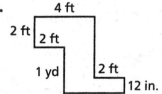

$P =$ _____

Solve the Factor Puzzles.

20.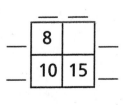

21.

48	56
	63

22.

15	35
12	

Subtract Whole and Decimal Numbers

Use the data in the table to answer the questions that follow.

Lakefront Summer Concerts

Musical Group	Date	Audience Size	Ticket Sales
Wink	May 5	47,591	$475,910
Fred's Garage	May 26	59,985	$599,850
The Insiders	June 8	51,872	$518,720
The Beat Masters	June 19	43,469	$434,690
Paparazzi	June 27	56,327	$563,270

1. Which musical group entertained the largest audience? *Show your work.*

   _____

2. How many total people were in the audience at the concerts during May? During June?

   May _____

   June _____

3. For each concert, 60,000 tickets could have been sold. How many tickets were not sold when The Insiders performed? When Paparazzi performed?

   The Insiders _____

   Paparazzi _____

4. What amount of money represents the total ticket sales for May? for June?

   May _____

   June _____

5. What pattern do you see between the audience size and the ticket sales? _____

6. What does this tell you about the cost of the tickets?

   _____

Name _____ Date _____

Remembering

Use the number 24,168.05 for exercises 1–6.

1. Increase the number by 1,000. _____

2. Write the number with 2 fewer tens. _____

3. Decrease the number by 3 hundredths. _____

4. Write the number with 5 more ten thousands.

   _____

5. Write the number with 9 more in the tenths place.

   _____

6. Increase the number by 500. _____

Use the decimal numbers below to answer the questions that follow.

   0.2698   2.698   0.02698   0.26980   26.980

7. Which number is the least? _____

8. Which number is the greatest? _____

9. Which two numbers are equivalent? _____

Write the equivalent measurement.

10. 36 in. = _____ ft   **11.** 24 ft = _____ yd   **12.** 36 in. = _____ yd

13. 2 yd = _____ in.   **14.** 4 ft = _____ in.   **15.** 8 yd = _____ ft

Calculate the perimeter (*P*) and the area (*A*) of each rectangle.

16.

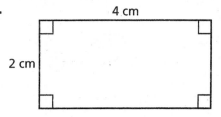

4 cm

2 cm

17.

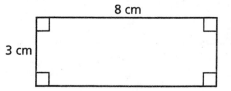

8 cm

3 cm

P = _____   *P* = _____

A = _____   *A* = _____

Place Value Word Problems

Use the Commutative Property to solve for n.

1. $26{,}184 + 1{,}546 = 1{,}546 + n$

$n =$ _____

2. $17.39 + 12.58 = 12.58 + n$

$n =$ _____

Regroup the numbers using the Associative Property. Then add.

3. $(389 + 700) + 300 =$

_____

4. $1.02 + (0.98 + 4.87) =$

_____

Use the Distributive Property to rewrite each problem so it has only two factors. Then solve.

5. $(8 \times 700) + (8 \times 300) =$

_____

6. $(25 \times 9) + (75 \times 9) =$

_____

Group the numbers to make the addition easier. Then add.

7.	8.	9.	10.
20,000	10,000	10.75	1.600
70,000	25,000	10.4	1.200
30,000	89,000	10.25	1.200
68,000	75,000	10.57	+ 1.479
+ 80,000	+ 90,000	+ 10.6	

Subtract.

11. $\$182.09 - 37¢ =$ _____

12. $\$5{,}287.32 - 59¢ =$ _____

13. $\$362 - 48¢ =$ _____

14. $6 \text{ m} - 0.03 \text{ m} =$ _____

15. $8 \text{ dm} - 0.5 \text{ dm} =$ _____

16. $4 \text{ m} - 0.032 \text{ m} =$ _____

Name _____ Date _____

Remembering

Use these decimal numbers to answer the questions that follow.

68.70 6.870 6.087 6.87 0.6870

1. Which number is the least? _____

2. Which number is the greatest? _____

3. Which two numbers are equivalent? _____

Compare. Write >, <, or =.

4. 0.09 ◯ 0.7

5. 0.30 ◯ 0.3

6. 0.86 ◯ 0.7

7. 0.461 ◯ 0.416

8. 1.9 ◯ 0.83

9. 0.5 ◯ 0.500

10. 1.26 ◯ 12.6

11. 7.00 ◯ 7

12. 2 ◯ 0.2

Solve.

Show your work.

13. What is the greatest 3-digit whole number you can make using the digits 5, 8, and 2 once? What is the least 3-digit whole number you can make?

_____

14. What is the smallest decimal number you can make using the digits 5, 0, 8, and 2 once?

_____

15. Cherise is growing a tomato plant for her science project. At the end of the first week, the plant was 4.7 cm tall. During the second week, the plant had grown 0.9 cm. How tall was the plant at the end of the second week?

_____

Properties and Strategies

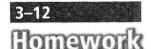

Name _____   Date _____

Use the information in each problem to make a pictograph.

1. The Horizon Book Company needs a pictograph showing the
   number of books sold this year. Using the information shown,
   make a pictograph. Give your graph a title and a key.

| Children | 500,000 |
| Adults | 700,000 |

Books for Children	
Books for Adults	
	Key: _____

2. The Melodic Music Company needs a pictograph showing the
   number of CDs sold this year. Using the information shown,
   make a pictograph. Remember to include the title and
   the key.

Rock	40,000
Country	30,000
Jazz	15,000
Classical	5,000

Rock	
Country	
Jazz	
Classical	
	Key: _____

3. Ask 2 questions about your pictograph for problem 2 and
   then answer them.

   _____

   _____

   _____

Remembering

Answer each question about the decimal numbers.

58.76	5.876	0.05876	5.8760	0.5876

1. Which number is the smallest?

_____

2. Which number is the greatest?

_____

3. Which two numbers are equivalent?

_____

Write each number.

4. seven tenths

_____

5. thirty million

_____

6. eight hundredths

_____

7. four million one

_____

8. forty-five thousand six

_____

9. seven hundred fifty thousand ten

_____

10. eighty thousand twenty-nine

_____

11. two thousandths

_____

For each measurement, write an equivalent length in decimeters (dm), centimeters (cm), and millimeters (mm).

12. 13.74 m _____ dm _____ cm _____ mm

13. 0.85 m _____ dm _____ cm _____ mm

Pictographs with Large Numbers

Name _____   **Date** _____

Homework

Round to the nearest ten.

1. 62 _____   2. 91 _____

Round to the nearest thousand.

3. 3,205 _____   4. 8,500 _____

Round to the nearest hundred.

5. 493 _____   6. 1,580 _____

Round to the nearest 10 thousand.

7. 50,926 _____   8. 75,612 _____

Decide whether a *safe* or an *ordinary* estimate is needed. Then estimate to find each answer.

Show your work.

9. Amy has 5,805 large beads and 3,950 small beads. About how many more large beads than small beads does Amy have?

_____

10. Lincoln School has 54 fifth-graders, and Elm School has 38 fifth-graders. The two schools will have a party together. Each fifth-grade student will get a balloon. About how many balloons should the teachers buy?

_____

11. In a parking garage, there are 598 cars and 214 vans. About how many vehicles are in the parking garage altogether?

_____

12. A sports shop sold $15,679 worth of roller blades and $16,231 worth of skateboards this year. About how much money did the shop make on these two items?

_____

Remembering

At the county fair each August, there is a contest to see who can grow the tallest sunflower. Below is a table that shows how tall each sunflower plant is.

1. Make a list showing whose plants got first place, second place, and third place.

Sunflower Growers

Arturo	4.781 m
Jan	5.935 m
Shen	6.105 m
Max	6.20 m
Madison	5.92 m
Alex	5.915 m

First Place _____

Second Place _____

Third Place _____

Solve.

2. Michaela, Simone, and Veronica want to buy T-shirts for the science club. If the club treasurer gives them $35.00, and they spend $27.50 on the T-shirts, how much money will they have left?

Show your work.

_____

3. Michaela, Simone, and Veronica want to buy special glitter paint with the leftover money. The paint is on sale. They can buy 3 tubes for $6.00. Do they have enough money to buy 3 tubes of paint? If so, how much money will they have left?

_____

Find the area of each right triangle.

4.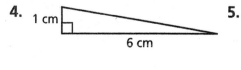
1 cm
6 cm

_____

5.
5 cm
4 cm

_____

6.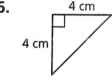
4 cm
4 cm

_____

Name_____ Date_____

A forest ranger estimated the number of trees in the forest and made this bar graph.

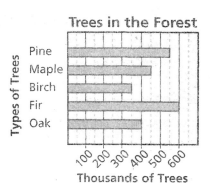

Trees in the Forest

Types of Trees: Pine, Maple, Birch, Fir, Oak

Thousands of Trees

1. About how many maple trees are in the forest?

_____

2. About how many fir and pine trees are there altogether?

_____

3. About how many more oak trees are there than birch trees?

_____

4. Write an estimate of the total number of trees in the forest.

_____

Make a bar graph.

The table below shows an estimate of the number of cats, dogs, and birds kept as pets in the United States.

5. Make a bar graph to show these data.
   Make your own scale.

Cats	59,000,000
Dogs	53,000,000
Birds	13,000,000

Common Pets in the United States

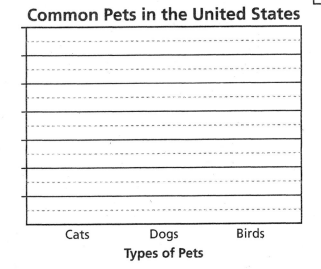

Cats   Dogs   Birds

Types of Pets

Name _____   **Date** _____

Remembering

Add or subtract. Use a separate sheet of paper.

1. 2,387,046 + 6,125,348 _____

2. 38.567 + 4.286 _____

3. 50,000 − 8,936.2 _____

4. 5.004 + 0.38 _____

5. 0.0852 − 0.039 _____

6. 5.004 − 0.38 _____

Use the pictograph to solve.

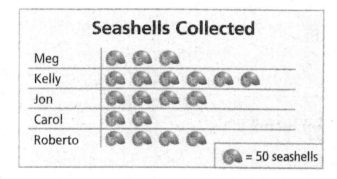

7. Who has more seashells than Meg?

_____

8. How many more seashells did Jon collect than Carol?

_____

9. How many seashells did Kelly collect?

_____

Solve the Factor Puzzles.

10.
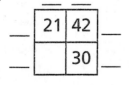

21	42
	30

11.

24	36
6	

12.

10	
14	56

Bar Graphs and Rounding

1. Round to the nearest whole number.

   a. 8.36 _____

   b. 18.7 _____

2. Round to the nearest hundredth.

   a. 58.635 _____

   b. 7.214 _____

3. Round to the nearest tenth.

   a. 24.316 _____

   b. 5.23 _____

4. Round to the nearest thousandth.

   a. 7.1488 _____

   b. 38.0769 _____

Copy and estimate each sum or difference.

5. $46.78 − $18.55

6. 12.3 + 4.7

7. 9.586 + 3.097

Solve.   *Show your work.*

8. A decimal number changed to 23.7 after it was rounded. Give a decimal number that is less than 23.7 and another that is greater than 23.7 that each round to 23.7. Explain to what place each number was rounded.

   _____

   _____

9. When Marla rounded 19.95 to the nearest tenth, she found the number changed to 20. Is this correct? Explain.

   _____

10. Peter decided that the total of a $24.55 pair of jeans and a $12.25 shirt was $26.80. Was Peter's answer reasonable? Explain why or why not.

    _____

11. Biruk wants to buy a book for $15.25 and a book for $4.85. He wants to pay with one $20 bill. Use estimation to decide if this is reasonable. Explain to what place value to round for an estimate that is useful in this situation.

    _____

    _____

    _____

Remembering

Add or subtract.

1. 41,253,270 + 6,050

2. 14,365,024 + 7,840,993

3. 5,000,000 − 563,000

4. 35,789,630 − 2,894

5. 83,918.7 + 605.357

6. 10,250 − 4,200.24

7. 9,473.2 + 851.69

8. 756.42 − 94.51

Use the Commutative Property to solve for n.

9. 98,551 + 2,841 = 2,841 + n

$n =$ _____

10. 65.18 + 75.43 = 75.43 + n

$n =$ _____

Use the Associative Property to regroup the numbers. Then add.

11. (496 + 800) + 200

_____

12. 2.25 + (0.75 + 8.57)

_____

Solve.

Show your work.

13. Nathaniel says his string project uses 7.5 ft of string. Kara says her project uses 7.52 ft of string. Who used the least amount of string? Explain how you know.

_____

14. Last month, Myles ran 14.55 miles while training for a marathon. Frances ran 0.6 miles farther than Myles. How far did Frances run last month?

_____

Round and Estimate with Decimal Numbers

Name _____ Date _____

Use the line graph below to answer the questions that follow.

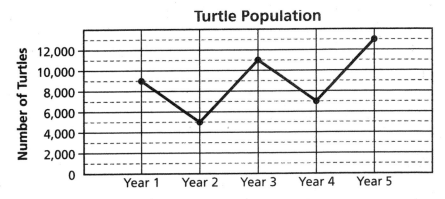

Turtle Population

1. The graph shows the turtle population at the end of each year during a 5-year period. What was the turtle population in Year 4? _____

2. How much greater was the population in Year 1 than in Year 2? _____

3. Which year represents the greatest turtle population? What was the population that year?

_____

Make a line graph.

4. The table at the right shows a store's inventory of kites at the end of 4 months. Make a graph below to show an estimate of the number of kites at the end of each month. Make your own scale and title.

January	135
February	382
March	673
April	424

_____

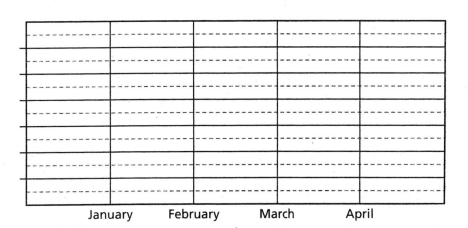

January   February   March   April

Remembering

Estimate the area and perimeter of each figure. Each side of each grid square represents 1 cm.

1.

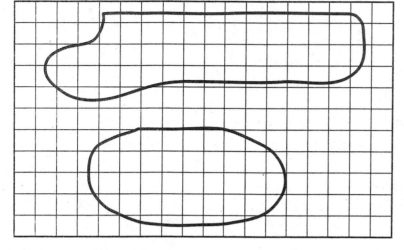

$P =$ _____

$A =$ _____

2.

$P =$ _____

$A =$ _____

Solve.

3. Chris counted the number of steps he took on his way to school. He took 943 steps to get to his friend's house, and then another 1,208 steps to get to school. How many steps did he take altogether?

_____

Show your work.

4. Devon cares for two puppies. One puppy weighs 8.54 pounds. The other puppy weighs 12.39 pounds. How much do the two puppies weigh altogether?

_____

Round each given decimal number to the nearest whole number, tenth, and hundredth.

5. 14.852 _____   _____   _____

6. 7.149 _____   _____   _____

7. 912.574 _____   _____   _____

8. 23.631 _____   _____   _____

Discrete and Continuous Data

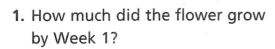

Name _____ **Date** _____

Jamal made a line graph to show the weekly growth of a flower he planted from a seed.

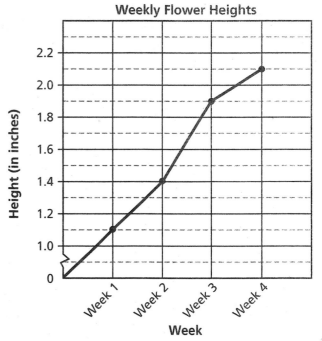

Weekly Flower Heights

1. How much did the flower grow by Week 1?

_____

2. How much did the flower grow between week 3 and week 4?

_____

3. The flower reached its maximum height on Week 4. What is the tallest this flower will grow?

_____

4. Between which two weeks did the flower grow the most?

_____

The table shows the amount of rainfall this month in 4 different cities.

Chester	0.20 cm
Creekside	0.10 cm
Merton	0.05 cm
Warner	0.25 cm

5. Make a bar graph showing this information. Remember to give your graph a title and a scale.

Chester   Creekside   Merton   Warner

Graphs With Decimal Numbers **79**

Remembering

Estimate.

Show your work.

1. The bird watchers of Pine County counted 2,956 cardinals, 3,204 finches, and 978 hawks this summer. About how many cardinals, finches, and hawks did they count in all?

_____

2. Anne-Marie has $125. She wants to buy a jacket for $94 and some boots for $32. Should she estimate the total with a safe estimate or an ordinary estimate? Does she have enough money?

_____

_____

_____

3. The Lightfoot Library has 31,823 books, but 9,625 are checked out right now. About how many books are still on the shelves?

_____

4. A toothbrush factory made 2,461,200 electric toothbrushes and 5,847,500 regular toothbrushes this week. About how many toothbrushes did the factory make in all?

_____

Write a decimal equivalent for each fraction.

5. $\frac{76}{100}$ 6. $\frac{349}{100}$ 7. $\frac{9}{100}$ 8. $\frac{5}{100}$ 9. $\frac{2}{10}$

_____   _____   _____   _____   _____

10. How many congruent isosceles triangles are inside the regular octagon? _____

11. What is the area of each triangle? _____

12. What is the area of the octagon? _____

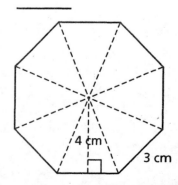

4 cm

3 cm

Graphs With Decimal Numbers

Homework

In your Math Journal or on a sheet of paper, write a word problem for each situation and answer the questions.

Situation 1

1. Write a word problem that represents a change situation.

2. Did you write a change plus or a change minus situation?

3. Is your situation an unknown result, unknown change, or unknown start?

Situation 2

4. Write a word problem that represents a collection situation.

5. Does your situation include an unknown total or an unknown partner?

6. Does you situation represent a take apart, put together, or no action situation?

Situation 3

7. Write a word problem that represents a comparison situation.

8. Does your situation have an unknown difference or an unknown quantity?

Solve these comparison problems.

Show your work.

9. Camille collected 13 shells from the beach. Her friend Sarah collected 10 times as many. How many shells did Sarah collect? _____

10. Last week, Armando read 285 pages of a book. This week, he read 196 pages. How many fewer pages did he read this week? _____

11. The Eiffel Tower in Paris is 300 meters tall. It is 253.5 meters taller than the Statue of Liberty. How tall is the Statue of Liberty? _____

Remembering

Add or subtract. Use a separate sheet of paper.

1. $17{,}092 - 3{,}746 =$

_____

2. $657.92 + 53.035 =$

_____

3. $62.004 - 48.65 =$

_____

4. $831.5 - 46.75 =$

_____

5. $190.98 + 256.3 =$

_____

6. $41.003 - 7.02 =$

_____

7. $24 - 0.04 =$

_____

8. $9.72 + 31 =$

_____

**Use the Distributive Property to rewrite the expressions.
Then multiply.**

9. $(7 \times 600) + (7 \times 400)$

_____

10. $(30 \times 6) + (70 \times 6)$

_____

Solve.   *Show your work.*

11. Antonia bought 6.25 yards of fabric for two school projects.
    She used 3.75 yards for the first project. She needs at least
    3 yards for her second project. Does Antonia have enough
    fabric? Explain how you can use estimation to find your answer.

    _____

    _____

12. Logan has 5.33 pounds of flour in his bakery. He bought
    11.59 pounds more flour. He needs at most 16 pounds of
    flour. Does Logan have enough flour? Explain how you
    can use estimation to find your answer.

    _____

    _____

Name _____ Date _____

Write a situation equation and a solution equation for each problem. Then solve the problem.

1. At the chicken ranch this morning there were 7,149 chicks. Later today some more chicks hatched. Now the ranch has 8,945 chicks. How many new chicks hatched today?

   _____   _____   _____

   Situation Equation   Solution Equation   Answer

2. The library had a large collection of books. Then the librarian ordered 2,000 more books. Now there are 12,358 books. How many books were there at the start?

   _____   _____   _____

   Situation Equation   Solution Equation   Answer

3. Rosa's parents collected $682 at their yard sale. They paid her for helping out that day. Now they have $662.25. How much money did Rosa's parents pay her?

   _____   _____   _____

   Situation Equation   Solution Equation   Answer

4. Marco sells caramel apples at the state fair. Today he sold 957 apples, and now he has 1,062 left to sell. How many caramel apples did Marco begin with?

   _____   _____   _____

   Situation Equation   Solution Equation   Answer

Find the unknown number. Use mental math if you can.

5. $80,000 + r = 82,000$ $r =$ _____

6. $0.005 + g = 0.105$ $g =$ _____

7. $r + 655 = 2,655$ $t =$ _____

8. $b + 0.36 = 25.36$ $b =$ _____

9. $6,500 = 7,000 - z$ $z =$ _____

10. $0.135 = 0.130 + c$ $c =$ _____

11. $f - 10,000 = 25,000$ $f =$ _____

12. $w - 2.5 = 0.3$ $w =$ _____

Remembering

Name the most sensible metric unit for each measurement.

1. The width of this button.

_____

2. The length of this pencil.

_____

3. The length of an ant.

_____

4. The longest dimension of your classroom.

_____

Write a whole or decimal number for each word name.

5. eight tenths

_____

6. twenty million

_____

7. five million, ten

_____

8. sixty-five thousand, four

_____

9. two hundred forty thousand, twelve

_____

10. six hundred four thousand

_____

Use the bar graph at the right to answer the following questions.

11. How many angelfish are in the aquarium?

_____

12. How many catfish and clown fish are there altogether?

_____

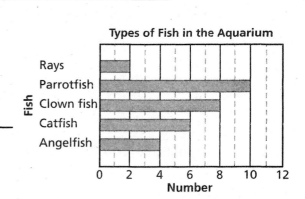

Situation and Solution Equations

Homework

Solve.   *Show your work.*

1. There are 476,092 fish in the city aquarium. That number of fish is 476,070 more fish than Nadia has in her aquarium. How many fish does Nadia have in her aquarium?

   _____

2. The Follett family traveled 2,145 miles this summer. They traveled 1,296 fewer miles than the Garcia family. How far did the Garcia family travel?

   _____

3. A 15-year-old boy built the largest house of cards on record. It was made of 15,714 cards. Today Michael built a house of cards that was made of 200 cards. How many more cards must he use to tie the record?

   _____

4. Maria wants to buy a new car. She will choose a green car or a silver car. The green car costs $16,898, and the silver car costs $1,059.75 less than the green car. What is the cost of the silver car?

   _____

5. A bakery has produced 5,285 loaves of bread so far this year. That number of loaves is 200 more loaves than the bakery produced last year. How many loaves of bread did the bakery produce last year?

   _____

Find the unknown number. Use mental math if you can.

6. $80,000 - q = 60,000$ $q =$ _____

7. $0.003 + p = 0.403$ $p =$ _____

8. $t - 8,500 = 9,000$ $t =$ _____

9. $b + 0.005 = 0.015$ $b =$ _____

10. $7,000,000 = 7,000,020 - z$ $z =$ _____

11. $37.96 = 39.96 - c$ $c =$ _____

12. $f - 986 = 12,000$ $f =$ _____

13. $w - 0.5 = 16$ $w =$ _____

Remembering

Write a situation equation and a solution equation for each problem. Then solve the problem.

1. There were 761 campers at a campground. After a number of campers went home, 659 campers remained at the campground. How many campers went home?

_____ _____ _____

Situation Equation   Solution Equation   Answer

2. After 143 new students arrived at Elm Street School, the enrollment was 1,356 students. How many students were enrolled before the new students arrived?

_____ _____ _____

Situation Equation   Solution Equation   Answer

3. April sold 200 stamps from her collection. Now she has 2,250 stamps. How many stamps were in her collection before the sale?

_____ _____ _____

Situation Equation   Solution Equation   Answer

Round to the nearest thousand.

4. 4,195 _____   5. 9,947 _____

6. 14,861 _____   7. 21,253 _____

Round to the nearest million.

8. 7,956,122 _____   9. 2,305,472 _____

10. 19,037,513 _____   11. 31,894,567 _____

Complete.

12. 48 in. = _____ ft   13. 36 ft = _____ yd   14. 7 yd = _____ ft

15. 3 yd = _____ in.   16. 2 ft = _____ in.   17. 36 in. = _____ yd

Comparison Problems

Name _____ **Date** _____

Complete one or more steps to solve each problem.   *Show your work.*

1. The regular price of an item is $9,985. The sale price of
   the item is $9,575. What is the difference between the
   sale price and the regular price of 10 items?

   _____

2. The Stein family plans to drive 125.7 miles to Middletown.
   They drive 62.5 miles before they have to go back
   10.2 miles for something they leave behind at a
   restaurant. How far from Middletown is the restaurant?

   _____

3. A toy factory made 15,000 toys and packed them in boxes
   of 10 each. The factory loaded 1,275 boxes on a delivery
   truck. How many boxes of toys were not loaded on
   the truck?

   _____

If the problem below has too much information, cross out the
extra information. If it has too little information, tell what
information is missing and add some possible missing information.
Then solve each problem.

4. Jillian has $125.67 saved for a stereo. The stereo costs $175
   and a television costs $295. She babysat for 4 hours this
   weekend and earned $7 an hour. How much more does
   she need to buy the stereo?

   _____

   _____

5. Michael ran a marathon to raise money for his favorite
   charity. Each sponsor agreed to pay $2 for each mile that
   he runs. He found a total of 6 sponsors. How much money
   did he raise?

   _____

   _____

Name _____ Date _____

Remembering

Round to the nearest 10,000 and the nearest 1,000.

1. 11,287 _____ _____

2. 45,732 _____ _____

3. 9,674 _____ _____

4. 89,135 _____ _____

Solve.   *Show your work.*

5. Last year Paco's bonsai tree was 6.75 centimeters tall. Today it is 8.40 centimeters tall. How much has the tree grown?

_____

6. This morning the temperature outside was 12.5°C. At noon it was 3.7 degrees warmer. What was the temperature at noon?

_____

7. A tomato seed is about 0.295 centimeters long. A cucumber seed is about 0.38 centimeters long.

Which seed is shorter? _____

How much shorter? _____

8. The Harrisons' dining room table with the table extension is 2.55 meters long. Without the extension the table is 2.25 meters long.

How long is the extension? _____

9. The perimeter of an equilateral triangle is 45 inches. A rectangle whose width is $\frac{1}{3}$ its length has a perimeter of 48 inches. Which figure has the *longest* side? Explain.

_____

_____

_____

_____

_____

_____

_____

_____

Two-Step Word Problems

Homework

1. **Connections** Lorenzo is a realtor and wants to become a member of the Million Dollar Club. To do this he must have at least $1 million in sales. So far, he has sold three homes for $256,900, $373,100, and $284,400. How can you quickly tell if these sales will allow him to be a member? If they can't, how much more does he need in sales?

_____

_____

_____

_____

_____

_____

_____

2. **Representation** Susan owns a card shop. She kept a record of the number of cards sold each month for one year. Then, she used a line graph to graph the data she collected. Explain what the line graph showed and how she might use the data.

_____

_____

_____

_____

_____

_____

_____

_____

_____

_____

3. **Communication** Hanna bought 4 pencils for 9¢ each, two notebooks for $1.58 each, and one pack of paper for $3.17 each. She paid with $10 and received $3.58 in change. Is the change correct? If not, identify the correct amount of change and why the error was made.

_____

_____

_____

_____

_____

_____

_____

4. **Reasoning and Proof** Can you draw a square that has an area and a perimeter that are not the same, such as, an area of 16 m² and a perimeter of 20 m? Explain your answer.

_____

_____

_____

_____

_____

_____

_____

_____

Name _____ **Date** _____

Remembering

Use the number 149,578.324 for exercises 1–6.

1. Increase the number by 5 more hundredths.

   _____

2. Decrease the number by 1 hundred thousand.

   _____

3. Decrease the number by 4 tens.

   _____

4. Increase the number by one hundred thirteen thousandths.

   _____

Solve.

5. Last week, Jillian drove 113.4 miles and 49.67 miles. So far this week, she has driven 152.89 miles. How many more miles will she have to drive this week to equal the miles driven last week?

   _____

Write a situation equation and a solution equation. Then solve.

6. The charity held a banquet as a fundraiser. After paying $1,796 in expenses from the money collected, the charity has $4,853 left. How much did the charity collect in all at the party?

   _____   _____   _____

   Situation Equation   Solution Equation   Answer

7. Skyler bought 214 more baseball cards at a flea market. He now has 567 baseball cards in his collection. How many baseball cards did he have before the purchase?

   _____   _____   _____

   Situation Equation   Solution Equation   Answer

Use Mathematical Processes

Homework

1. Use your ruler. Draw two lines that intersect. Label the lines and their point of intersection.

2. Name all the lines in your drawing.

   _____

3. Name four rays in your drawing.

   _____

4. Name four angles in your drawing.

   _____

5. Name two pairs of vertical angles formed by the intersecting lines below.

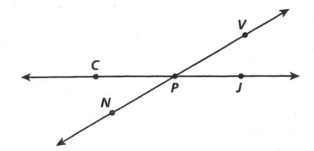

   _____

   _____

Use this diagram for exercises 6–9.

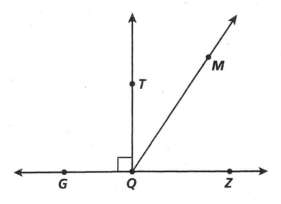

6. Which angles are complementary angles?

   _____

7. Which angles are supplementary angles?

   _____

8. Which angle is a straight angle?

   _____

9. Which angles are right angles?

   _____

Name _____ **Date** _____

Remembering

Solve.

1. 28 ÷ 4 = _____ **2.** 2 × 9 = _____ **3.** 54 ÷ 6 = _____ **4.** 8 × 0 = _____

5. 5 × 5 = _____ **6.** 63 ÷ 7 = _____ **7.** 3 × 4 = _____ **8.** 20 ÷ 5 = _____

9. 81 ÷ 9 = _____ **10.** 12 × 1 = _____ **11.** 15 ÷ 3 = _____ **12.** 6 × 5 = _____

13. 3 × 7 = _____ **14.** 18 ÷ 2 = _____ **15.** 7 × 6 = _____ **16.** 45 ÷ 9 = _____

17. 80 ÷ 8 = _____ **18.** 4 × 8 = _____ **19.** 0 ÷ 4 = _____ **20.** 9 × 1 = _____

21. Ah Lam and George worked on a puzzle from 5:27 P.M. to 7:11 P.M. How long did they work on the puzzle?

_____

22. Deacon's baby brother began napping at 12:17 P.M. He slept for 2 hours and 12 minutes. What time did he wake up?

_____

23. Rebecca and her friends finished watching a movie at 2:25 P.M. The movie was 1 hour and 43 minutes long. At what time did they start the movie?

_____

24. The Diaz family left to visit with friends at 10:43 A.M. They arrived at their friends' home at 1:09 P.M. How long was the trip?

_____

Name _____ **Date** _____

Homework

Complete each statement.

1. The total of the angle measures of a _____
   is always 180°.

2. The total of the angle measures of a _____
   is always 360°.

Write the measure of the unknown angle.

3.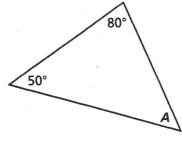

_____

4.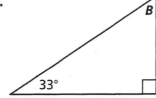

_____

5.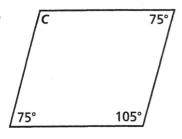

_____

6.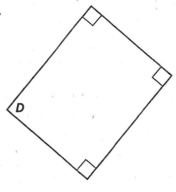

_____

7. One angle measure in an isosceles triangle is 100°.
   What is the measure of each of the other angles?

_____

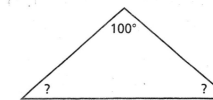

8. Two angle measures in a parallelogram are 80°.
   What is the measure of each of the other angles?

_____

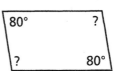

Remembering

Solve.

1. $2 \times 3 =$ _____   2. $77 \div 7 =$ _____   3. $8 \times 6 =$ _____   4. $10 \div 1 =$ _____

5. $49 \div 7 =$ _____   6. $10 \times 4 =$ _____   7. $4 \div 2 =$ _____   8. $7 \times 0 =$ _____

9. $4 \times 4 =$ _____   10. $64 \div 8 =$ _____   11. $1 \times 3 =$ _____   12. $12 \div 3 =$ _____

13. $10 \div 2 =$ _____   14. $8 \times 3 =$ _____   15. $6 \div 1 =$ _____   16. $2 \times 10 =$ _____

17. $11 \times 1 =$ _____   18. $72 \div 8 =$ _____   19. $7 \times 5 =$ _____   20. $0 \div 6 =$ _____

21. The Smiths hiked a trail marked "2 hours and 30 minutes." They took a 20-minute break. If they arrived at the end of the trail at 5:15 P.M., at what time did they start their hike?

_____

22. A play runs for 1 hour and 56 minutes. Part way through the play, there is a 15-minute break. If the play started at 4:30 P.M., what time will it finish?

_____

23. Kuri watched a movie that was 2 hours and 13 minutes long. She stopped the movie for 17 minutes. If she started watching at 11:30 A.M., at what time was her movie finished?

_____

Homework

In each row, circle all of the figures that look congruent.

1.

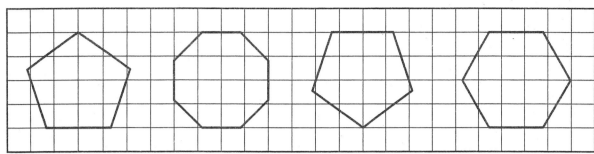

2.

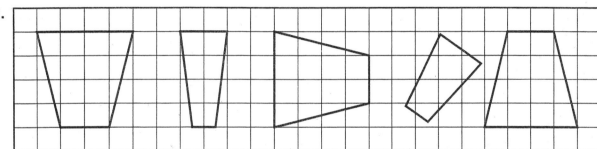

3.

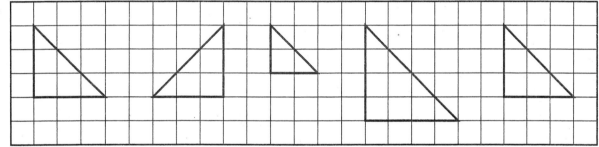

Write *always*, *sometimes*, or *never* to complete each statement.

4. A quadrilateral _____ has exactly two congruent angles.

5. A quadrilateral _____ has exactly three congruent angles.

6. Draw a figure that is congruent to the figure below.

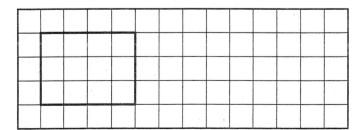

Name _____ Date _____

Remembering

Solve.

1. $0.123 + 1.30 =$ _____
2. $4.50 - 3.50 =$ _____
3. $1.27 + 2.40 =$ _____

4. $10.405 - 9.10 =$ _____
5. $2.8 + 2.7 =$ _____
6. $5.6 - 1.2 =$ _____

7. $3.08 + 4.10 =$ _____
8. $10.39 - 8.40 =$ _____
9. $8.54 + 2.039 =$ _____

10. $15.45 - 10.157 =$ _____
11. $0.87 + 0.10 =$ _____
12. $12.78 - 3.43 =$ _____

13. $7.609 - 2.01 =$ _____
14. $18.0 - 15.5 =$ _____
15. $20.05 + 10.05 =$ _____

16. $13.93 - 10.70 =$ _____
17. $9.7 + 1.2 =$ _____
18. $10.19 - 3.2 =$ _____

Complete the statements.

19. The total of the measures of two _____ angles is 180°.

20. The total of the measures of two _____ angles is 90°.

21. A _____ is a quadrilateral with two pairs of parallel sides.

22. A _____ is a quadrilateral with four right angles.

23. A _____ is a set of points forming a straight path extending infinitely in opposite directions.

24. A _____ is part of a line beginning at an endpoint and extending infinitely in one direction.

25. Two rays that share an endpoint form a(n) _____.

Write true or false.

26. A quadrilateral can have each of 4 angles a different measure. _____

27. A ray extends infinitely in both directions. _____

28. A polygon has sides that are line segments. _____

Compare and Contrast Polygons

Homework

The measure of each shaded angle is given. Write the measure of each angle that is not shaded.

1.

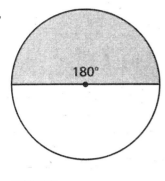

180°

____

2.

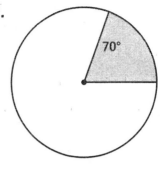

70°

____

3.

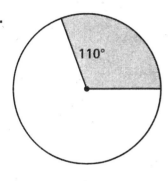

110°

____

4.

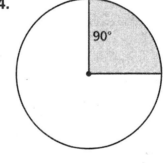

90°

____

5. Draw the figure after a turn of 180° clockwise.

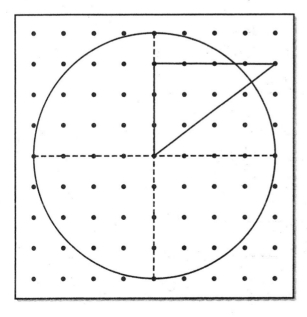

6. Draw the figure after a turn of 90° counterclockwise.

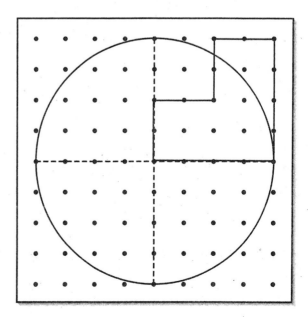

Remembering

Solve.

1. 4.09 + 4.38 = _____

2. 5.6 − 1.8 = _____

3. 16.0 + 2.316 = _____

4. 3.34 + 9.01 = _____

5. 11.70 − 10.358 = _____

6. 8.87 − 4.56 = _____

7. 0.43 + 1.07 = _____

8. 14.4 − 6.2 = _____

9. 14.34 + 11.48 = _____

10. 7.40 + 1.93 = _____

11. 13.4 − 6.28 = _____

12. 8.7 − 4.3 = _____

Solve the Factor Puzzles.

13.

72	
27	15

14.

	6
28	8

15.

8	16
	72

Complete the statements.

16. A _____ angle has a measure of 180°.

17. A(n) _____ angle has a measure less than 90°.

18. A(n) _____ angle has a measure greater than 90° and less than 180°.

19. _____ angles are pairs of opposite and congruent angles formed by intersecting lines.

20. A _____ angle has a measure of 90°.

21. _____ lines are always the same distance apart.

22. Lines that form right angles at the point of intersection are _____ lines.

23. _____ lines are lines that form acute or obtuse angles at the point of intersection.

Circles and Angles

Name _____ **Date** _____

Homework

1. In the space below, draw a figure that has at least one line of symmetry.

. . . .

. . . .

. . . .

. . . .

. . . .

. . . .

. . . .

. . . .

. . . .

. . . .

Consider these letters of the alphabet.

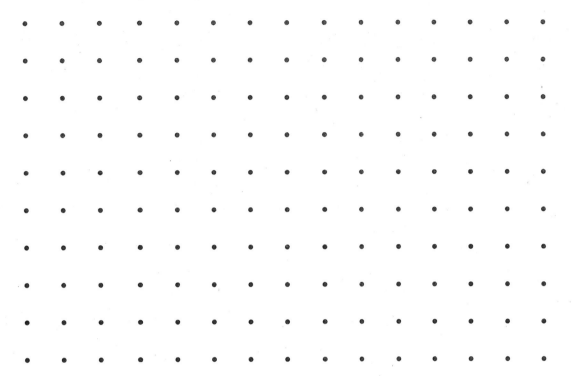

2. Which letters have line symmetry?

_____

_____

3. Which letters have rotational symmetry?

_____

_____

4. Which letters have line symmetry and rotational symmetry?

_____

_____

Remembering

Solve for the unknown number.

1. $1.4 + a = 5.7$ _____

2. $e - 1 = 1.75$ _____

3. $b + 0.25 = 1$ _____

4. $2.54 - m = 1.50$ _____

5. $5.6 + c = 6.0$ _____

6. $n - 3.7 = 1.7$ _____

7. $p + 10.01 = 10.45$ _____

8. $3.9 - d = 1.2$ _____

9. $0.5 + s = 0.8$ _____

10. $t - 4.13 = 0.40$ _____

11. $y + 0.8 = 4.1$ _____

12. $5.87 - h = 4.33$ _____

13. $7.4 + r = 9.5$ _____

14. $f - 9.7 = 4.3$ _____

15. $x + 1.88 = 4.91$ _____

16. $8.69 - g = 5.82$ _____

17. $10.04 + k = 11.00$ _____

18. $w - 5.0 = 11.73$ _____

19. What is the measure of the base of a triangle that has a height of 8 centimeters and an area of 24 square centimeters? Explain your thinking.

_____

_____

_____

_____

20. What is the measure of the length of a rectangle that has a width of 2 meters and a perimeter of 14 meters? Explain your thinking.

_____

_____

_____

_____

Round each decimal to the nearest whole number.

21. 12.3 _____

22. 25.6 _____

23. 19.8 _____

24. 10.45 _____

25. 99.9 _____

26. 100.09 _____

27. 41.67 _____

28. 35.70 _____

29. 50.51 _____

Homework

Use the circle graph to answer questions 1–3.

Annual Honolulu Weather

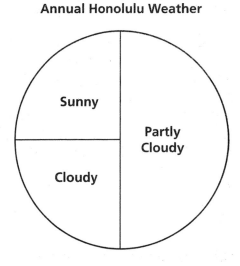

1. Which types of days occur equally often, according to the graph?

   _____

2. If you visited Honolulu for ten days, how many of those days would you expect it to be partly cloudy? Explain your reasoning.

   _____

   _____

   _____

   _____

3. Out of the 365 days in a year, about how many sunny days would you expect in Honolulu? How do you know?

   _____

   _____

   _____

4. Last night, Sharise studied for 60 minutes. The table below shows the subjects she studied and how long she studied each subject. Show the data on this circle graph.

Time Spent Studying

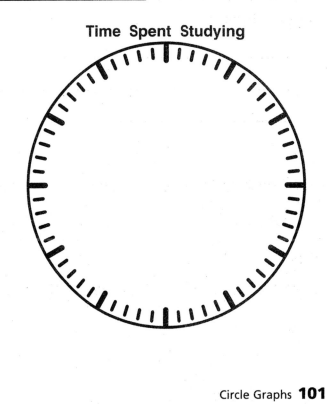

Time Spent Studying	
Subject	**Time**
Science	20 minutes
Reading	30 minutes
Spelling	10 minutes

Remembering

Use the line graph to answer each question.

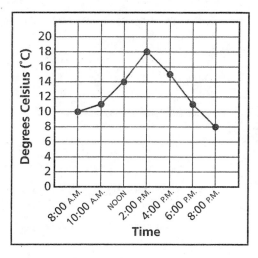

1. What was the temperature at 10:00 A.M.? _____

2. What was the temperature at noon? _____

3. What was the temperature at 4:00 P.M.? _____

4. At what time was the temperature 18°C? _____

5. What is the highest temperature? _____

6. What is the lowest temperature? _____

Find the perimeter of each figure.

7.

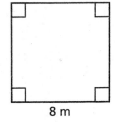

8 m

8.

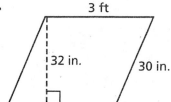

3 ft

32 in.

30 in.

9.

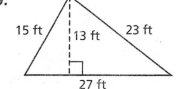

15 ft   13 ft   23 ft

27 ft

_____   _____   _____

10. What is the measure of the side length of a square that has an area of 49 square centimeters? Explain your thinking.

_____

_____

_____

11. What is the measure of the base of a triangle that has side lengths of 3 meters and 2 meters, and a perimeter of 9 meters? Explain your thinking.

_____

_____

_____

Homework

Use the given measures to estimate the circumference of each circle. Use 3 for π.

1.

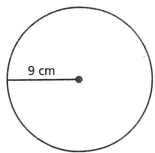

9 cm

_____

2.

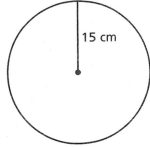

6 in.

_____

3.

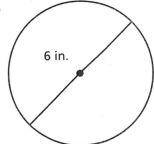

15 cm

_____

4. The circumference of a circle is 24 meters. About how long is a diameter of that circle?

_____

5. The circumference of a circle is 30 inches. About how long is a radius of that circle?

_____

Name _____ **Date** _____

Remembering

Solve for the unknown.

1. $z + 0.02 = 0.94$ _____

2. $12.4 - b = 8.5$ _____

3. $3.46 + d = 4.10$ _____

4. $p - 8.0 = 4.9$ _____

5. $m + 0.57 = 0.61$ _____

6. $2.44 - w = 1.00$ _____

7. $14.1 + e = 16.0$ _____

8. $n - 3.00 = 7.29$ _____

9. $a + 0.3 = 1.2$ _____

10. $8.56 - h = 2.50$ _____

11. $4.4 + h = 5.5$ _____

12. $s - 8.21 = 5.47$ _____

13. $r + 14.1 = 18.7$ _____

14. $7.8 - x = 6.9$ _____

15. $0.51 + t = 1.00$ _____

16. $y - 0.4 = 0.1$ _____

17. $c + 7.16 = 9.01$ _____

18. $1.32 - f = 0.74$ _____

Find the area of each shaded region. Explain your thinking.

19.

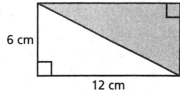

6 cm

12 cm

_____

_____

_____

_____

_____

20.

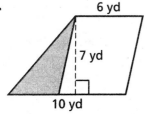

6 yd

7 yd

10 yd

_____

_____

_____

_____

_____

21.

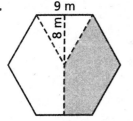

9 m

8 m

_____

_____

_____

_____

Circumference

Name _____ **Date** _____

Homework

Write an equation that shows the total of all the unit fractions.
Each bar is 1 whole.

1.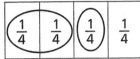

_____

2.

_____

Write an equation that shows the total of the circled parts.

3.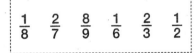

_____

4.

_____

Add.

5. $\frac{1}{8} + \frac{4}{8} =$ _____

6. $\frac{2}{7} + \frac{3}{7} =$ _____

7. $\frac{3}{9} + \frac{2}{9} + \frac{1}{9} + \frac{2}{9} =$ _____

8. Circle the unit fractions.

$$\frac{1}{8} \quad \frac{2}{7} \quad \frac{8}{9} \quad \frac{1}{6} \quad \frac{2}{3} \quad \frac{1}{2}$$

9. Put hats on $\frac{3}{5}$ of the heads.

10. This car is $\frac{1}{5}$ of the train.
    Use rectangles to draw the whole train.

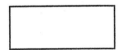

Use the circle graph to answer questions 11–12.

11. What fraction of the clothes are hats? _____

12. What fraction of the clothes are shirts? _____

13. I practiced soccer for $\frac{1}{4}$ hour and volleyball for $\frac{2}{4}$ hour.
    What fraction of an hour did I practice? _____

14. The porch floor has 9 identical boards. Jody painted 4 boards
    and Chris painted 3 boards. What fraction of the porch floor
    have they painted so far? _____

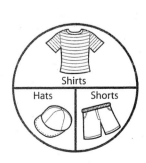

Build Unit Fractions **105**

Name _____

Date _____

Remembering

Find the unknown numbers.

1. $3d = 21$

$d =$ _____

2. $4d + 1 = 17$

$d =$ _____

3. $z = (8 \times 8) + (2 \times 5)$

$z =$ _____

4. $7 \times (6 + 3) = t$

$t =$ _____

5. $63 \div s = 7$

$s =$ _____

6. $\frac{1}{6}k = 8$

$k =$ _____

7. $32 + p = 40$

$p =$ _____

8. $v \div 7 = 56$

$v =$ _____

9. $4r - 4 = 8$

$r =$ _____

Find the perimeter and area.

10.

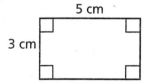

5 cm

3 cm

$P =$ _____

$A =$ _____

11.

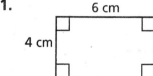

6 cm

4 cm

$P =$ _____

$A =$ _____

12.

2 cm

7 cm

$P =$ _____

$A =$ _____

Solve.

Show your work.

13. A group of scientists discovered 9 stegosaurus footprints and 6 times as many tyrannosaurus footprints. How many dinosaur footprints were there altogether?

_____

14. The scientists discovered 21 tyrannosaurus eggs. Some eggs were broken. There were 6 times as many unbroken eggs as broken eggs. How many eggs were not broken?

_____

Build Unit Fractions

Homework

Circle the greater fraction. Then write the correct sign (> or <) between them.

1. $\frac{1}{3}$ $\frac{1}{4}$

2. $\frac{1}{9}$ $\frac{1}{7}$

3. $\frac{1}{98}$ $\frac{1}{99}$

4. $\frac{5}{7}$ 1

5. 1 $\frac{7}{8}$

6. 1 $\frac{51}{52}$

7. $\frac{5}{6}$ $\frac{4}{6}$

8. $\frac{51}{68}$ $\frac{53}{68}$

9. $\frac{2}{5}$ $\frac{2}{8}$

10. $\frac{1}{10}$ $\frac{1}{2}$

11. $\frac{9}{10}$ $\frac{9}{100}$

12. $\frac{3}{5}$ $\frac{3}{4}$

13. Claire and Ramona each have a banana the same size. Claire cuts hers into fourths. Ramona cuts hers into sixths. Whose banana has bigger pieces?

Show your work.

_____

14. Jorge rode his bicycle $\frac{2}{5}$ of a mile. Andrew rode his $\frac{4}{5}$ of a mile. Julio rode his $\frac{3}{5}$ of a mile. Who rode the farthest?

_____

15. At a basketball game, Tessa scored $\frac{1}{10}$ of the points, Erica scored $\frac{1}{12}$ of the points, and Kenya scored $\frac{1}{9}$ of the points. Who scored the most points?

_____

16. Tony and Kurt are reading the same book. Tony has read $\frac{136}{200}$ of the book. Kurt has read $\frac{124}{200}$ of the book. Who has read more of it?

_____

Remembering

Solve the Factor Puzzles.

1.

	__	__
__	7	
__	28	36

__ __

2.

	5
16	8

3.

40	56
	35

4.

12	14
60	

5.

3	
18	24

6.

	21
20	35

7.

16	32
	24

8.

40	55
32	

Find the perimeter and area.

9.

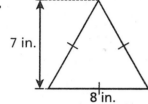

7 in.

8 in.

P = _____

A = _____

10.

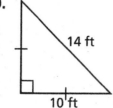

14 ft

10 ft

P = _____

A = _____

11.

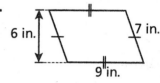

6 in.   7 in.

9 in.

P = _____

A = _____

Solve.

Show your work.

12. At your lemonade stand you charge $0.50 for a half cup and $0.75 for a full cup. At the end of the day, you see that 12 cups have been used and you have made $8.00. How many of each size of drink did you sell?

_____

13. Anna is 3 years older than Laura. The product of their ages is double the sum of their ages. How old are they?

_____

_____

Compare Fractions

Homework

Name _____ **Date** _____

Add or subtract.

1. $\frac{1}{6} + \frac{4}{6} =$ _____

2. $\frac{3}{7} + \frac{2}{7} + \frac{1}{7} =$ _____

3. $\frac{3}{5} - \frac{1}{5} =$ _____

Find n or d.

4. $\frac{7}{8} - \frac{2}{8} = \frac{n}{8}$

   $n =$ _____

5. $\frac{3}{4} - \frac{1}{4} = \frac{2}{d}$

   $d =$ _____

6. $\frac{4}{15} + \frac{6}{15} + \frac{2}{15} = \frac{n}{15}$

   $n =$ _____

7. $\frac{2}{d} + \frac{2}{d} + \frac{2}{d} + \frac{2}{d} = \frac{8}{15}$

   $d =$ _____

8. $\frac{5}{12} + \frac{2}{12} + \frac{3}{12} = \frac{10}{d}$

   $d =$ _____

9. $\frac{1}{d} + \frac{1}{d} + \frac{1}{d} + \frac{1}{d} + \frac{1}{d} = \frac{d}{d}$

   $d =$ _____

Circle the greater fraction.

10. $\frac{1}{5}$ $\frac{1}{9}$

11. $\frac{3}{d}$ $\frac{7}{d}$

12. $\frac{8}{d}$ $\frac{6}{d}$

13. What is $\frac{n}{d}$? _____

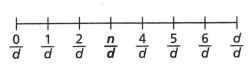

14. What fraction is circled? _____

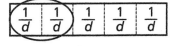

15. What fraction of the class likes winter or summer best? _____

16. What fraction of the class likes fall best? _____

17. Use the circle graph to find d.

$\frac{3}{4} + \frac{2}{d} = 1$ $d =$ _____

Favorite Seasons

18. The grade 5 class sold cheese for a fundraiser. What fraction of the orders did each of the four students take?

_____

_____

_____

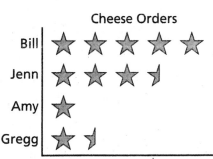

Cheese Orders

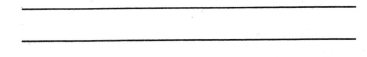
= 4 orders

Name _____ **Date** _____

Remembering

Add or subtract.

1. 0.75 + 0.2 = _____

2. 3.5 + 2.5 = _____

3. 0.5 − 0.2 = _____

4. 0.175 + 0.250 = _____

5. 5.835 + 1.35 = _____

6. 3.7 − 1.6 = _____

7. 0.072 − 0.03 = _____

8. 0.001 + 0.959 = _____

9. 8.206 + 1.5 = _____

10. 3.504 − 1.25 = _____

11. 4.0 − 0.8 = _____

12. 6.34 − 2.28 = _____

Find the area of the shaded region.

13.

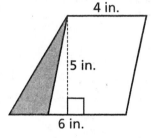

4 in.

5 in.

6 in.

_____

14.

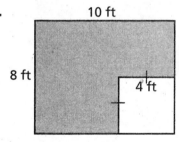

10 ft

8 ft

4 ft

_____

Use the bar graph to solve problems 15–17.

15. How many students in the class have at least 1 brother or sister?

_____

16. How many more students have 1 brother or sister than have 3?

_____

17. The number of students with 2 children in the family is double the number of students with how many children in the family?

_____

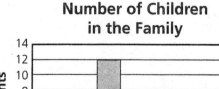

Number of Children in the Family

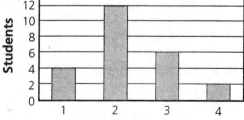

Students

Children in Family

Subtract Fractions

Homework

Add or subtract.

1. $\frac{4}{7} - \frac{1}{7} =$ _____

2. $\frac{6}{52} + \frac{4}{52} =$ _____

3. $\frac{8}{15} + \frac{7}{15} =$ _____

4. $\frac{5}{60} + \frac{12}{60} =$ _____

5. $\frac{6}{37} + \frac{6}{37} =$ _____

6. $\frac{50}{100} - \frac{40}{100} =$ _____

Find *n* or *d*.

7. $1 - \frac{7}{13} = \frac{n}{d}$

$\frac{n}{d} =$ _____

8. $1 - \frac{5}{40} = \frac{n}{d}$

$\frac{n}{d} =$ _____

9. $\frac{5}{8} + \frac{n}{d} = 1$

$\frac{n}{d} =$ _____

10. $\frac{3}{16} + \frac{n}{d} = 1$

$\frac{n}{d} =$ _____

11. $\frac{20}{25} + \frac{n}{d} = 1$

$\frac{n}{d} =$ _____

12. $\frac{150}{200} + \frac{n}{d} = 1$

$\frac{n}{d} =$ _____

Solve.

13. Hannah's joke made $\frac{25}{32}$ of the class laugh. What fraction of the class did not laugh at her joke?

_____

14. Tyler's joke made $\frac{28}{32}$ of the class laugh. What fraction of the class did not laugh at his joke?

_____

15. Who told the funnier joke?

_____

16. In Mrs. Lopez' class, $\frac{9}{24}$ of the students take the bus to school and $\frac{8}{24}$ come in a car. The rest of the students walk to school. What fraction of the students walk?

_____

Name _____ **Date** _____

Remembering

Find the unknown.

1. $6b = 42$

$b =$ _____

2. $5c + 1 = 36$

$c =$ _____

3. $d = (4 \times 5) + (2 \times 9)$

$d =$ _____

4. $64 \div s = 8$

$s =$ _____

5. $\frac{1}{6}m = 9$

$m =$ _____

6. $28 + p = 32$

$p =$ _____

7. $7(5 + 3) = t$

$t =$ _____

8. $k = 4(6 + 3)$

$k =$ _____

9. $6v = 72$

$v =$ _____

Label each angle as acute, obtuse, or right.

10.

11.

12.

13.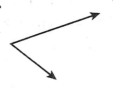

14.

_____ _____ _____ _____ _____

Solve.

15. The bookstore staff sold 700 books in one week. If they sold the same number of books each day, how many books had they sold after 3 days?

_____

16. The grade 5 students are raising money for a trip that will cost $175. Students have taken orders for 92 buckets of frozen cookie dough at a price of $6.00 each. If the students have to pay $4.00 for each bucket, will they make enough money for their trip?

_____

Fractional Addends of Ones

Homework

What fraction of each group of ice cream cones has a cherry?

1.
_____

2.
_____

3.
_____

4. Answer the Puzzled Penguin's letter.

Dear Math Student,

I just learned that $\frac{1}{3}$ of the students in my class play soccer. My friend in another class says that $\frac{1}{3}$ of the students in her class also play soccer. I said, "Oh, then the same number of students play soccer in each class." She answered, "No, I don't think that's true."

Now I'm confused. If the same **fraction** of students play soccer, wouldn't that mean that the same **number** of students play soccer? Who do you think is right? Can you explain this to me?

Thank you,

Puzzled Penguin

_____

_____

_____

_____

_____

_____

_____

_____

_____

_____

Remembering

Name _____ **Date** _____

1. 692 + 463 = _____

2. 1,843 + 199 = _____

3. 567 + 4,968 = _____

4. 746 − 99 = _____

5. 2,420 − 398 = _____

6. 62,685 − 810 = _____

7. 6,874 + 552 = _____

8. 7,502 + 2,539 = _____

9. 29,463 + 14,054 = _____

10. 3,985 − 1,775 = _____

Find the perimeter and area of each figure.

11.

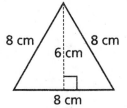

8 cm   8 cm
6 cm
8 cm

P = _____

A = _____

12.

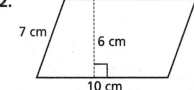

7 cm   6 cm
10 cm

P = _____

A = _____

13.

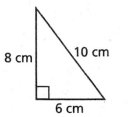

8 cm   10 cm
6 cm

P = _____

A = _____

14.

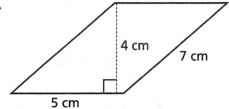

4 cm   7 cm
5 cm

P = _____

A = _____

Solve.

15. Hayley has twice as many stamps in her collection as Kevin does. Kevin has three times as many stamps as Jen. If Kevin has 60 stamps, how many do the three friends have altogether?

_____

16. Jon has 32 books on his shelf. He has 7 times the number of mystery books as science fiction. How many of each kind does he have?

_____

Relate Fractions and Wholes

Name the mixed number shown by the shaded parts.

   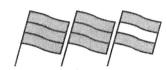

1. _____   2. _____   3. _____

Write the mixed number as an improper fraction.

4. $2\frac{1}{3}$ = _____   5. $4\frac{2}{5}$ = _____   6. $3\frac{3}{4}$ = _____   7. $1\frac{5}{8}$ = _____

Write the improper fraction as a mixed number.

8. $\frac{7}{6}$ = _____   9. $\frac{8}{3}$ = _____   10. $\frac{9}{2}$ = _____   11. $\frac{10}{7}$ = _____

Complete. Give the answer as a mixed number.

12. $\frac{3}{5} + \frac{4}{5}$ = _____   13. $\frac{6}{4} + \frac{3}{4}$ = _____

14. $\frac{2}{9} + \frac{8}{9}$ = _____   15. $7 + \frac{2}{3}$ = _____

Solve.   *Show your work.*

16. Alicia walked $\frac{7}{8}$ mile on Saturday and $\frac{6}{8}$ mile on Sunday.
    How far did she walk over the weekend? Give the
    answer as a mixed number.

    _____

17. The dark chain is $\frac{5}{12}$ yard long. The white one is
    $\frac{9}{12}$ yard long. How long will they be if they are
    joined? Give the answer as a mixed number.

    _____

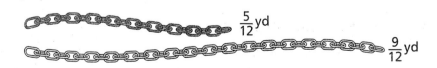

$\frac{5}{12}$ yd

$\frac{9}{12}$ yd

Remembering

Solve.

1. The dog has gone $\frac{5}{8}$ of the way across the yard. How much farther does it have to go to reach the gate? _____

2. The cat has gone $\frac{7}{16}$ of the way across the yard. How much farther does it have to go to reach the gate? _____

3. I cleaned $\frac{6}{9}$ of my room, and my friend cleaned $\frac{2}{9}$ of my room. How much of my room do we still have to clean? _____

4. Mrs. Spencer's class is signing up to play sports. $\frac{8}{26}$ of the students want to play soccer and $\frac{12}{26}$ want to play basketball. The rest of the students want to play baseball. What fraction of the students wants to play baseball? _____

Solve the Factor Puzzles.

5.

5	
25	35

6.

	6
12	8

7.

30	27
	18

8.

	64
36	72

9.

9	12
21	

10.

4	
10	25

Fractions Greater Than One

Homework

Complete each equation. Express answers as mixed numbers.

1. $\frac{3}{5} + \frac{4}{5} =$ ____

2. $\frac{6}{4} + \frac{3}{4} =$ ____

3. $4\frac{2}{9} + 2\frac{7}{9} =$ ____

4. $1\frac{7}{8} + 3\frac{3}{8} =$ ____

5. $4\frac{1}{2} + 5\frac{1}{2} =$ ____

6. $3\frac{1}{7} + 2\frac{1}{7} =$ ____

7. $1\frac{5}{7} + 1\frac{3}{7} =$ ____

8. $50\frac{1}{3} + 50\frac{1}{3} =$ ____

9. A group of campers hiked for $5\frac{3}{4}$ hours today and $6\frac{3}{4}$ hours yesterday. How many hours did they hike in all? _____

10. What fractional parts are shown on the number line below? _____

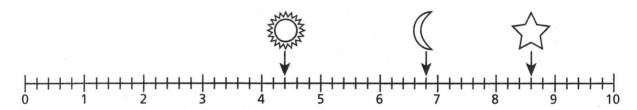

11. What mixed number is marked by the sun? _____

12. What mixed number is marked by the moon? _____

13. What mixed number is marked by the star? _____

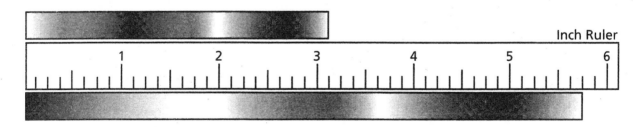

14. What fractional parts are shown on the inch ruler above? _____

15. How long is the ribbon on top? _____

16. How long is the ribbon on the bottom? _____

17. If you place the two ribbons end-to-end, how long are they? _____

Name _____ **Date** _____

Remembering

Add.

1. 363.12
   + 422.51

2. 86,435.717
   + 3,385.122

3. 1,382,104.4050
   + 34,208,010.6334

Subtract.

4. 945.3
   − 412.1

5. 12,532.36
   − 10,801.45

6. 9,112,001.880
   − 8,750,500.224

Solve.   *Show your work.*

7. Sebastián is wrapping a present for his friend. He has 5 kinds of ribbon, 4 types of wrapping paper, and 2 styles of bows. How many different ways can he wrap the present? _____

8. The Mahoney family stayed at the seashore for 18 days. They stayed 3 times as long as the Adorno family. How long did the Adorno family stay? _____

9. Lisle planted 4 rows of tomatoes with 6 tomato plants in each row. He also planted 3 rows of squash with 7 squash plants in each row. How many plants did Lisle plant in all? _____

10. Which triangles are equilateral? _____

11. Which triangles are isosceles? _____

12. Which triangles are scalene? _____

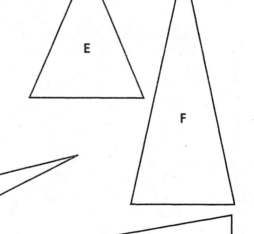

Add Fractions Greater Than One

Homework

Subtract.

1. $1\frac{7}{9} - \frac{4}{9} =$ ___

2. $4\frac{6}{7} - 2\frac{5}{7} =$ ___

3. $6\frac{4}{5} - 3\frac{2}{5} =$ ___

4. $25\frac{5}{8} - 10\frac{1}{8} =$ ___

5. $2 - \frac{1}{3} =$ ___

6. $5\frac{3}{8} - 2\frac{7}{8} =$ ___

7. $2\frac{1}{6} - 1\frac{5}{6} =$ ___

8. $7\frac{2}{5} - 3\frac{3}{5} =$ ___

Solve.   *Show your work.*

9. I made a clay snake $9\frac{5}{8}$ inches long, but a section $1\frac{7}{8}$ inches long broke off. How long is the snake now?

_____

10. Deacon had $12\frac{1}{3}$ ounces of juice, but he drank $3\frac{2}{3}$ ounces. How much juice is left?

_____

How long will each log be after a piece is cut off? Check your answer by adding the lengths of the two pieces.

11. cut off $3\frac{2}{6}$ feet $10\frac{5}{6}$ feet total

___ feet left

12. cut off $4\frac{3}{4}$ feet $7\frac{1}{4}$ feet total

___ feet left

13. cut off $6\frac{2}{9}$ feet $11\frac{4}{9}$ feet total

___ feet left

14. cut off $3\frac{2}{5}$ feet $6\frac{2}{5}$ feet total

___ feet left

Name _____ **Date** _____

Remembering

Write > or < to show which is greater.

1. 209 _____ 290

2. 30,502 _____ 30,052

3. 128,779 _____ 127,999

4. 360.099 _____ 306.990

5. 41,772.012 _____ 41,770.228

6. 100.096 _____ 100.10

Solve. Use multiplication or division.

Show your work.

7. Jenny prepared 4 rows for bean plants. She can fit 16 bean plants in each row. How many bean plants can she grow?

_____

8. A school bus can carry 60 students. How many buses should a school order to take 520 students on a trip?

_____

9. A hummingbird's heart beats about 4 times in one second while it is resting. At this rate, how many times does its heart beat in one hour? in one day?

_____

Label each triangle acute, right, or obtuse. Briefly explain.

10.

_____

_____

11.

_____

_____

12.

_____

_____

13.

_____

_____

Subtract Mixed Numbers

Homework

Subtract.

1. $\frac{4}{5} - \frac{1}{5} =$ ____

2. $9\frac{5}{8} - 3\frac{3}{8} =$ ____

3. $5\frac{1}{6} - 2\frac{5}{6} =$ ____

4. $18\frac{4}{9} - 10\frac{5}{9} =$ ____

5. $3 - \frac{1}{4} =$ ____

6. $6\frac{3}{8} - 2\frac{7}{8} =$ ____

7. $2\frac{1}{3} - 1\frac{2}{3} =$ ____

8. $6\frac{5}{7} - 3\frac{3}{7} =$ ____

Solve.   *Show your work.*

9. Cory planned to practice the piano for $1\frac{1}{4}$ hours but he spent $\frac{3}{4}$ hour playing computer games. How long did he actually practice the piano?

   _____

10. Hala made $\frac{4}{10}$ of the hits at the baseball game and Ernestina made $\frac{1}{10}$. Who made more hits? How many more?

    _____

The campers at Tall Pines Camp saw some animal tracks in the woods. They measured them and made a table showing all the different lengths. Use the table to complete exercises 11–15.

Animal Track	Length
Raccoon	$1\frac{2}{8}$ in.
Fox	$3\frac{1}{8}$ in.
Deer	$1\frac{6}{8}$ in.
Moose	$5\frac{7}{8}$ in.

11. Which track is longer, the raccoon track or the fox track? by how much?

    _____

12. How much shorter is the deer track than the moose track?

    _____

13. How much longer is the fox track than the deer track?

    _____

14. How much shorter is the raccoon track than the deer track?

    _____

15. List the animal tracks in order from the longest to the shortest.

    _____

Name _____ **Date** _____

Remembering

Find the unknown number in each equation.

1. $s = 4 + (3 \times 9)$ $s =$ _____   **2.** $12 = t - 7$ $t =$ _____

3. $k = 28 - (2 \times 6)$ $k =$ _____   **4.** $(14 - 9) \times 3 = m$ $m =$ _____

5. $y = (112 - 94) \times 4$ $y =$ _____   **6.** $36 = b + 12$ $b =$ _____

7. $h - 15 = 52$ $h =$ _____   **8.** $70 = p + (3 \times 6)$ $p =$ _____

Solve.

Show your work.

9. Lina has $20 with her. She buys 3 items that cost
$6.98, $4.49, and $7.75. Can she also buy a bottle of
juice for $1.29?

_____

10. Asim is 11 years old. He went on the bus with his mom,
his aunt, his two younger brothers, and his aunt's
7-year-old daughter. Tickets cost $1.60 for an adult and
$0.80 for a child. How much did the trip cost?

_____

11. Graph the data in the table on the circle below.
Don't forget to label the graph.

_____

Favorite Fruit	
Fruit	**Number**
Orange	16
Banana	2
Apple	4
Grape	8
Other	6

Comparison Situations

Homework

The workers at Willow Green Animal Shelter recently took in four new animals. They decided to measure each animal and record the measurements in a table. Use this table to complete exercises 1–4.

1. Which is longer, the pig or the dog? how much longer?

_____

2. How much shorter is the duck than the cat?

_____

3. How much longer is the dog than the duck?

_____

4. How much shorter is the cat than the pig?

_____

Animal	Length
Duck	$1\frac{5}{12}$ ft
Cat	$2\frac{8}{12}$ ft
Dog	$3\frac{10}{12}$ ft
Pig	$3\frac{4}{12}$ ft

Troy and Francisco decided to make gingerbread people using this recipe. Use it to complete exercises 5–9.

5. Troy has $\frac{3}{4}$ cup of sugar and Francisco has $\frac{2}{4}$ cup. How much sugar do they have in all?

_____

6. Will they have any sugar left after making the cookies? How much?

_____

7. Troy and Francisco have $\frac{3}{4}$ cups of flour. How much more do they need?

_____

8. At the party, the girls ate $\frac{5}{8}$ of the cookies and the boys ate $\frac{3}{8}$. How many cookies are left?

_____

9. Troy and Francisco started with 1 pound of butter. How much do they have now?

_____

Gingerbread People
$\frac{1}{4}$ pound butter
1 cup sugar
$\frac{1}{4}$ teaspoon salt
$2\frac{1}{4}$ cups flour
1 cup molasses
$1\frac{3}{4}$ teaspoons soda
$2\frac{1}{4}$ teaspoons ginger
2 eggs

Name _____

Date _____

Remembering

Circle the greater fraction in each pair. Write a greater than (>) or less than (<) sign between them.

1. $\dfrac{6}{700}$ $\bigcirc$ $\dfrac{4}{700}$

2. $3\dfrac{4}{8}$ $\bigcirc$ $3\dfrac{7}{8}$

3. $7\dfrac{9}{10}$ $\bigcirc$ $7\dfrac{5}{10}$

4. $10\dfrac{1}{4}$ $\bigcirc$ $9\dfrac{8}{4}$

Find each unknown number.

5. $7a = 56$ $a =$ _____

6. $9 \times d = 81$ $d =$ _____

7. $42 \times 0 = m$ $m =$ _____

8. $27 \div 3 = a$ $a =$ _____

9. $36 \div 12 = q$ $q =$ _____

10. $n \times 5 = 75$ $n =$ _____

11. $y \times 4 = 48$ $y =$ _____

12. $72 = 8h$ $h =$ _____

Find the perimeter of each figure.

Show your work.

13.

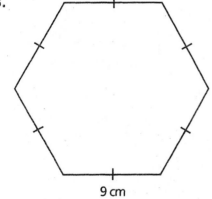

9 cm

Perimeter = _____

14.

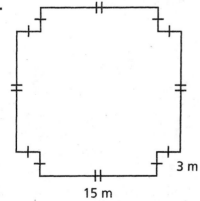

3 m

15 m

Perimeter = _____

Mixed Practice with Like Fractions

Homework

1. Write a chain of equivalent fractions for the shaded parts.

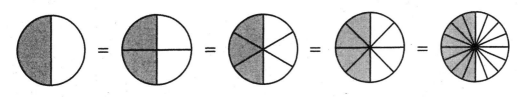

_____ = _____ = _____ = _____ = _____

Use the number lines to complete exercises 2–7.

Fourths

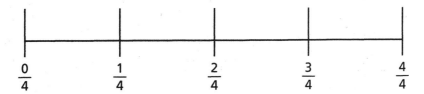

Eighths

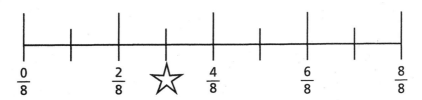

Twelfths

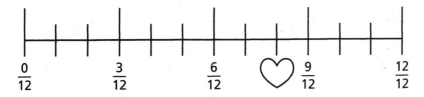

2. What fraction is marked by the star? _____

3. What fraction is marked by the heart? _____

4. If you have $\frac{3}{4}$ cup of flour, how many eighths do

you have? _____

5. If you have $\frac{3}{12}$ of an orange, how many fourths do

you have? _____

6. Which is larger, $\frac{3}{4}$ or $\frac{10}{12}$? _____

7. Give two equivalent fractions for $\frac{6}{8}$. _____

Name _____ Date _____

Remembering

Add.

1. 4,560 + 52,973 = _____

2. 581,002 + 26,596 = _____

3. 4,300,129 + 3,426 = _____

4. 321,589 + 1,000,000 = _____

5. 8,601,308 + 585,434 = _____

6. 2,474,767 + 5,687,136 = _____

Subtract.

7. 398,000 − 213,546 = _____

8. 5,439,456 − 1,217,388 = _____

9. 984,305 − 411,900 = _____

10. 1,473,862 − 24,540 = _____

11. 846,549 − 2,308 = _____

12. 7,458,100 − 3,457 = _____

Round to the nearest thousand.

13. 14,541 = _____

14. 1,543,200 = _____

15. 5,081 = _____

16. 800,760 = _____

17. 3,894,956 = _____

18. 27,403 = _____

This graph represents a survey of students who were asked to name their favorite type of movie.

19. Which types of movie are equally popular? _____

20. Which type of movie is twice as popular as romance movies? _____

21. If 50 students named action as their favorite type of movie, how many students named horror as their favorite? _____

Favorite Movies

Show your work.

Solve.

22. The Carsons drove 654 km on Monday, 792 km on Tuesday, and 517 km on Wednesday. How many kilometers did they drive in total over the 3 days?

_____

23. Otis is 3,750 days old and Casey is 4,539 days old. How many days older than Otis is Casey?

_____

Discover Equivalent Fractions

Homework

Name _____ **Date** _____

1. Write a chain of equivalent fractions for the shaded parts.

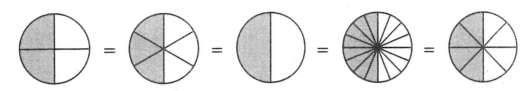

_____ = _____ = _____ = _____ = _____

Write the multiplier or divisor for each pair of equivalent fractions.

2. $\frac{4}{12} = \frac{1}{3}$

Divisor = _____

3. $\frac{2}{9} = \frac{6}{27}$

Multiplier = _____

4. $\frac{6}{60} = \frac{1}{10}$

Divisor = _____

5. $\frac{3}{10} = \frac{15}{50}$

Multiplier = _____

6. $\frac{21}{56} = \frac{3}{8}$

Divisor = _____

7. $\frac{5}{7} = \frac{30}{42}$

Multiplier = _____

8. $\frac{4}{16} = \frac{1}{4}$

Divisor = _____

9. $\frac{5}{9} = \frac{25}{45}$

Multiplier = _____

10. $\frac{10}{60} = \frac{1}{6}$

Divisor = _____

11. $\frac{3}{7} = \frac{18}{42}$

Multiplier = _____

12. $\frac{24}{56} = \frac{3}{7}$

Divisor = _____

13. $\frac{5}{6} = \frac{35}{42}$

Multiplier = _____

Complete each exercise about the pairs of fraction bars.

14. What equivalent fractions are shown? _____

15. Identify the multiplier. _____

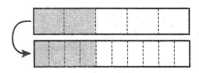

16. What equivalent fractions are shown? _____

17. Identify the divisor. _____

18. Write a chain with at least six equivalent fractions.

_____ = _____ = _____ = _____ = _____ = _____

Name _____   **Date** _____

Remembering

Solve.

1.   1,000.98
   +   265.03
	2. 100,289
	   − 91,460
		3. 312,642
		   + 89,435

4.   10.651
   −   8.092
	5. 0.354
	   + 9.717
		6. 12.603
		   − 2.711

Find the area of each triangle.

7.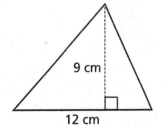

8.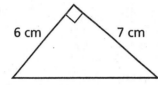

9.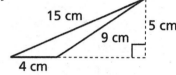

A = _____   A = _____   A = _____

Solve.   *Show your work.*

10. A restaurant has 60 plates. One night, 9 groups of
people with 6 people in each group ate dinner at the
restaurant. How many plates were still clean at the end
of the night?

_____

11. Clara has a garden that is 7 feet wide and 4 feet long.
She has 30 tomato plants to put in the garden. Each
plant needs 1 square foot of space. How many leftover
plants will Clara have?

_____

12. Carol's bookshelf has 4 shelves with 6 books on each.
Her brother Robert has 3 shelves with 7 books on each.
How many books do they have altogether?

_____

Equivalent Fractions and Multipliers

Name _____ **Date** _____

Find _n_ or _d._

1. $\frac{3}{4} = \frac{n}{12}$ $n =$ _____

2. $\frac{1}{5} = \frac{n}{30}$ $n =$ _____

3. $\frac{6}{42} = \frac{n}{7}$ $n =$ _____

4. $\frac{4}{16} = \frac{2}{d}$ $d =$ _____

5. $\frac{2}{7} = \frac{n}{49}$ $n =$ _____

6. $\frac{3}{5} = \frac{30}{d}$ $d =$ _____

7. $\frac{21}{28} = \frac{n}{4}$ $n =$ _____

8. $\frac{7}{63} = \frac{1}{d}$ $d =$ _____

Answer the questions about the circle graph. Simplify your answers.

Rows of Garden Vegetables

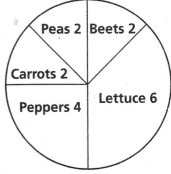

9. What fraction of the vegetables are peppers? _____

10. What fraction of the vegetables are beets? _____

11. What fraction of the vegetables are lettuce? _____

12. Arnetta planted the lettuce and the peppers. What fraction of the vegetables did she plant? _____

Answer the questions about the bar graph. Simplify your answers.

13. How many balloons are there altogether? _____

14. What fraction of the balloons are red? _____

15. What fraction of the balloons are white? _____

16. What fraction of the balloons are blue? _____

17. Estevan filled 20 balloons. Did he fill more or less than half? _____ How do you know?

_____

_____

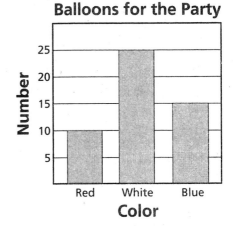

Balloons for the Party

Name _____   **Date** _____

Remembering

Find the unknown number in each equation.

1. $6r + 2 = 56$

   $r =$ _____

2. $3(7 + 2) = f$

   $f =$ _____

3. $(8 \times 5) + (3 \times 7) = k$

   $k =$ _____

4. $3 + 2t = 13$

   $t =$ _____

5. $9(6 - 1) = g$

   $g =$ _____

6. $(4 \times 6) - (5 \times 2) = b$

   $b =$ _____

7. $4s - 6 = 30$

   $s =$ _____

8. $a(5 + 6) = 88$

   $a =$ _____

9. $c + (9 \times 3) = 30$

   $c =$ _____

Draw all the lines of symmetry for each figure.

10.

11.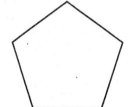

12.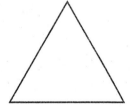

Solve each word problem.

Show your work.

13. Cooper has arranged 20 marbles into groups of 5. How many more marbles does he need to have 6 groups of 5 marbles? _____

14. Sheila baked 100 muffins for 5 families to share equally. Each family has 4 people in it. How many muffins will each person receive? _____

Solve the Factor Puzzles.

15.

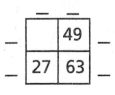

16.

30	48
	24

17.

54	48
45	

Solve Equivalence Problems

Homework

Add or subtract.

1. $\frac{1}{3} + \frac{1}{2} =$ _____

2. $\frac{7}{10} + \frac{1}{5} =$ _____

3. $\frac{2}{9} - \frac{1}{6} =$ _____

4. $\frac{5}{32} + \frac{1}{4} =$ _____

5. $\frac{5}{6} - \frac{2}{3} =$ _____

6. $\frac{5}{11} + \frac{1}{2} =$ _____

7. $\frac{13}{16} - \frac{3}{4} =$ _____

8. $\frac{3}{7} + \frac{1}{3} =$ _____

9. $\frac{11}{12} - \frac{3}{8} =$ _____

Solve.

Show your work.

10. Leona grew $\frac{7}{8}$ of an inch this year. Her sister Myra grew $\frac{3}{4}$ of an inch.

    Who grew more? _____

    How much more? _____

11. Sack A has 16 horns and 14 harmonicas. Sack B has 7 horns and 8 harmonicas. You are hoping for a harmonica.

    Which sack will you draw from? _____

    Why? _____

    _____

12. For breakfast, Oliver drank $\frac{5}{16}$ of a pitcher of juice. His brother Joey drank $\frac{3}{8}$ of the pitcher of juice. How much did they drink together?

    _____

13. If the pitcher in exercise 12 held exactly 1 quart of juice, how much is left?

    _____

Name _____ **Date** _____

Remembering

Find the area.

1.

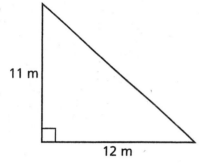

5 cm

12 cm

$A = $ _____

2.

11 m

12 m

$A = $ _____

Solve for *n* or for *d*.

3. $\frac{1}{6} = \frac{n}{24}$ _____

4. $\frac{3}{4} = \frac{15}{d}$ _____

5. $\frac{9}{54} = \frac{1}{d}$ _____

6. $\frac{10}{18} = \frac{n}{9}$ _____

7. $\frac{3}{7} = \frac{18}{d}$ _____

8. $\frac{3}{5} = \frac{n}{40}$ _____

9. $\frac{27}{36} = \frac{n}{4}$ _____

10. $\frac{14}{49} = \frac{2}{d}$ _____

11. $\frac{5}{6} = \frac{n}{48}$ _____

12. $\frac{1}{3} = \frac{20}{d}$ _____

13. $\frac{21}{56} = \frac{3}{d}$ _____

14. $\frac{20}{25} = \frac{n}{5}$ _____

Solve.

Show your work.

15. A truck is 5.4 m tall. It drives under a bridge that is 6.2 m tall. How much space is there between the top of the truck and the bridge?

_____

16. A classroom is 10 yards long. The floor is being tiled with new square tiles that are each 10 inches long. How many tiles are needed to make one row the length of the classroom?

_____

Add and Subtract Unlike Fractions

Homework

Add or subtract. Give your answers in the simplest form.

1. $7\frac{1}{2}$
   $+\ 6\frac{5}{8}$

2. $2\frac{3}{5}$
   $+\ 5\frac{1}{4}$

3. $5\frac{3}{8}$
   $+\ 2\frac{3}{4}$

4. $3\frac{4}{15}$
   $-\ 1\frac{1}{5}$

5. $9\frac{5}{6}$
   $-\ 4\frac{1}{8}$

6. $1\frac{1}{9}$
   $+\ 3\frac{5}{8}$

7. $8\frac{1}{6}$
   $-\ 2\frac{7}{12}$

8. $6\frac{7}{9}$
   $-\ 4\frac{2}{3}$

9. $3\frac{9}{14}$
   $-\ 1\frac{2}{7}$

Solve. Give your answer in the simplest form.

Show your work.

10. Last year my elm tree was $8\frac{5}{6}$ feet tall. This year it is $10\frac{1}{12}$ feet tall. How much did it grow in one year?

_____

11. Luis rode his bicycle $2\frac{3}{10}$ miles before lunch. He rode $1\frac{1}{4}$ miles after lunch. How far did Luis ride altogether?

_____

12. Carrie spent $2\frac{1}{2}$ hours trimming bushes and $1\frac{1}{4}$ hours weeding the garden. She is supposed to work in the yard for 5 hours. How much longer does she need to work?

_____

Remembering

Name _____ **Date** _____

Multiply or divide. Try to do these in your head.

1. $3\frac{1}{4} + 2\frac{3}{4} =$ _____

2. $2\frac{3}{4} - \frac{1}{4} =$ _____

3. $3\frac{2}{5} + 4\frac{4}{5} =$ _____

4. $6\frac{6}{7} - 5\frac{2}{7} =$ _____

5. $8\frac{2}{3} + 1\frac{2}{3} =$ _____

6. $5\frac{6}{7} - 1\frac{2}{7} =$ _____

7. $3\frac{3}{5} + 3\frac{3}{5} =$ _____

8. $7\frac{7}{8} - 3\frac{3}{8} =$ _____

9. $5\frac{3}{8} + 3\frac{5}{8} =$ _____

Find the area and perimeter.

10.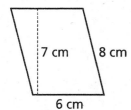

P = _____

A = _____

11.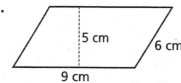

P = _____

A = _____

12.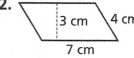

P = _____

A = _____

Solve the Factor Puzzles.

13.

12	
27	45

14.

	42
45	63

15.

18	48
	56

16.

	49
12	21

17.

36	48
	56

18.

30	48
45	

Solve with Unlike Mixed Numbers

Homework

Name _____ Date _____

1. Write a chain of equivalent fractions for the shaded parts of the circles below.

_____ = _____ = _____ = _____ = _____

Add or subtract. Give your answer in the simplest form.

2. $\frac{2}{5} + \frac{1}{3} =$ _____   3. $\frac{2}{3} - \frac{1}{6} =$ _____   4. $\frac{13}{16} - \frac{3}{4} =$ _____

5. $\frac{2}{9} + \frac{1}{4} =$ _____   6. $\frac{9}{14} - \frac{2}{7} =$ _____   7. $\frac{3}{32} + \frac{3}{4} =$ _____

A gumball machine has 4 kinds of gumballs. There are 36 red ones, 24 white ones, 18 blue ones, and 12 black ones.

8. What is the total number of gumballs in the machine?

_____

9. What fraction of the gumballs are red? Simplify the fraction.

_____

10. What fraction of the gumballs are black? Simplify the fraction.

_____

11. Pang's favorite flavors are blue and black. What is the probability that he will get one of these flavors?

Give your answer in the simplest form. _____

12. Tessa's favorite flavors are red and white. What is the probability that she will get one or the other of these flavors?

Give your answer in the simplest form. _____

13. **Challenge** Suppose Tessa put in a coin and got a red gumball. If she puts in another coin, what is the probability that she will get another red gumball? Can you simplify your answer?

_____

Remembering

What mixed number is shown by each shaded part?

1.

2.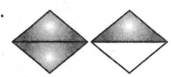

3.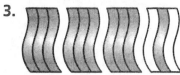

_____   _____   _____

Answer the questions about the bar graph. Give your answers as simple fractions.

4. How many cookies are there altogether? _____

5. What fraction of the cookies are chocolate chip? _____

6. What fraction of the cookies are oatmeal? _____

7. What fraction of the cookies are peanut butter? _____

8. Melanie baked 25 cookies. Did she bake more or less than half of the cookies? _____
   How do you know? _____

   _____

   _____

Cookies for the Bake Sale

Which metric unit would you use to measure each item?

9. the length of your shoe _____

10. the length of your classroom _____

11. the distance across your state _____

12. the length of your street _____

13. the circumference of a dinner plate _____

Solve. Simplify your answers if possible.

1. What is the probability that the arrow will land on a shaded section of the spinner?

   _____

   What is the probability that the arrow will land on a white section?

   _____

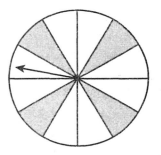

2. If you take one of these donuts from a box, what is the probability that you will get a chocolate one?

   _____

   What is the probability that you will get a vanilla one?

   _____

3. If you take a ring from a box with 8 silver rings and 12 gold rings, what is the probability that you will get a silver ring?

   _____

   What is the probability that you will get a gold ring?

   _____

4. This board game is called *Dungeons and Crowns*. If you land on one of the dark corner squares, you will be thrown in a dungeon. If you land on one of the squares with a star, you will be crowned monarch.

   What is the probability that you will be thrown in a dungeon?

   _____

   What is the probability that you will be crowned monarch?

   _____

Name _____ **Date** _____

Remembering

Add or subtract. Simplify. Try to do these in your head.

1. $4\frac{1}{3} + 1\frac{2}{3} =$ _____

2. $2\frac{4}{6} - 1\frac{4}{6} =$ _____

3. $3\frac{5}{10} + 1\frac{1}{10} =$ _____

4. $5\frac{3}{4} - 2\frac{1}{4} =$ _____

5. $2\frac{1}{3} + 6\frac{1}{3} =$ _____

6. $10\frac{6}{7} - 5\frac{4}{7} =$ _____

7. $1\frac{5}{8} + 2\frac{4}{8} =$ _____

8. $9\frac{4}{6} - 3\frac{2}{6} =$ _____

9. $3\frac{2}{9} + 4\frac{1}{9} =$ _____

10. $5\frac{4}{5} - 4\frac{1}{5} =$ _____

11. $3\frac{2}{8} + 5\frac{7}{8} =$ _____

12. $7\frac{3}{10} - 3\frac{2}{10} =$ _____

There are 360° in a circle. What fraction of a circle is each angle? Simplify your answers.

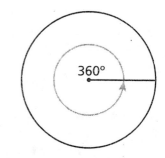

13. 90° _____

14. 45° _____

15. 180° _____

16. 120° _____

17. 60° _____

18. 30° _____

19. 10° _____

20. 5° _____

21. The 2004 population of six states is shown in the bar graph.

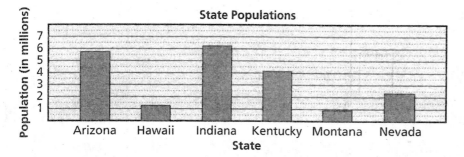

Estimate the population of each state to the nearest million.

_____

_____

_____

_____

Probability and Equivalent Fractions

Homework

Name _____ **Date** _____

Match the equivalent forms.

A. $\frac{1}{2}$ **B.** 0.2   **C.** 0.$\overline{3}$ **D.** $\frac{3}{4}$

1. 0.75 _____   **2.** $\frac{1}{3}$ _____   **3.** $\frac{2}{10}$ _____   **4.** 0.5 _____

Complete the number line by writing each missing fraction and decimal in the given boxes.

5.

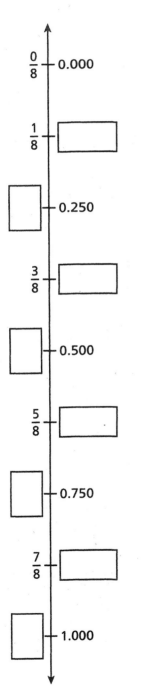

6.

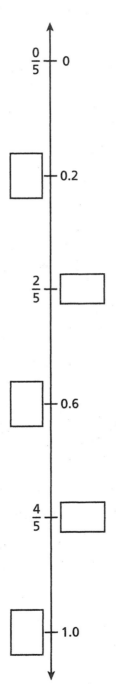

7.

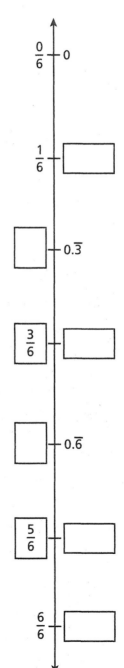

Name _____   **Date** _____

Remembering

Solve for the unknown.

1. $5.67 - 3.86 = a$

   $a =$ _____

2. $11{,}402.7 - b = 1{,}889.1$

   $b =$ _____

3. $14.18 + v = 15.07$

   $v =$ _____

4. $n - 79.069 = 83.801$

   $n =$ _____

5. $1{,}450.9 + 87.12 = e$

   $e =$ _____

6. $394.621 - 206.45 = c$

   $c =$ _____

7. $y - 3.021 = 6.979$

   $y =$ _____

8. $4.753 + m = 6.033$

   $m =$ _____

9. $r(4 + 56) = 60$

   $r =$ _____

10. $(9 \times 7) + (8 \times 2) = d$

    $d =$ _____

11. $7j + 2 = 30$

    $j =$ _____

12. $7g - 2 = 33$

    $g =$ _____

Solve.

13. The students all have the same book to read. Khalil finished reading $\frac{6}{10}$ of the book. Laurence finished reading $\frac{3}{4}$ of the book. Nahlia read $\frac{3}{5}$ of the book. Who has read the same amount of the book? Explain.

    _____

14. Jake ran 2.59 miles on Monday and 3.68 miles on Tuesday. Which day did he run the most? By how many more miles?

    _____

15. For the yearbook, Patricia had taken 1,501 pictures from two school field trips. She took 768 pictures on the first field trip. How many pictures did she take on the second field trip?

    _____

Fractional and Decimal Equivalencies

Homework

Compare. Write >, <, or =.

1. $\frac{5}{6}$ ◯ $\frac{5}{8}$

2. $\frac{7}{10}$ ◯ $\frac{9}{10}$

3. $\frac{8}{10}$ ◯ $\frac{4}{5}$

4. $\frac{3}{4}$ ◯ $\frac{7}{12}$

5. $2\frac{5}{12}$ ◯ $3\frac{1}{12}$

6. $4\frac{5}{16}$ ◯ $4\frac{7}{16}$

7. $21\frac{2}{3}$ ◯ $21\frac{2}{5}$

8. $5\frac{3}{8}$ ◯ $5\frac{5}{16}$

9. $6\frac{6}{8}$ ◯ $6\frac{3}{4}$

10. $\frac{2}{5}$ ◯ 0.4

11. $\frac{1}{3}$ ◯ 0.3

12. 0.758 ◯ $\frac{3}{4}$

13. 9.58 ◯ $9\frac{7}{12}$

14. $11\frac{1}{8}$ ◯ 11.12

15. $7\frac{5}{6}$ ◯ 7.83

Write the numbers in order from greatest to least.

16. $\frac{3}{5}$ $\frac{3}{4}$ $2\frac{4}{5}$ $\frac{7}{10}$ $2\frac{17}{20}$ _____

17. $\frac{5}{6}$ $\frac{2}{3}$ $3\frac{5}{9}$ $\frac{17}{18}$ $3\frac{1}{6}$ _____

Write the numbers in order from least to greatest.

18. $5\frac{2}{3}$ 5.6 $\frac{5}{6}$ 0.83 $5\frac{3}{4}$ _____

19. $7\frac{1}{2}$ $\frac{3}{8}$ 0.37 7.52 $\frac{31}{4}$ _____

Compare and Order Fractions and Decimals **141**

Name _____   **Date** _____

Remembering

Write the measure of the unknown angle.

1.

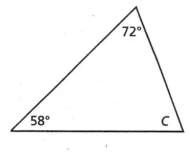

_____

2.

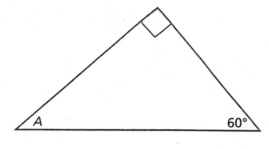

_____

3.

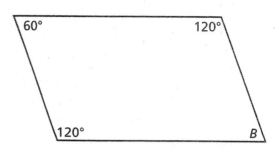

_____

4.

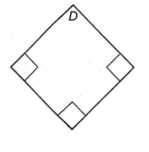

_____

Solve.   *Show your work.*

5. Tanya and Antoine both have a sheet of paper that is the same size. Tanya folds her paper into eighths. Antoine folds his paper into tenths. Who has more folds? Who has larger folded areas?

_____

6. Darren finished $\frac{5}{6}$ of his homework. Ophelia finished $\frac{1}{6}$ less than Darren. How much of Ophelia's homework did she finish? Simplify your answer.

_____

7. A rug covers $\frac{1}{4}$ of the floor. The area of the rug is 10 ft². What is the area of the floor?

_____

Compare and Order Fractions and Decimals

Name _____ **Date** _____

Homework

Decide if each addend is closer to 0 or closer to 1. Then estimate the sum or difference.

1. $\frac{2}{5} + \frac{4}{7}$

Estimate: _____

2. $\frac{13}{20} - \frac{3}{10}$

Estimate: _____

3. $\frac{13}{18} + \frac{1}{2}$

Estimate: _____

Estimate by rounding each number to the nearest whole number. Then add or subtract.

4. $3\frac{5}{8} - 1\frac{1}{2}$

Estimate: _____

5. $6\frac{4}{9} + 5\frac{7}{12}$

Estimate: _____

6. $7\frac{11}{18} - 4\frac{1}{15}$

Estimate: _____

The list below shows the variety of flour used in four recipes and the amounts.

Amounts of Flour Used (lb = pound)

Flour A 4.4 lb   Flour B 5.7 lb

Flour C 5.1 lb   Flour D 4.9 lb

Decide if each amount is closer to a whole pound or to a half pound. Then *estimate* the total amount of flour used.

7. B + C _____

8. A + D _____

Solve.

9. Estimate the difference $8\frac{7}{12} - 4\frac{7}{8} - \frac{4}{10}$.
Explain how you found the answer.

_____

_____

Remembering

Use the diagram below to answer exercises 1–6.

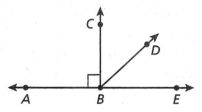

1. Which angles are complementary?

_____

2. Which angles are supplementary?

_____

_____

3. Which angle is a straight angle?

_____

4. Which angles are right angles?

_____

5. Which angles are acute angles?

_____

6. Which angle is an obtuse angle?

_____

Solve.

7. Belle planted 7 marigolds in each of the 8 rows in her garden. Then she planted 2 tulips in each of the rows. If she bought 60 marigolds in all, does she have any remaining? If so, how many?

_____

8. Lionel has three times as many DVDs as Brad. Brad has half as many DVDs as Iris. If Iris has 20 DVDs, how many DVDs do they have in all?

_____

_____

9. A triangle has a base of 5 cm and a height of 10 cm. A square has a side of 5 cm. Which figure has the greatest area?

_____

Homework

1. **Connections** A square rug is placed on top of a rectangular floor. The rug has a perimeter of 16 ft. The floor has a perimeter of 28 ft and a length of 6 ft. How much of the floor is not covered by the rug? Show your work.

_____

2. **Representation** Manuel needs a length of pipe that is 0.6 ft long. He has a piece of pipe that is $\frac{3}{5}$ ft long. Does he have enough pipe? Use a number line to help you decide.

_____

3. **Communication** Madison completed 36 out of 60 bracelets in time for the school craft fair. She says she has at least $\frac{4}{5}$ of the bracelets completed. Is this correct? Explain why or why not.

_____

_____

4. **Reasoning and Proof** Is it possible to draw a circle with a circumference of 30 in. inside a square with an area of 100 in.²? Explain. Draw a picture to prove your answer. Use 3 for π.

_____

_____

_____

Name _____ **Date** _____

Remembering

Compare. Use >, <, or =.

1. 3,467,080 $\bigcirc$ 34,670,800

2. 521,987 $\bigcirc$ 521,887

3. 1,746.8 $\bigcirc$ 1,746.80

4. $\frac{1}{4}$ $\bigcirc$ $\frac{1}{2}$

5. $\frac{5}{6}$ $\bigcirc$ $\frac{2}{3}$

6. $468\frac{1}{5}$ $\bigcirc$ $4,680\frac{1}{5}$

7. $15\frac{3}{8}$ $\bigcirc$ $15\frac{7}{10}$

8. $23\frac{6}{10}$ $\bigcirc$ 23.5

9. $9\frac{5}{8}$ $\bigcirc$ 9.62

10. $14\frac{2}{3}$ $\bigcirc$ 14.68

Solve. Give your answer in the simplest form.   *Show your work.*

11. Tom is training for a marathon. On Monday, he walked $1\frac{3}{4}$ miles to and from a park. On Tuesday, he walked $2\frac{1}{8}$ miles to and from another park. How far did Tom walk altogether?

_____

12. The circumference of a circle is 24 m. What is the radius of the circle? Use 3 for π.

_____

13. A round pool has a distance of 30 ft around it. About how wide is the widest part of the pool? Use 3 for π.

_____

Use Mathematical Processes

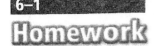
Solve. *Show your work.*

1. The inside of a refrigerator is 6 feet tall, 3 feet wide, and 2 feet deep. How many cubic feet of space are inside the refrigerator?

   _____

2. Isabel wants to estimate the volume of her bedroom, if her bedroom was empty. Her bedroom measures 4 meters long, 3 meters wide, and 3 meters tall. What is the volume of Isabel's bedroom?

   _____

3. Miguel is painting letters of the alphabet on cubes. He will paint one letter of the alphabet on each face of each cube. He knows that there are 26 letters in the alphabet. How many cubes will he need if he paints each letter once? How many faces on the last cube will be empty?

   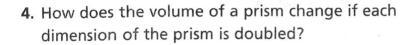

   _____

4. How does the volume of a prism change if each dimension of the prism is doubled?

   _____

5. A rectangular prism has a length of 4 cm and a width of 5 cm. The volume of the prism is 200 cu cm. The height of the prism is unknown. Explain how to find the height of the prism. Then give the height.

   _____

   _____

   _____

   _____

   _____

Remembering

Use multiplication to write three fractions equivalent to each given fraction.

1. $\frac{2}{3}$

2. $\frac{3}{5}$

3. $\frac{5}{8}$

4. $\frac{9}{10}$

_____   _____   _____   _____

Add or subtract.

5. $\frac{2}{3} + \frac{3}{5} =$ _____

6. $\frac{9}{10} + \frac{3}{5} =$ _____

7. $\frac{5}{8} + \frac{9}{10} =$ _____

8. $\frac{5}{8} + \frac{2}{3} =$ _____

Calculate the area of each figure in square centimeters.

9.
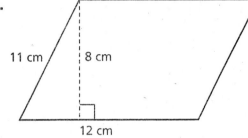

11 cm   8 cm

12 cm

_____

10.
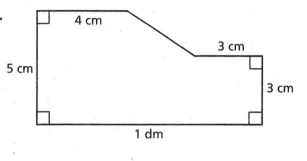

4 cm

3 cm

5 cm

3 cm

1 dm

_____

Draw a picture to help you solve each problem.

A right triangle has sides of 6 cm, 8 cm, and 1 dm.

11. What is its perimeter in centimeters? _____

12. What is its area in square centimeters? _____

Solve the Factor Puzzles.

13.
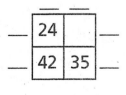

24	
42	35

14.

	21
72	63

15.

30	48
	40

Cubic Units and Volume

Homework

For each question, write whether you would measure for length, area, or volume.

1. The amount of space inside a moving van _____

2. The number of tiles needed to cover a bathroom floor _____

3. The distance from a porch to a tree _____

4. The amount of water a tank holds _____

5. The height of a flagpole _____

Solve.

6. A box is 5 inches long, 4 inches wide, and 1 inch deep. How much space is inside the box?

   _____

7. Aponi built a toy chest for her niece. It has a volume of 12 cubic feet. The chest is 3 feet long and 2 feet wide. How deep is it?

   _____

8. The rug in Alan's room has an area of 18 square feet. He is planning to buy another rug that is twice as long and twice as wide. What is the area of the new rug?

   _____

9. Each drawer in Monique's nightstand has a volume of 6 cubic decimeters. Each drawer in her dresser is twice as long, twice as wide, and twice as deep. What is the volume of one of Monique's dresser drawers?

   _____

10. Fong and Daphne built these structures. Who used more cubes? How many more?

    _____

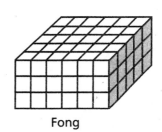

Fong

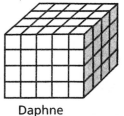

Daphne

Name _____ **Date** _____

Remembering

1. List the leaves in order from the longest to the shortest.

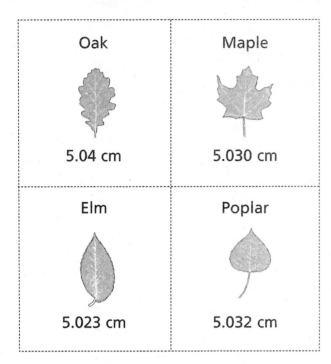

Oak	Maple
5.04 cm	5.030 cm
Elm	Poplar
5.023 cm	5.032 cm

Longest _____

_____

_____

Shortest _____

Add. Write the answer as a decimal and as a fraction.

	Decimal	**Fraction**
2. 0.8 + 0.09	_____	_____
3. 0.32 + 0.4	_____	_____
4. 0.51 + 0.07	_____	_____
5. 0.006 + 0.2	_____	_____
6. 0.409 + 0.5	_____	_____

Relate Length, Area, and Volume

Solve.

1. 3 kL = _____ L

2. 2,500 mL = _____ L

3. 5,000 L = _____ kL

4. 1.5 L = _____ mL

5. 12 kL = _____ L

6. 7,500 mL = _____ L

7. 2 pt = _____ qt

8. 4 qt = _____ gal

9. 2 c = _____ pt

10. 3 qt = _____ pt

11. 1 qt = _____ c

12. 5 gal = _____ qt

Write a fraction.

13. What fraction of 1 gallon is 1 quart?

   _____

14. What fraction of 1 liter is 1 milliliter?

   _____

15. What fraction of 1 kiloliter is 1 liter?

   _____

16. What fraction of 1 pint is 1 cup?

   _____

Solve.   *Show your work.*

17. Cesar bought 2 bags of flour that each weighed a
    kilogram and another bag that weighed 500 grams.
    How many grams of flour did he buy?

   _____

18. Samantha saw two bottles of ketchup at the store for
    the same price. One bottle contained a liter of ketchup,
    and the other contained 750 milliliters of ketchup. Which
    bottle was the better bargain?

   _____

19. A pitcher is full of lemonade. Which unit of capacity best
    describes the amount of lemonade in the pitcher? Explain.

   _____

   _____

   _____

Remembering

What is the area of each figure?

1.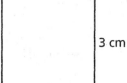

3 cm

_____

2.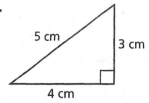

5 cm   3 cm

4 cm

_____

3.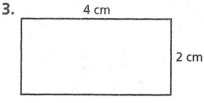

4 cm

2 cm

_____

4. Look again at the figures above. Which figure has the greatest perimeter?

_____

Solve. Write your answers in simplest form.

5. What fraction of 1 foot is 2 inches?

_____

6. What fraction of 1 yard is 18 inches?

_____

For exercise 7, write fractions in simplest form.

7. A paper bag contains 12 marbles. The marbles are identical, except for color. The bag contains 5 red marbles, 4 white marbles, and 3 blue marbles.

   What is the probability of reaching into the bag and without looking, choosing:

   a white marble?

   _____

   a blue marble?

   _____

   a red marble or a white marble?

   _____

   a marble that is not white?

   _____

   a red marble, a white marble, or a blue marble?

   _____

Measures of Capacity

Homework

Complete.

1. 3 g = _____ mg

2. 50 kg = _____ g

3. 2,000 mg = _____ g

4. 2 kg = _____ g

5. 1,500 mg = _____ g

6. 7,500 g = _____ kg

7. 1 lb = _____ oz

8. 2 T = _____ lb

9. 32 oz = _____ lb

10. 1,000 lb = _____ T

11. 4 lb = _____ oz

12. 10,000 lb = _____ T

Write a mixed number in simplest form to represent each number of ounces.

13. 40 oz = _____ lb

14. 50 oz = _____ lb

15. 44 oz = _____ lb

16. 68 oz = _____ lb

17. 22 oz = _____ lb

18. 94 oz = _____ lb

Solve.   *Show your work.*

19. At a garden center, grass seed sells for $8 per pound. Kalil spent $10 on grass seed. What amount of seed did he buy?

_____

20. Irina estimates that she is carrying 3 kg in her book bag. If her lunch has a mass of 500 g, what is the mass of everything else in her book bag?

_____

21. A pickup truck is carrying 500 pounds of cargo. When empty, the truck weighs $2\frac{1}{2}$ tons. What is the weight of the truck and its cargo in tons?

_____

22. At a grocery store, salted peanuts in the shell cost 30¢ per ounce. Is $5.00 enough money to buy 1 pound of peanuts? If it is, what amount of money will be left over?

_____

Remembering

Draw and label each figure. Use your ruler or protractor.

1. ray *AB*

2. line segment *YN*

3. perpendicular lines *CQ* and *DX*

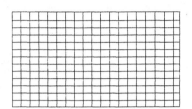
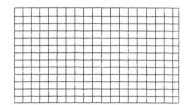
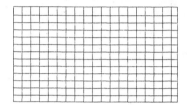

Find each missing angle measure.

4.

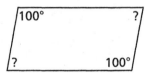

_____

5.

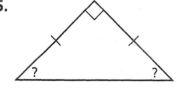

_____

Compare. Write >, <, or =.

6. 27 ◯ 31

7. 54 ◯ 80

8. 106 ◯ 101

9. 330 ◯ 303

10. $\frac{1}{2}$ ◯ $\frac{5}{10}$

11. $\frac{1}{3}$ ◯ $\frac{2}{3}$

12. $\frac{7}{8}$ ◯ $\frac{3}{8}$

13. $\frac{1}{1}$ ◯ $\frac{3}{3}$

14. $\frac{3}{4}$ ◯ $\frac{7}{8}$

15. $\frac{3}{15}$ ◯ $\frac{1}{5}$

16. $\frac{5}{6}$ ◯ $\frac{1}{2}$

17. $\frac{1}{4}$ ◯ $\frac{1}{3}$

Solve.

18. Three eighths of the interior of a figure is shaded.
What fraction of the interior of the figure is not shaded?

_____

Use the information in the table to complete the exercises below.

Metric	Customary
kilo = 1,000	1 pint (pt) = 2 cups (c)
milli = $\frac{1}{1,000}$	1 quart (qt) = 2 pints
	1 gallon (gal) = 4 quarts
1 gram (g) = 1,000 milligrams (mg)	1 pound (lb) = 16 ounces (oz)
1 kiloliter (kL) = 1,000 liters (L)	1 ton (T) = 2,000 pounds

1. 12 pt = _____ gal _____ qt

2. 2 L 5 mL = _____ mL

3. 2 lb 4 oz = _____ oz

4. 2,500 L = _____ kL _____ L

5. 2 kg 100 g = _____ g

6. 2 gal 1 pt = _____ c

7. 95 oz = _____ lb _____ oz

8. 3,675 mg = _____ g _____ mg

Add or subtract.

9.   4 qt 1 pt
   + 3 qt 1 pt
   _____

10.   4 pt
   − 2 pt 1 c
   _____

11.   6 gal 3 qt
   + 4 gal 2 qt
   _____

12.   13 g
   − 10 g 700 mg
   _____

13.   7 T 1,200 lb
   + 4 T   800 lb
   _____

14.   18 lb   3 oz
   − 17 lb 14 oz
   _____

15.   6 g   550 mg
   + 2 g 1,850 mg
   _____

16.   15 kL 750 L
   + 14 kL 250 L
   _____

17.   13 gal 1 qt
   −   9 gal 2 qt
   _____

Remembering

Find *n* or *d*.

1. $\frac{3}{10} = \frac{n}{90}$ $n =$ _____

2. $\frac{4}{9} = \frac{36}{d}$ $d =$ _____

3. $\frac{6}{8} = \frac{3}{d}$ $d =$ _____

4. $\frac{24}{56} = \frac{n}{7}$ $n =$ _____

5. $\frac{35}{45} = \frac{n}{9}$ $n =$ _____

6. $\frac{6}{7} = \frac{54}{d}$ $d =$ _____

Add or subtract. Give your answers in the simplest form.

7. $7\frac{2}{3} - 5\frac{1}{6}$

8. $9\frac{3}{4} + 7\frac{3}{8}$

9. $2\frac{3}{7} + 1\frac{1}{2}$

10. $7\frac{3}{4} - 3\frac{5}{6}$

11. $4\frac{3}{5} + 2\frac{1}{2}$

12. $6 - 1\frac{7}{10}$

13. $5\frac{2}{3} - 3\frac{6}{7}$

14. $6\frac{2}{3} + 5\frac{5}{8}$

15. $8\frac{5}{6} + 1\frac{5}{12}$

Solve. Give your answer in the simplest form.

16. Out of 3 whole pizzas, $1\frac{7}{10}$ pizzas were eaten.
How much pizza is left?

_____

17. Francesca has $\frac{16}{7}$ ft of string for her kite. Jason has
$2\frac{3}{4}$ ft of string for his kite. Katie has more string than
either Francesca or Jason. How much string could
Katie have? Explain your answer.

_____

Homework

Name _____ **Date** _____

°C   °F

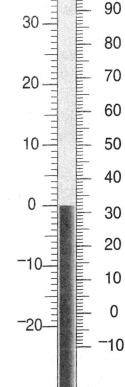

1. Ice is forming outside. What temperature in degrees Fahrenheit can it not be? in degrees Celsius?

_____

2. Give the related temperature.
   5°C is related to _____ °F.   86°F is related to _____ °C.

3. The temperature in the morning was 18°C. By noon, the temperature had risen 13°. What was the temperature at noon?

_____

4. The low temperature of the day was –7°F. The high temperature of the day was 12° higher. What was the high temperature of the day?

_____

5. The 10 P.M. temperature was 6°C. The 10 A.M. temperature was –2°C. How many degrees did the temperature change from 10 P.M. to 10 A.M.? Was the change an increase or a decrease?

_____

6. What tools and units can be used to measure the weight and the mass of a book? Explain.

_____

_____

The stem-and-leaf plot shows hourly morning temperatures. Use it to answer each question.

7. How many of the temperatures are above freezing?

_____

8. How many of the temperatures are warmer than 15°F?

_____

Hourly Temperatures (°F)	
Stem	Leaf
0	5
1	0 4 6
2	3

Legend: 1|0 means 10°F.

Remembering

Compare. Write >, <, or =.

1. $\frac{70}{70}$ ◯ 1

2. $\frac{4}{9}$ ◯ $\frac{8}{9}$

3. $\frac{5}{6}$ ◯ $\frac{8}{9}$

4. $6\frac{13}{13}$ ◯ 7

5. $4\frac{7}{10}$ ◯ $3\frac{9}{10}$

6. $14\frac{6}{7}$ ◯ $14\frac{3}{7}$

7. $9\frac{1}{2}$ ◯ $9\frac{3}{4}$

8. $12\frac{4}{5}$ ◯ $12\frac{2}{3}$

9. $9\frac{2}{5}$ ◯ $8\frac{9}{5}$

10. $24\frac{1}{3}$ ◯ $23\frac{11}{6}$

11. $4\frac{5}{6}$ ◯ $4\frac{3}{4}$

12. $3\frac{2}{3}$ ◯ $2\frac{7}{4}$

Order the following from least to greatest.

13. $\frac{12}{12}$, $1\frac{5}{12}$, $\frac{11}{12}$, $1\frac{1}{12}$, $\frac{19}{12}$

_____

14. 0.75, 0.749, 0.7, 0.707

_____

15. $\frac{2}{3}$, $\frac{1}{4}$, $\frac{1}{6}$, $\frac{7}{12}$

_____

Solve.

16. Karla is choosing a writing tool from Box A with 12 pencils and 8 pens. Pablo is choosing a writing tool from Box B with 7 pencils and 3 pens. Who has the better chance of choosing the pencil? Why?

_____

_____

Name _____ **Date** _____

Homework

Complete.

1. $1\frac{1}{2}$ days = _____ hours

2. 5 min 27 sec = _____ sec

3. 28 months = _____ years
   _____ months

4. $1\frac{1}{2}$ hr = _____ min

5. 49 hr = _____ days _____ hour

6. 248 min = _____ hr _____ min

7. 28 days = _____ weeks

8. $3\frac{1}{4}$ min = _____ sec

Solve.

9. It takes Dan 25 minutes to walk to work. If he arrived at work at 6:40 A.M., when did he leave his house?

   _____

10. Soccer practice is 2 hours 10 minutes long. What time did practice start if it ended at 1:05 P.M.?

    _____

11. Karolinka went to sleep at 9:45 P.M. and awoke at 6:30 A.M. How long did Karolinka sleep?

    _____

12. The movie started at 11:35 A.M. and was 2 hours 25 minutes long. What time did the movie end?

    _____

13. Sara gave a presentation at the Science Fair from 8:12 A.M. through 11:02 A.M. Between those times, a 35-minute lunch was given. What was the actual length of Sara's presentation?

    _____

14. On Saturday, Colby studied from 10:35 A.M. to 11:30 A.M., from 11:55 A.M. to 2:30 P.M., and from 3:15 P.M. to 5:40 P.M. What is a reasonable estimate of the length of time he studied on Saturday?

    _____

Remembering

Compare. Write >, <, or =.

1. $0.4 \bigcirc 0.40$

2. $0.7 \bigcirc 0.07$

3. $0.54 \bigcirc 0.543$

4. $1.6 \bigcirc 1.599$

5. $32.853 \bigcirc 32.851$

6. $0.8 \bigcirc \frac{4}{5}$

7. $\frac{1}{4} \bigcirc 0.26$

8. $\frac{9}{10} \bigcirc 0.899$

9. $23\frac{2}{5} \bigcirc 23.41$

10. $10\frac{1}{2} \bigcirc 10.52$

11. $5.3 \bigcirc 5\frac{3}{4}$

12. $66.2 \bigcirc 65\frac{6}{5}$

Order the following from greatest to least.

13. $3\frac{1}{6}, 2\frac{5}{3}, 3\frac{5}{8}, 3\frac{3}{4}$ _____

14. $0.5, \frac{5}{6}, 0.7, \frac{2}{3}$ _____

15. $4\frac{3}{5}, 4.1, 4\frac{1}{2}, 4.2$ _____

Solve. Use 3 for π.

16. The circumference of a circle is 18 ft. About how long is the diameter of the circle?

_____

17. Circle A has a circumference of 24 m. Circle B has a radius of 5 m. Which circle has the greater circumference?

_____

Homework

Solve.

1. $\begin{array}{r} 40 \\ \times\ 20 \\ \hline \end{array}$

2. $\begin{array}{r} 400 \\ \times\ \ 20 \\ \hline \end{array}$

3. $\begin{array}{r} 400 \\ \times\ 200 \\ \hline \end{array}$

4. $\begin{array}{r} 4,000 \\ \times\ \ \ 200 \\ \hline \end{array}$

5. $\begin{array}{r} 80 \\ \times\ 60 \\ \hline \end{array}$

6. $\begin{array}{r} 800 \\ \times\ \ 60 \\ \hline \end{array}$

7. $\begin{array}{r} 800 \\ \times\ 600 \\ \hline \end{array}$

8. $\begin{array}{r} 8,000 \\ \times\ 6,000 \\ \hline \end{array}$

9. $\begin{array}{r} 70 \\ \times\ 20 \\ \hline \end{array}$

10. $\begin{array}{r} 900 \\ \times\ \ 40 \\ \hline \end{array}$

11. $\begin{array}{r} 800 \\ \times\ 700 \\ \hline \end{array}$

12. $\begin{array}{r} 6,000 \\ \times\ \ \ 700 \\ \hline \end{array}$

Solve.

Show your work.

13. A tortoise walks 27 miles in a year. At this rate, how many miles will this tortoise walk in 10 years?

    _____

14. If the tortoise lives to be 100 years old, how many miles will it walk during its lifetime?

    _____

15. Every month, Paolo earns $40 for walking his neighbor's dog after school. How much does he earn from this job in one year?

    _____

16. There are 60 seconds in a minute and 60 minutes in an hour. How many seconds are there in an hour?

    _____

17. An elephant eats about 250 pounds of food each day. About how much food does an elephant eat in 1,000 days?

    _____

Name _____ **Date** _____

Remembering

Complete each Factor Puzzle.

1.

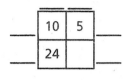

2.

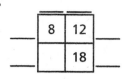

3.

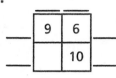

4.

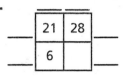

5.

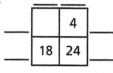

6.

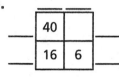

Solve.

Show your work.

7. A box shaped like a rectangular prism is 6 inches long, 4 inches wide, and 2 inches tall. What is the volume of the box?

_____

8. Sandwiches are arranged on 3 trays. Each tray holds 4 sandwiches along the width and 5 sandwiches along the length. How many sandwiches are there in total?

_____

9. A shipping crate measures 4 m long, 3 m wide, and 2 m deep. What volume of goods will fit in the crate?

_____

For each question, write whether you would measure for *length*, *area*, or *volume*. Write the number of measurements you need to make.

10. How far is it from your house to the street? _____

11. How much paper is needed to cover a table? _____

12. How much water will fit in a container shaped like a rectangular prism? _____

Shift Patterns in Multiplication

Name _____ **Date** _____

Solve the first problem with Rectangle Sections. Solve the other problems using any method you like. Use a separate sheet of paper.

1.

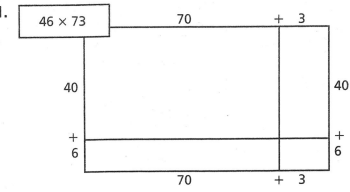

2. 84
   × 19

3. 67
   × 53

4. 91
   × 28

Solve.

Show your work.

5. Kamini needs to know the area of her yard so that she can buy the right amount of grass seed. The yard is 26 feet by 19 feet. What is the area of Kamini's yard in square feet?

_____

6. A restaurant has 16 crates of juice. Each crate holds 12 gallons of juice. How many gallons of juice are there altogether?

_____

7. Mr. Jackson is taking 23 students to see a movie. Tickets for the movie cost 75 cents. How much money will Mr. Jackson spend on student tickets?

_____

8. There are usually 20 school days in a month. Grace has band practice for 60 minutes every day after school. How many minutes does she usually practice each month?

_____

Name _____ **Date** _____

Remembering

Write these decimal numbers as fractions.

1. 0.67 = _____

2. 0.3 = _____

3. 0.08 = _____

4. 0.259 = _____

5. 0.004 = _____

6. 0.75 = _____

Use the cubes to answer the following questions.

The edges of a cube are each 4 inches long.

7. What is the area of each face? _____

8. What is the volume of the cube? _____

A cube has a volume of 27 cubic centimeters.

9. What is the length of each edge? _____

10. What is the area of each face? _____

One face of a cube has an area of 4 square feet.

11. What is the length of each edge? _____

12. What is the volume of the cube? _____

Complete each Factor Puzzle.

13.

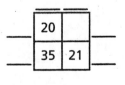

20	
35	21

14.

72	56
	35

15.

15	40
24	

The Area Model for Multiplication

Name _____ **Date** _____

Homework

Solve. Use any method.

1. 78
    × 26

2. 93
    × 42

3. 39
    × 84

4. 56
    × 71

The table shows how many newspapers are delivered each week by three paper carriers. **Use the table to answer the questions. Use 1 year = 52 weeks.**

Papers Delivered Each Week

Jameel	93
Clare	97
Mason	98

Show your work.

5. How many papers does Jameel deliver in a year?

_____

6. How many papers does Clare deliver in a year?

_____

7. How many more papers does Mason deliver each week than Clare?

_____

8. How could you find how many papers Mason delivers in a year without doing any multiplication? What is the answer?

_____

_____

_____

Solve.

9. Ray needs to know the area of his floor so he can buy the right amount of carpet. The floor is 21 feet by 17 feet. What is the area of the floor?

_____

10. Maria is buying flowers. Each tray of flowers costs $24. If she buys 15 trays, what will the total cost be?

_____

Remembering

Solve.

Show your work.

1. Martha and Andy ordered a chicken pot pie to share. Andy ate $\frac{1}{3}$ of the pie, and Martha ate $\frac{1}{2}$ of the pie. Who ate more pie? How do you know?

_____

2. How much of the pie did they eat altogether?

_____

3. Look at the two spinners. Which spinner gives you a better chance of landing on a dark space? How do you know?

A   B

_____

_____

4. The White Wolf Trail is $18\frac{9}{10}$ miles long. The Elk Trail is $15\frac{3}{5}$ miles long. How much longer is the White Wolf Trail?

_____

Complete.

5. 750 mL = _____ L

6. 2 kL = _____ L

7. 1.5 L = _____ mL

8. 4,000 L = _____ kL

9. 2,500 mL = _____ L

10. 3 kL = _____ L

Solve.

Show your work.

11. Ricky mixed 500 milliliters of red paint with 750 milliliters of blue paint. How many liters of purple paint did he make?

_____

Multiply Two-Digit Numbers

Homework

Solve. You will need a separate sheet of paper for some of the exercises.

1. 87 × 10	**2.** 23 × 40	**3.** 112 ×200
4. 852 × 56	**5.** 938 × 76	**6.** 768 × 34
7. 592 × 643	**8.** 475 × 245	**9.** 318 × 146

Melissa works at Sunny Fields grocery store. Her job is to count the grocery items in the storage room at the end of each day.

Solve.   *Show your work.*

10. There are 34 boxes of soup with 20 cans in each box. How many cans of soup are there?

_____

11. There are 68 cartons of eggs with a dozen eggs in each carton. How many eggs are there?

_____

12. There are 75 boxes of lemons with 48 lemons in each box. How many lemons are there?

_____

13. There are 478 bags of peanuts with 125 peanuts in each bag. How many peanuts are there?

_____

Name _____ **Date** _____

Remembering

Tell whether each triangle is *acute*, *obtuse*, or *right*.

1.

_____

2.

_____

3.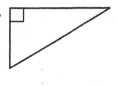

_____

4.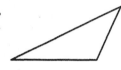

_____

Solve. Watch the signs.

5. $\frac{2}{5} + \frac{1}{2} =$ _____

6. $\frac{2}{3} - \frac{1}{9} =$ _____

7. $\frac{3}{8} - \frac{1}{4} =$ _____

8. $\frac{2}{7} + 3 =$ _____

9. $\frac{1}{4} + \frac{2}{3} =$ _____

10. $\frac{3}{5} - \frac{1}{4} =$ _____

11. $6\frac{1}{4} + \frac{1}{2} =$ _____

12. $2\frac{5}{8} - 1\frac{3}{8} =$ _____

13. $5\frac{1}{7} - 3\frac{2}{7} =$ _____

Solve.

Show your work.

14. A sandbox is 6 feet long, 5 feet wide, and $\frac{1}{2}$ foot deep. What is the volume of the sandbox?

_____

15. A box has the shape of a cube. Each edge is 4 centimeters long. What is the volume of the box?

_____

Multiply with Larger Numbers

Homework

Solve. You will need a separate sheet of paper.

1. 65
    × 40

2. 79
    × 42

3. 713
    × 60

4. 184
    × 50

5. 47
    × 55

6. 945
    × 32

7. 126
    × 85

8. 186
    × 125

9. 305
    × 273

The table shows the sizes of Farmer Reuben's fields. Use the table and a separate sheet of paper to help you answer each question.

	Corn Field	435 feet by 62 feet
	Wheat Field	731 feet by 120 feet
	Barley Field	256 feet by 194 feet

10. What is the area of the corn field?

_____

11. What is the area of the wheat field?

_____

12. What is the area of the barley field?

_____

13. How many square feet of land did Farmer Reuben plant in all?

_____

Remembering

Name _____

Date _____

Write each mixed number as an improper fraction.

1. $4\frac{1}{3} =$ _____

2. $2\frac{2}{5} =$ _____

3. $3\frac{3}{4} =$ _____

4. $1\frac{2}{7} =$ _____

5. $4\frac{1}{2} =$ _____

6. $2\frac{2}{9} =$ _____

Write each improper fraction as a mixed number.

7. $\frac{6}{5} =$ _____

8. $\frac{7}{3} =$ _____

9. $\frac{9}{2} =$ _____

10. $\frac{16}{5} =$ _____

11. $\frac{13}{4} =$ _____

12. $\frac{11}{3} =$ _____

Use these figures for problems 13–15.

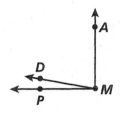

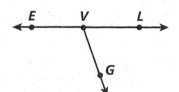

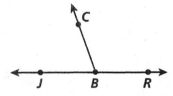

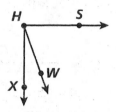

13. Name two straight angles.

_____   _____

14. Name two pairs of complementary angles.

_____   _____

15. Name two pairs of supplementary angles.

_____   _____

Homework

Solve. Use a separate sheet of paper or work in your Math Journal.

1. $\begin{array}{r} 93 \\ \times\ 60 \\ \hline \end{array}$

2. $\begin{array}{r} 84 \\ \times\ 50 \\ \hline \end{array}$

3. $\begin{array}{r} 26 \\ \times\ 89 \\ \hline \end{array}$

4. $\begin{array}{r} 35 \\ \times\ 74 \\ \hline \end{array}$

5. $\begin{array}{r} 95 \\ \times\ 68 \\ \hline \end{array}$

6. $\begin{array}{r} 86 \\ \times\ 57 \\ \hline \end{array}$

7. $\begin{array}{r} 407 \\ \times\ 95 \\ \hline \end{array}$

8. $\begin{array}{r} 398 \\ \times\ 76 \\ \hline \end{array}$

9. $\begin{array}{r} 729 \\ \times\ 93 \\ \hline \end{array}$

10. $\begin{array}{r} 948 \\ \times\ 75 \\ \hline \end{array}$

11. $\begin{array}{r} 825 \\ \times\ 573 \\ \hline \end{array}$

12. $\begin{array}{r} 796 \\ \times\ 948 \\ \hline \end{array}$

Solve.

Show your work.

13. Kim is baking cookies for the school bake sale. She can bake 24 cookies on each cookie tray. How many cookies can she bake on 12 trays?

_____

14. The dimensions of the Cloverville soccer field are 110 meters by 75 meters. What is the area of this soccer field?

_____

15. A package of spaghetti weighs 454 grams. William needs 16 packages for a pasta party. How many grams of spaghetti will he have altogether?

_____

16. The Eagle Express is a fast train with 18 cars. Each car has 135 seats. What is the most amount of people who can ride on the Eagle Express at once if one person sits on each seat?

_____

17. A passenger airplane flies 968 miles every day. If there are 365 days in a year, how many miles does the airplane fly each year?

_____

Name _____

Date _____

Remembering

Solve.

1. Hurricanes have winds of about 150 miles per hour. Tornadoes have winds about twice as fast. How fast are tornado winds?

   _____

2. The Udder Delight Dairy Farm has 39 barns, and there are 368 cows in each barn. How many cows are there on the farm in all?

   _____

3. The Marble Pillar Hotel has 48 floors with guest rooms. There are 52 guest rooms on each floor. How many guest rooms are there at the hotel?

   _____

4. Armando earns $296 a week. If he works 52 weeks in a year, how much money will he earn this year?

   _____

Complete each Factor Puzzle.

5.

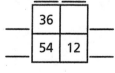

	36	
	54	12

6.

48	42
	35

7.

	32
45	72

Multiplication Practice

Name _____ **Date** _____

Homework

Solve. You may need a separate sheet of paper.

1. 0.9
    × 7

2. 0.6
    × 80

3. 0.004
    × 9

4. 0.05
    × 70

5. 0.16
    × 7

6. 7.0
    × 8

7. 0.09
    × 30

8. 0.007
    × 60

9. 0.17
    × 81

10. 940
     × 0.2

11. 3.43
     × 7

12. 0.29
     × 86

13. 0.015
     × 93

14. 0.721
     × 546

15. 0.268
     × 379

Three runners started making a table for April to show how far they run every day, every week, and the entire month.

Show your work.

16. They are not sure how to multiply the decimal numbers. Finish the table for them.

Runner	Miles Per Day	Miles Per Week	Miles in April
Cedric	0.6	$7 \times 0.6 =$	$30 \times 0.6 =$
Shannon	2.4		
Regina	1.75		

17. May has 31 days. What strategy could they use for finding out how far each runner will run during the month of May?

   _____

   _____

   _____

18. Give the total miles in May for each runner below.

   Cedric: _____   Shannon: _____   Regina: _____

Remembering

Solve. You may need a separate sheet of paper.

1. 50
   × 20

2. 500
   × 20

3. 500
   × 200

4. 5,000
   × 20

5. 5,000
   × 200

6. 30 × 60 = _____

7. 300 × 60 = _____

8. 3,000 × 600 = _____

Use the diagrams for problems 9–12.

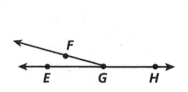 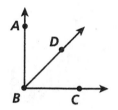

9. Name a straight angle. _____

10. Name a right angle. _____

11. Name a pair of complementary angles. _____

12. Name a pair of supplementary angles. _____

Solve.   *Show your work.*

13. Robyn mixed 500 milliliters of sparkling water with
    1,250 milliliters of juice to make punch. How many
    liters of punch did she make?

    _____

14. A recipe for 12 muffins requires $2\frac{3}{4}$ cups of flour.
    Henry wants to make 6 muffins. How many cups of
    flour does he need?

    _____

Multiply Decimals with Whole Numbers

Homework

Solve.

1. $0.3 \times 0.6 =$ _____

2. $0.4 \times 0.07 =$ _____

3. $0.003 \times 0.8 =$ _____

4. $5 \times 0.07 =$ _____

5. $0.002 \times 0.3 =$ _____

6. $0.05 \times 0.09 =$ _____

7.
$$\begin{array}{r} 1.8 \\ \times\ \ 6 \\ \hline \end{array}$$

8.
$$\begin{array}{r} 0.23 \\ \times\ \ 40 \\ \hline \end{array}$$

9.
$$\begin{array}{r} 0.014 \\ \times\ \ 0.9 \\ \hline \end{array}$$

10.
$$\begin{array}{r} 0.36 \\ \times\ 0.82 \\ \hline \end{array}$$

11. Circle the two multiplications that have the same product.

3×0.2　　　0.03×0.02　　　0.03×0.2　　　0.3×0.002　　　0.03×2

Solve using mental math.

12. $82 \times 0.001 =$ _____

13. $385 \times 0.1 =$ _____

14. $2,194 \times 0.001 =$ _____

Solve.

Show your work.

15. The sunlit zone of the ocean has a depth of about 600 feet. The dark zone, where there is no light at all, begins at 5.5 times that depth. At what depth does the dark zone of the ocean begin?

_____

16. Lauren has 9.9 meters of ribbon. She is cutting it into 100 equal pieces. That is the same as multiplying 9.9 by 0.01. How long will each piece of ribbon be?

_____

17. A furlong is a unit of measure used in horse racing. Every year, horses race 10 furlongs in the Kentucky Derby. One furlong is equal to 0.125 mile. How long is the Kentucky Derby in miles?

_____

Name _____ **Date** _____

Remembering

Cross out the number that does _not_ mean the same as the others.

1. 8/10   0.8 $\frac{4}{5}$ 0.08

2. 0.25 $\frac{1}{4}$ $\frac{3}{9}$ 0.250

Find the unknown angle measure of each triangle.

3.

∠CDB = _____

4.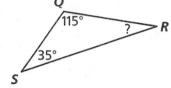

∠QRS = _____

Solve.   _Show your work._

5. Each month, Mary pays $250 on a car loan. How much will she have paid after 10 months?

   _____

6. Jeremy is buying pizzas for a party. A large pizza costs $12. How much will 18 large pizzas cost?

   _____

7. There are 60 seconds in one minute. How many seconds are there in 45 minutes?

   _____

Complete each Factor Puzzle.

8.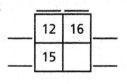

9.
24	15
	10

10.
28	
36	9

Multiply by Decimals

Homework

Solve.

1.
$$\begin{array}{r} 4.8 \\ \times\ 100 \\ \hline \end{array}$$

2.
$$\begin{array}{r} 2.9 \\ \times\ 0.3 \\ \hline \end{array}$$

3.
$$\begin{array}{r} 0.56 \\ \times\ \ \ 20 \\ \hline \end{array}$$

4.
$$\begin{array}{r} 0.069 \\ \times\ \ \ 0.7 \\ \hline \end{array}$$

5.
$$\begin{array}{r} 2.6 \\ \times\ 3.4 \\ \hline \end{array}$$

6.
$$\begin{array}{r} 3.8 \\ \times\ 0.051 \\ \hline \end{array}$$

7.
$$\begin{array}{r} 1.75 \\ \times\ 4.9 \\ \hline \end{array}$$

8.
$$\begin{array}{r} 3.42 \\ \times\ 1.67 \\ \hline \end{array}$$

Solve.   *Show your work.*

9. Hector and his family will be on vacation for 28 days.
   Hector's friend Paco will take care of Hector's rabbits.
   The rabbits eat 0.34 kilogram of food each day. How
   many kilograms of rabbit food will Hector need to
   leave with Paco?

   _____

10. Room temperature is about 72°F. The average
    temperature on Venus is about 12.5 times that much.
    What is the average temperature on Venus in °F?

    _____

11. The Sunrise Café gets tea bags in boxes of 1,000. If the
    café charges $1.75 for each cup of tea, and each cup of
    tea gets one tea bag, how much money does the café
    make for each box of 1,000 teabags?

    _____

12. If a box of tea bags costs $95, how much money does
    the café actually make after they have used up the box?

    _____

Remembering

Circle each fraction that is equivalent to $\frac{3}{6}$.

1. $\frac{4}{5}$ $\frac{6}{3}$ $\frac{6}{12}$ $\frac{13}{16}$

2. $\frac{1}{2}$ $\frac{1}{6}$ $\frac{1}{4}$ $\frac{1}{3}$

Find each unknown angle measure.

3.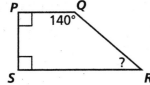

    ∠QRS = _____

4.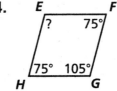

    ∠HEF = _____

Solve. You may need a separate sheet of paper.

5.   35
   × 30

6.   67
   × 13

7.   145
   × 62

8.   143
   × 30

9.   75
   × 18

10.   234
   × 73

11.   539
   × 200

12.   532
   × 421

13.   286
   × 34

14.   96
   × 73

15.   427
   × 393

16.   468
   × 300

17.   47
   × 14

18.   308
   × 271

19.   294
   × 176

20.   875
   × 30

Name _____ **Date** _____

Homework

Round to the nearest tenth.

1. 0.38 _____   2. 0.94 _____   3. 0.621 _____   4. 0.087 _____

Round to the nearest hundredth.

5. 0.285 _____   6. 0.116 _____   7. 0.709 _____   8. 0.563 _____

Write an estimated answer for each problem. Then find and write each exact answer.

Estimated Answer	**Exact Answer**

9. $38 \times 92 \approx$ _____ × _____ ≈ _____ $38 \times 92 =$ _____

10. $8.1 \times 4.2 \approx$ _____ × _____ ≈ _____ $8.1 \times 4.2 =$ _____

11. $7.65 \times 0.99 \approx$ _____ × _____ ≈ _____ $7.65 \times 0.99 =$ _____

12. $3.8 \times 6.02 \approx$ _____ × _____ ≈ _____ $3.8 \times 6.02 =$ _____

Solve.

Show your work.

13. A factory makes 394 motorcycles each week. If there are 52 weeks in a year, how many motorcycles will the factory make in a year?

   Estimate: _____

   Exact answer: _____

14. Suppose you want to buy 3 CDs for $18.95 each. Should you make a safe estimate or an ordinary estimate to find out if you have enough money? What would be a good estimate of how much money you will need? If you have $55, do you have enough money?

   _____

   _____

   _____

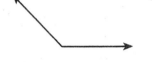

Write each fraction as a decimal.

1. $\frac{1}{4}$ _____

2. $\frac{9}{10}$ _____

3. $\frac{4}{8}$ _____

4. $\frac{2}{5}$ _____

Write each decimal as a fraction.

5. 0.2 _____

6. 0.15 _____

7. 0.5 _____

8. 0.75 _____

Label each angle as *acute*, *right*, *obtuse*, or *straight*.

9.

_____

10.

_____

Angelo kept track of the high temperature every day for a week.
He made a line graph of the data. Use the graph to answer each
question.

11. Which day had the highest temperature?

_____

12. Did the temperature increase or decrease
from Wednesday to Thursday?

_____

13. How much did the temperature change
from Thursday to Friday?

_____

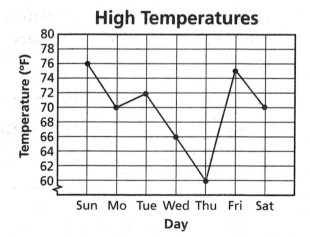

High Temperatures

Estimate Products

Name _____ **Date** _____

Homework

Find each product. You may need a separate sheet of paper.

1.   57
      × 0.31

2.   0.29
      ×   74

3.   7.6
      × 8.3

4.   0.35
      ×   94

5.   0.048
      × 0.92

6.   0.605
      × 0.81

7.   847
      × 0.13

8.   915
      × 0.24

Solve.

Show your work.

9. Josefina is buying 10 pounds of salmon, which costs $6.78 per pound. How much will the salmon cost?

_____

10. It is 9.2 miles between Mr. Rossi's place of work and his home. Because he comes home for lunch, he drives this distance 4 times a day. How far does Mr. Rossi drive each day?

_____

11. Mr. Rossi works 20 days a month. How far does he drive in a month?

_____

Round to the nearest tenth.

12. 0.37 _____

13. 0.59 _____

14. 0.91 _____

15. 0.75 _____

Round to the nearest hundredth.

16. 0.367 _____

17. 0.195 _____

18. 0.742 _____

19. 0.655 _____

Name   **Date**

Remembering

Find each product. You may need a separate sheet of paper. Use mental math where you can.

1. $\begin{array}{r} 72 \\ \times\ 90 \\ \hline \end{array}$

2. $\begin{array}{r} 18 \\ \times\ 29 \\ \hline \end{array}$

3. $\begin{array}{r} 245 \\ \times\ 92 \\ \hline \end{array}$

4. $\begin{array}{r} 416 \\ \times\ 72 \\ \hline \end{array}$

5. $0.5 \times 100 = \underline{\hspace{1.5cm}}$

6. $0.03 \times 1,000 = \underline{\hspace{1.5cm}}$

7. $0.24 \times 10 = \underline{\hspace{1.5cm}}$

8. $0.2 \times 3 = \underline{\hspace{1.5cm}}$

9. $0.04 \times 5 = \underline{\hspace{1.5cm}}$

10. $0.001 \times 8 = \underline{\hspace{1.5cm}}$

11. $\begin{array}{r} 0.01 \\ \times\ 0.6 \\ \hline \end{array}$

12. $\begin{array}{r} 0.5 \\ \times\ 20 \\ \hline \end{array}$

13. $\begin{array}{r} 0.54 \\ \times\ 0.7 \\ \hline \end{array}$

14. $\begin{array}{r} 0.301 \\ \times\ 0.9 \\ \hline \end{array}$

Use your ruler and draw all of the lines of symmetry.

15.

16.
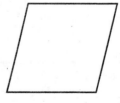

17.
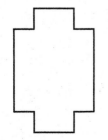

18.
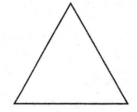

Multiplication Practice

Homework

Complete each division. Check your answer.

1. 5)4,820

2. 8)7,548

3. 9)7,535

4. 3)2,958

5. 7)5,857

6. 6)5,556

7. 7)6,945

8. 8)5,624

9. 4)3,254

Solve. Then estimate using compatible numbers to check the solution.

Show your work.

10. Mrs. Wong drove from Chicago to St. Louis 8 times last month. Altogether she drove 2,376 miles. How far is it from Chicago to St. Louis?

_____

11. Jay has 6,200 beads. He is making bracelets with 9 beads each. How many bracelets can he make? How many beads will be left?

_____

12. There are 5,280 feet in a mile. There are 3 feet in a yard. How many yards are there in a mile?

_____

13. The Pencil Pal factory wraps pencils in packages of 6. Today there are 5,750 pencils to be packaged. How many packages will there be? How many pencils will be left over?

_____

_____

Name _____ **Date** _____

Remembering

Solve each exercise.

1. $\frac{7}{8} - \frac{1}{4} =$ _____

2. $\frac{4}{9} + \frac{1}{3} =$ _____

3. $\frac{5}{8} - \frac{1}{2} =$ _____

4. $\frac{3}{5} - \frac{3}{10} =$ _____

5. $\frac{1}{2} + \frac{3}{4} =$ _____

6. $\frac{1}{3} - \frac{1}{6} =$ _____

Use the word *ray*, *angle*, or *line* to name each figure.

7.

$\overrightarrow{BC}$ _____

8.

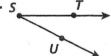

$\angle TSU$ _____

9.

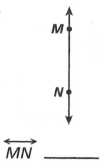

$\overleftrightarrow{MN}$ _____

Solve.

Show your work.

10. Mrs. Carranza is planting flowers in her garden. If she plants 11 rows with 14 flowers in each row, how many flowers will she plant?

_____

11. Grant is packing books into boxes. So far, he has packed 17 boxes with 24 books in each box. How many books has he packed so far?

_____

12. Malik does sit-ups every day. He did 125 sit-ups each day for 30 days. How many sit-ups did he do in those 30 days?

_____

Divide Whole Numbers by One Digit

Name _____   **Date** _____

Solve each division exercise. You may need a separate sheet of paper.

1. $9\overline{)6.57}$

2. $5\overline{)36.41}$

3. $4\overline{)9.584}$

4. $6\overline{)207.9}$

5. $3\overline{)80.07}$

6. $7\overline{)654.5}$

7. $8\overline{)4.184}$

8. $2\overline{)7.006}$

9. $6\overline{)5.16}$

Solve.

Show your work.

10. Teresa bought 8 roses for $10.32. How much did she pay for each rose?

_____

11. Barry's dog Cubby is 1.26 meters long. Cubby is 7 times as long as Douglas's guinea pig Taffy. How long is Taffy?

_____

12. Farmer Sanchez has 469.62 acres of land. He will divide it into 9 equal fields for spring planting. How many acres will there be in each field?

_____

13. Six friends will stay at a cabin in the woods this weekend. The cabin is 148.5 miles away from home. Each person will drive one sixth of the distance. How far will each person drive?

_____

Divide Decimal Numbers by One Digit **185**

Name _____ **Date** _____

Remembering

Write each decimal as a fraction in simplest form.

1. $0.58 =$ _____

2. $0.4 =$ _____

3. $0.07 =$ _____

4. $0.376 =$ _____

5. $0.009 =$ _____

6. $0.285 =$ _____

Find each unknown angle measure.

7.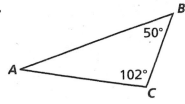

$\angle A =$ _____

8.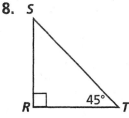

$\angle S =$ _____

9.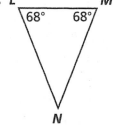

$\angle N =$ _____

Solve.

Show your work.

10. Paolo earns $5.15 per hour at his after-school job. How much will he earn if he works 6 hours one week?

_____

11. Frankie is training for a track meet. Each day, he runs 3.25 miles. How far will he run in one week (7 days)?

_____

12. Carlie is carrying 4 textbooks home. Each book weighs 2.09 pounds. How much do her textbooks weigh altogether?

_____

Divide Decimal Numbers by One Digit

Homework

1. Circle the one that does *not* mean the same as the others.

0.75 $\frac{3}{4}$ 0.750 $4\overline{)3.00}$ $\frac{75}{100}$ $3\overline{)4.00}$ $\frac{6}{8}$

Solve.   *Show your work.*

2. Clayton walks $\frac{5}{8}$ mile to school each day. Melinda walks 0.65 mile. Who walks farther? How much farther?

_____

3. In Veronica's art class 5 out of 9 people speak Spanish. What decimal number shows what part of the class speaks Spanish?

_____

4. Jake has decided to save $\frac{1}{8}$ of the money he earns each week. After he has earned $100, how much will he have saved?

_____

Complete each division. Add zeros if needed.

5. $8\overline{)5}$ **6.** $4\overline{)217}$ **7.** $7\overline{)36.05}$ **8.** $9\overline{)865.8}$

9. $5\overline{)241}$ **10.** $8\overline{)434}$ **11.** $9\overline{)2}$ **12.** $9\overline{)650.07}$

13. Look back at exercises 5–12. Which exercise has an answer that is a repeating decimal?

_____

Remembering

Answer each question about the bar graph.

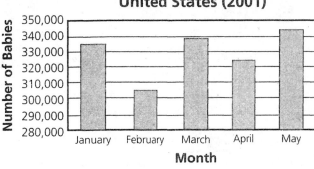

**Babies Born in the
United States (2001)**

Solve.

1. About how many babies were born in April?

_____

2. About how many more babies were born in January than in
February?

_____

3. In which month were the most babies born? About how many
babies were born that month?

_____

Find each unknown angle measure.

4.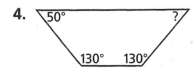

5.

6.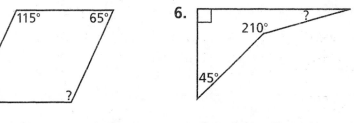

_____   _____   _____

Express Fractions as Decimals

Name _____ **Date** _____

Divide.

1. $39\overline{)2{,}886}$

2. $81\overline{)7{,}533}$

3. $68\overline{)4{,}967}$

4. $72\overline{)4{,}968}$

5. $28\overline{)2{,}520}$

6. $33\overline{)1{,}287}$

7. $46\overline{)1{,}426}$

8. $55\overline{)990}$

Solve.

Show your work.

9. The lunchroom has enough seats for 168 students. Each class has 24 students. How many classes can eat in the lunchroom at the same time?

_____

10. Mrs. Randall bought tickets to the art museum for all the fifth-grade students. Each ticket cost $12, and the total cost of the tickets was $1,152. How many fifth-grade students are there?

_____

11. The Harmony Hotel has a total of 1,596 rooms. There are 42 rooms on each floor. How many floors does the Harmony Hotel have?

_____

Remembering

Round to the nearest tenth.

1. 0.76 _____   2. 0.245 _____   3. 0.309 _____   4. 0.92 _____

Round to the nearest hundredth.

5. 0.087 _____   6. 0.245 _____   7. 0.309 _____   8. 0.432 _____

Round to the nearest thousandth.

9. 0.2908 _____   10. 0.6541 _____   11. 0.7556 _____   12. 0.9429 _____

Estimate the circumference of each circle. Use 3 for π.

13.

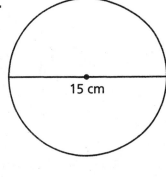

15 cm

_____

14.

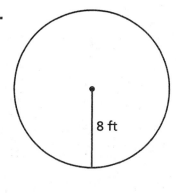

8 ft

_____

Solve.   *Show your work.*

15. David spent $216 on photo albums. Each album cost $24. How many albums did he buy?

_____

16. An apple orchard received a shipment of 320 apple trees. The trees will be planted in 12 rows of 26 trees each. How many trees will be left over?

_____

Explore Dividing by Two-Digit Whole Numbers

Name _____ **Date** _____

Homework

Divide.

1. $34\overline{)7,276}$

2. $85\overline{)6,120}$

3. $73\overline{)4,309}$

4. $38\overline{)3,576}$

5. $57\overline{)4,722}$

6. $26\overline{)7,903}$

7. $65\overline{)5,918}$

8. $69\overline{)1,796}$

Solve.

Show your work.

9. A carousel factory has 1,252 carousel horses. 48 horses are placed on each carousel.

   How many carousels can the factory build? _____

   How many horses will be left over? _____

10. Farmer Parson collected 1,183 chicken eggs this morning. He will put them in cartons that hold a dozen eggs each.

    How many cartons will he fill? _____

    How many eggs will be left over? _____

11. Write a division word problem using 7,903 and 26.

    _____

    _____

    _____

Remembering

Solve.

Show your work.

1. Caleb has 1,976 pennies. He has 576 fewer pennies than Alec. Alec has 358 more pennies than Jacob. How many pennies does Jacob have?

   _____

2. Martha has $60 to buy a coat. A blue coat costs $57.98, and a red coat is $8.23 less than the blue one. How much change will Martha get if she buys the red coat and there is no tax?

   _____

3. Maya delivered 2,250 newspapers in April last year. That is 450 papers more than she delivered this April. She earns 8¢ for each paper she delivers. How much did she earn this April?

   _____

Find the volume of each rectangular prism.

4.

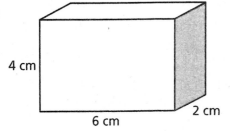

4 cm
6 cm
2 cm

$V =$ _____

5.

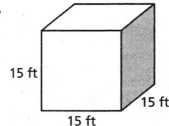

15 ft
15 ft
15 ft

$V =$ _____

Too Large, Too Small, or Just Right?

Solve. Circle the choice that tells how you gave your answer.   *Show your work.*

1. A Ferris wheel holds 48 people. There are 823 people with tickets to ride the Ferris wheel. How many times will the Ferris wheel need to be run to give everyone a ride?

   _____

   | whole number only | round up | mixed number | decimal | remainder only |

2. Bananas cost 89 cents each at the fruit stand. Isabel has $11.75. How many bananas can she buy?

   _____

   | whole number only | round up | mixed number | decimal | remainder only |

3. The 15 members of the Running Club made $1,338 selling magazines. They will divide the money equally. How much should each runner get?

   _____

   | whole number only | round up | mixed number | decimal | remainder only |

4. There are 524 goldfish in the fish pond. They will be put in indoor tanks for the winter. If each tank holds 45 fish, how many tanks will be needed?

   _____

   | whole number only | round up | mixed number | decimal | remainder only |

5. Mr. Lopez made 339 ounces of strawberry jam. He plans to divide the jam equally among his 12 cousins. How many ounces of jam will each cousin get?

   _____

   | whole number only | round up | mixed number | decimal | remainder only |

Remembering

Multiply.

1.	65	2.	79	3.	713	4.	184
	× 38		× 42		× 60		× 56

For each question, write whether you would measure for *length*, *area*, or *volume*. Write the number of measurements you would make.

5. How much sand is in a sand box? _____

6. How long is a fence? _____

7. How much material is needed for a tablecloth? _____

8. How long is one wall of your classroom? _____

Solve.   *Show your work.*

9. Henry had $20. He bought a hat for $5.99 and a
   baseball for $3.50. How much did Henry have left?

   _____

10. Georgia made 3 trays of cookies. Each tray had
    12 cookies. She then wrapped the cookies in packages
    of 6 each. How many packages did she wrap?

    _____

11. Ralph picked 6 baskets of corn. Each basket held 30 ears
    of corn. He put 9 ears in each bag he wanted to sell.
    How many bags did he have?

    _____

12. Sierra had $35.00. She earned $8.00 raking leaves,
    $15.00 shoveling snow, and the rest babysitting. How
    much did Sierra earn babysitting?

    _____

Interpret Remainders

Homework

Solve.   *Show your work.*

1. Nella and Lydia are hiking 15 miles today. After every 0.5 mile, they will stop and rest. How many times will they rest during the hike?

   _____

2. A cookie cutter shark is 0.4 meter long, and a thresher shark is 6 meters long. How many times as long as the cookie cutter shark is the thresher shark?

   _____

3. At a large wedding, the cakes were cut into hundredths, so each piece was 0.01 of a whole cake. If there were 12 cakes, how many pieces were there?

   _____

4. A millimeter is 0.001 of a meter. How many millimeters are there in 7 meters?

   _____

5. Paco saves $0.75 each day for a new bicycle helmet. He has saved $36. For how many days has Paco been saving?

   _____

Solve.

6. $0.9\overline{)63}$

7. $0.08\overline{)72}$

8. $0.007\overline{)42}$

9. $0.6\overline{)420}$

10. $0.4\overline{)372}$

11. $0.6\overline{)534}$

12. $0.26\overline{)884}$

13. $0.71\overline{)1,136}$

Remembering

Circle the fraction that is *not* equivalent to $\frac{2}{5}$.

1. $\frac{4}{10}$ $\frac{20}{50}$ $\frac{6}{20}$ $\frac{10}{25}$

Circle the fraction that is *not* equivalent to $\frac{3}{12}$.

2. $\frac{1}{4}$ $\frac{6}{24}$ $\frac{12}{48}$ $\frac{9}{30}$

Write each improper fraction as a mixed number.

3. $\frac{18}{5} =$ _____

4. $\frac{25}{4} =$ _____

5. $\frac{66}{10} =$ _____

6. $\frac{10}{3} =$ _____

7. $\frac{23}{6} =$ _____

8. $\frac{38}{12} =$ _____

Use the cubes to answer questions 9–12.

The edges of a cube are 6 inches long.

9. What is the area of each face? _____

10. What is the volume of the cube? _____

6 in.

A cube has a volume of 125 cu cm.

11. What is the length of each edge? _____

12. What is the area of each face? _____

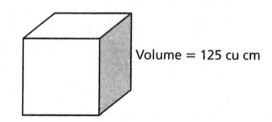

Volume = 125 cu cm

13. The Eiffel Tower is about 324 meters high. The Sears Tower is 442 meters high. How much higher is the Sears Tower? _____

14. Estimate to find the combined heights of both buildings in meters. _____

Multiply. You may need a separate sheet of paper.

15.   65
    × 38

16.   79
    × 42

17.   713
    × 60

18.   184
    × 56

Divide Whole Numbers by Decimal Numbers

Divide.

1. $0.07\overline{)4.2}$ 2. $0.8\overline{)2.4}$ 3. $0.05\overline{)4.8}$ 4. $0.24\overline{)2.064}$

5. Circle the division that does *not* have the same answer as the others.

   $54 \div 6$ $5.4 \div 0.6$ $0.54 \div 0.6$ $0.54 \div 0.06$ $0.054 \div 0.006$

Solve.   *Show your work.*

6. A beekeeper collected 7.6 liters of honey. She will pour it into bottles that each hold 0.95 liter. How many bottles will she fill?

   _____

7. A very small dinosaur, the microraptor, was only 1.3 feet long. One of the largest dinosaurs, the diplodocus, was about 91 feet long. How many times as long as the microraptor was the diplodocus?

   _____

8. Tomorrow in the town of Eastwood there will be a big race that is 5.25 kilometers long. A water station will be set up every 0.75 kilometer, including at the finish line. How many water stations will there be?

   _____

9. Marisol's bedroom has an area of 29.76 square meters. The length of the room is 6.2 meters. What is its width?

   _____

Solve.   *Show your work.*

1. Jessie and Jeff are planting seeds. Jessie said she planted
   $\frac{3}{8}$ of the seeds and Jeff said he planted $\frac{2}{3}$ of the seeds.
   Is this possible? Explain why or why not.

   _____

   _____

2. Ruth needs $3\frac{1}{4}$ yards of fabric to make a small quilt.
   She has $1\frac{7}{8}$ yards in her fabric box. How much more
   fabric does she need to buy?

   _____

3. Jorge ran $6\frac{1}{4}$ miles on Monday. On Tuesday he ran
   $\frac{3}{4}$ mile less. How far did he run on Tuesday?

   _____

Complete.

kiloliter (kL)	hectoliter (hL)	dekaliter (dkL)	**liter (L)**	deciliter (dL)	centiliter (cL)	milliliter (mL)
1,000 L	100 L	10 L	1 L	0.1 L	0.01 L	0.001 L

$\times\ 10 \longleftarrow\ \times\ 10 \longleftarrow\ \times\ 10 \longleftarrow\qquad \longrightarrow\ \div\ 10 \longrightarrow\ \div\ 10 \longrightarrow\ \div\ 10$

5. 2kL = _____ L   **6.** 3,000 mL = _____ L   **7.** 4,500 L = _____ kL

8. 6.5 L = _____ mL   **9.** 9.5 kL = _____ L   **10.** 400 mL = _____ L

Divide with Two Decimal Numbers

Homework

Divide.

1. $0.7\overline{)35}$

2. $0.06\overline{)24}$

3. $0.8\overline{)0.64}$

4. $0.03\overline{)18}$

5. $3\overline{)33}$

6. $0.05\overline{)0.65}$

7. $12\overline{)72}$

8. $0.04\overline{)11.56}$

9. $8\overline{)216}$

10. $0.8\overline{)490.4}$

11. $28\overline{)2,380}$

12. $0.033\overline{)5.148}$

Solve. Explain how you know your answer is reasonable.

Show your work.

13. Georgia works as a florist. She has 93 roses to arrange in vases. Each vase holds 6 roses. How many roses will Georgia have left over?

_____

_____

14. Julia is jarring peaches. She has 25.5 cups of peaches. Each jar holds 3 cups. How many jars will Julia need to hold all the peaches?

_____

_____

15. The area of a room is 137.5 square feet. The length of the room is 12.5 feet. What is the width of the room?

_____

_____

Name _____   **Date** _____

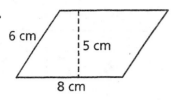

Find the perimeter and the area.

1.

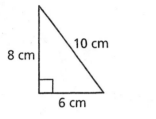

6 cm
5 cm
8 cm

P = _____

A = _____

2.

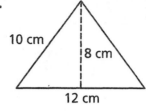

10 cm
8 cm
12 cm

P = _____

A = _____

3.

10 cm
8 cm
6 cm

P = _____

A = _____

4.

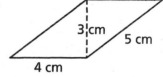

3 cm
5 cm
4 cm

P = _____

A = _____

Imagine you spin the spinner one time.
Write each probability as a fraction.

5. What is the probability of landing on a 1?

_____

6. What is the probability of landing on a 2?

_____

7. What is the probability of landing on a 3?

_____

8. What is the probability of landing on a 4?

_____

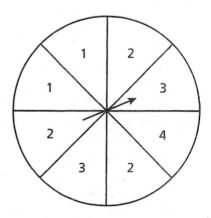

Division Practice

Name _____ Date _____

Multiply or divide. You may need a separate sheet of paper.

1. $1.5 \times 5 =$ _____

2. $0.4 \times 0.05 =$ _____

3. $0.004 \times 0.03 =$ _____

4.
$$\begin{array}{r} 0.55 \\ \times\ 0.07 \\ \hline \end{array}$$

5.
$$\begin{array}{r} 0.25 \\ \times\ 0.12 \\ \hline \end{array}$$

6.
$$\begin{array}{r} 22.3 \\ \times\ 6.2 \\ \hline \end{array}$$

7.
$$\begin{array}{r} 20.8 \\ \times\ 0.26 \\ \hline \end{array}$$

8. $0.3\overline{)0.108}$

9. $0.11\overline{)407}$

10. $0.67\overline{)32.16}$

11. $0.44\overline{)105.6}$

For each problem, decide whether you need to multiply or divide. Then solve. Explain how you know your answer is reasonable.

Show your work.

12. Harriet makes yo-yos. She needs 38 inches of string for each yo-yo. How many yo-yos can she make with 875 inches of string? How many inches of string will be left over?

_____

_____

13. Roberto will save $\frac{1}{6}$ of his allowance each day. If he gets $2.00 a day, about how much money will he save each day? Round your answer to the nearest penny.

_____

_____

14. Raisins cost $0.97 per pound. Michael bought $15.52 worth of raisins. How many pounds of raisins did he buy?

_____

_____

Name _____ Date _____

Remembering

Add or subtract.

1. $3.145 + 0.34$

2. $55.893 - 5.06$

_____

_____

3. $29.007 + 9.897$

4. $14.035 - 7.9$

_____

_____

5. $76.35 + 2.389$

6. $37.007 - 2.87$

_____

_____

Solve.

Show your work.

ounce (oz)	pound (lb)	ton (T)
1 lb = 16 oz	1 lb	1 T = 2,000 lb

5. A puppy weighs $4\frac{1}{2}$ pounds. What is the weight of the puppy in ounces?

_____

6. Truck A is carrying 2.5 tons of cargo. Truck B is carrying 4,500 pounds of cargo. Which truck is carrying more?

_____

Distinguish Between Multiplication and Division

Homework

"Meals on Wheels" is a program that delivers meals to elderly people who cannot leave their homes or prepare meals easily. The table at the right shows the number of meals delivered for 5 weeks in two different small cities.

Meals Delivered		
	City A	City B
Week 1	190	250
Week 2	190	230
Week 3	200	240
Week 4	210	230
Week 5	220	220

Use the table to solve exercises 1–5.

1. Draw two separate graphs or one double graph on grid paper for the data in the table.

2. Compare the shapes of the graphs. What trends do you see?

   _____

   _____

   _____

3. Find the mode of the data for each city.

   _____

4. Which city had the greater range?

   _____

5. Compare the mean number of meals delivered in the 5 weeks by each city. Which is greater? How much greater?

   _____

   _____

6. A line graph begins at a value of 4, increases very quickly to a maximum value, and then decreases back to 0 quickly. Make a drawing of the graph. Then write a story or problem the graph could represent.

   _____

   _____

   _____

Remembering

Solve. Check your work.

1. $26\overline{)1{,}547}$

2. $15\overline{)1{,}632}$

3. $68\overline{)5{,}527}$

4. $2{,}606 \div 34 =$ _____

5. $2{,}492 \div 89 =$ _____

6. $2{,}684 \div 57 =$ _____

7. $0.4\overline{)136}$

8. $1.6\overline{)76.8}$

9. $0.38\overline{)11.4}$

10. $477 \div 0.03 =$ _____

11. $145.8 \div 2.7 =$ _____

12. $193.52 \div 0.82 =$ _____

Solve. Explain how you know your answer is reasonable.

13. At the Sports Awards banquet, each table seats 12 people. The caterer expects 2,415 people to attend the banquet. How many tables are needed to seat everyone?

   _____

14. A decorator has 10 rolls of wallpaper. Each roll is 24 feet long. She wants to hang the wallpaper in strips 7.8 feet long. How many full strips can she hang?

   _____

15. Golf balls are sold in "sleeves" of 6 balls. The sleeves are then packed 12 sleeves to a carton. A manufacturer has 20,581 golf balls. How many cartons could the manufacturer fill?

   _____

     Statistics and Graphing

Homework

1. Connections

Ms. Colby wants to buy a bingo game for a party. She needs 35 cards. Which of the following is the best buy? Why?

Fun Shop: $5 for 10 + $5 shipping

Game Place: $12 for 30 + $4 shipping

Discount Haven: $21 for 40 + $5 shipping

_____

_____

_____

_____

2. Reasoning and Proof

x	0	2	3	5	6
y	3	7	9	11	15

One value in the function table above is wrong. Which is it? Explain your reasoning and write the correct number.

_____

_____

_____

_____

3. Communication

On a special day at the local ballpark, every 7th ticket had a coupon for a free soft drink. Every 13th ticket had a coupon for a free hotdog. If 1,890 people bought tickets for the game, how many people won a hot dog and a soft drink? Explain.

_____

_____

_____

_____

4. Representation

Order the following fractions from least to greatest. Make a drawing to show how you know you are correct.

$$\frac{2}{3}, \frac{1}{2}, \frac{1}{3}, \frac{3}{4}, \frac{1}{8}$$

_____

Name _____ **Date** _____

Remembering

Solve. Check your work.

1. $17 \overline{)1{,}604}$

2. $28 \overline{)3{,}789}$

3. $49 \overline{)5{,}723}$

4. $7{,}264 \div 34 =$ _____

5. $5{,}808 \div 81 =$ _____

6. $7{,}432 \div 50 =$ _____

7. $0.8 \overline{)530.4}$

8. $2.3 \overline{)485.3}$

9. $5.7 \overline{)649.8}$

10. $252 \div 0.09 =$ _____

11. $27.6 \div 0.015 =$ _____

12. $158.56 \div 0.032 =$ _____

Solve. Explain how you know your answer is reasonable.

13. The cars of the roller coaster hold 48 people on each trip through the loops. How many trips are needed to let 3,162 people each have a ride?

_____

14. Powdered vitamins for dogs are sold in pre-measured packets that weigh 0.03 pound. How many packets can be filled from a 50-pound bag of the vitamins?

_____

15. For the school dance, chairs are set up along one wall of the gym. Each chair is 20.4 inches wide. The wall of the gym is 125 feet long. How many chairs will fit along the wall?

_____

Use Mathematical Processes

Name _____ Date _____

Homework

Write in exponential form.

1. $5 \times 5 \times 5 \times 5$

_____

2. $2 \times 2 \times 2 \times 6 \times 6 \times 6$

_____

3. $8 \times 8 \times 8 \times 8 \times 8$

_____

4. $3 \times 3 \times 7$

_____

5. $4 \times 4 \times 9 \times 9 \times 9$

_____

6. $7 \times 7 \times 7 \times 7 \times 2 \times 2$

_____

Simplify.

7. $4^2 \times 3$ _____

8. 9^3 _____

9. $5^3 \times 2$ _____

Solve for n.

10. $5^n = 25$ _____

11. $n^3 = 8$ _____

12. $10^n = 100$ _____

Make a drawing on grid paper to find the square root of each number.

13. $\sqrt{36}$ _____

14. $\sqrt{9}$ _____

15. $\sqrt{4}$ _____

Write *prime* or *composite* for each number.

16. 50 _____

17. 64 _____

18. 5 _____

19. 88 _____

20. 43 _____

21. 19 _____

Make a factor firework to find the prime factorization of each number.

22. 28 _____

23. 42 _____

24. 60 _____

Name _____ Date _____

Remembering

Divide.

1. 124 ÷ 3.2 = _____   2. 371 ÷ 1.4 = _____   3. 93 ÷ 0.75 = _____

4. 5.5)‾561   5. 0.12)‾75   6. 2.6)‾1,183

Solve.

7. A packing company packs peanuts in bags. Each bag holds 9 ounces of peanuts. They currently have a 3,482-pound supply of peanuts to pack. How many bags can they fill? (Hint: Remember 1 pound = 16 ounces.)

   _____

8. Another packing company packs 12 ounces of pickles in each jar. They have a supply of 5,216 pounds of pickles. How many jars can they fill with these pickles?

   _____

9. A large can of peaches serves 6 people. How many cans of peaches would be needed to serve 287 people?

   _____

10. Paper plates are sold in packs of 24. How many packs of paper plates should be purchased if 305 people are expected to show up for a picnic?

    _____

11. At the aquarium, the penguins are put into smaller pools at night to protect them. Each smaller pool holds 12 penguins. The aquarium has 129 penguins in all. How many smaller pools do they need for the penguins?

    _____

12. It takes 32 pieces of paper to print a brochure for Pierre's Poodle Grooming Salon. Paper comes in packs of 500 sheets called a *ream*. How many reams are needed to print 152 brochures?

    _____

Exponents

Homework

Tell which operation to perform first.

1. $8 \times (13 - 7)$

_____

2. $2 + 7 \times 9$

_____

3. $13 - 30 \div 5$

_____

4. $(16 - 7) \div 3$

_____

5. $48 \div 4 \times 3$

_____

6. $7 \times (4 + 2)$

_____

Simplify. Use the Order of Operations.

7. $3 \times (16 \div 4) - 9$

_____

8. $3 \times (5 + 2)$

_____

9. $12 - 8 + 7$

_____

10. $(16 - 8) \times 4 + 1$

_____

11. $5 + 5 \times 9$

_____

12. $50 - (6 + 4) \times 3$

_____

Solve.

13. $18 - (56 \div 8) \times 2 =$ _____

14. $9 \times 2 \div 3 + 1 =$ _____

15. $(15 - 7) \div 4 =$ _____

16. $6 \times (21 \div 3) =$ _____

Insert parentheses if needed to make each equation true.

17. $8 \times 8 - 4 = 60$

18. $5 + 10 \times 2 = 30$

19. $6 + 8 \div 7 = 2$

20. $7 - 6 \div 3 = 5$

21. $28 \div 9 - 5 = 7$

22. $6 \times 4 + 4 = 48$

Remembering

Convert each measurement.

1. 4 quarts, 2 cups = _____ cups

2. 5 pounds, 6 ounces = _____ ounces

3. 1 kilogram, 300 grams = _____ grams

4. 4 liters, 250 milliliters = _____ milliliters

5. 3 quarts, 7 cups = _____ cups

6. 12 pounds, 8 ounces = _____ ounces

Multiply or divide.

7. $0.96 \div 0.2 =$ _____

8. $5.1 \times 1.7 =$ _____

9. $25.2 \div 3.5 =$ _____

10.   9.7
   $\times\ 3.04$

11. $1.6 \overline{)13.2}$

12.   4.29
   $\times\ 0.57$

Solve.

13. Ed started work at 8:45 A.M. He stopped for lunch at 12:00 P.M. and went back to work at 12:45 P.M. He quit for the day at 6:15 P.M. How long did Ed work on this day?

_____

14. In the morning, the temperature was at a low of 38°F. During the day, the temperature rose 27 degrees. What was the high temperature for the day?

_____

15. Avery has a 3-week vacation. He plans to drive across the country and back, a total of 4,898 miles. About how many miles should Avery average per day on his trip?

_____

16. As it turned out, Avery spent 5 hours per day driving and drove a total of 5,565 miles. What was his average speed for the hours he drove?

_____

Order of Operations

Homework

Solve each equation.

1. $12 = 1.5 \times p$

$p =$ _____

2. $150 = 18 + y$

$y =$ _____

3. $81 \div d = 3$

$d =$ _____

4. $k - 18 = 29$

$k =$ _____

5. $\frac{3}{4} + a = 2\frac{1}{2}$

$a =$ _____

6. $16n = 224$

$n =$ _____

Use two steps to solve each equation.

7. $14 = 2w + 6$

$w =$ _____

8. $35 \div (c + 2) = 7$

$c =$ _____

9. $7h + 3 = 45$

$h =$ _____

10. $(r \div 4) - 3 = 7$

$r =$ _____

11. $3m - 4 = 11$

$m =$ _____

12. $3 \cdot (t + 36) = 150$

$t =$ _____

Write situation and solution equations to solve each problem.

13. Diana wants to play the tuba in a marching band. Her goal is to practice 5 hours each week. It is Thursday and she has practiced for $3\frac{1}{2}$ hours. How much longer must she practice to meet her weekly goal?

Situation Equation: _____

Solution Equation: _____

14. Doug orders a $20 video game and 8 game cases from an online game store. If the total is $32, how much does each game case cost?

Situation Equation: _____

Solution Steps: _____

_____

Name _____ Date _____

Remembering

Convert each measurement.

1. 13 days, 2 hours = _____ hours

2. 9 hours, 12 minutes = _____ minutes

3. 28 minutes, 4 seconds = _____ seconds

4. 17 hours, 5 minutes = _____ minutes

Decide whether you need to multiply or divide. Then solve.

5. The football team needs new shoulder pads for the players. There are 64 players on the team, and each set of pads costs $132.79. How much will the team spend on shoulder pads?

   _____

6. Against their rival school, the football team gained a total of 781.75 yards on 53 plays. What was the average gain per play?

   _____

7. At the last game, the coach provided 2 quarts, 1 cup of sports drink for each of the 64 players. How many cups of sports drink did he provide in all?

   _____

8. The team equipment manager used 5 quarts of paint when he painted the team name on the helmets. How many cups of paint were used?

   _____

9. To go to a game at another school, the entire team, 12 coaches, 8 cheerleaders, and 50 members of the band traveled by bus. Each bus held 45 people. How many buses were needed?

   _____

10. Over the last 22 seasons, the team has scored a total of 6,028 points. What is the average number of points scored in a season?

    _____

Solve Equations

Name _____ Date _____

Homework

Substitute the given value for the variable to evaluate each expression.

1. $(15 \div y) - 5$ for $y = \frac{1}{3}$

_____

2. $n \cdot (47 - 19)$ for $n = 10$

_____

3. $(3 + 1.4) - (s \cdot 0.2)$ for $s = 6$

_____

4. $(18 + 32) \cdot (b \div 3)$ for $b = 57$

_____

5. Is $a - 0.15 = 0.25$ true for $a = 0.4$?

_____

6. Is $61 = 3(k + 1)$ true for $k = 20$?

_____

Choose the values of the variable that make each inequality true.

7. $18 \geq w + 7$

   a. $w = 7$ **b.** $w = 11$ **c.** $w = 25$ **d.** $w = 28$

8. $\frac{2}{3} < t \div 15$

   a. $t = 1$ **b.** $t = 5$ **c.** $t = 10$ **d.** $t = 15$

Choose the expression or inequality that represents each situation.

9. Daren is 4 years younger than his sister. If Daren's age is shown by d, which expression shows his sister's age?

   a. $4 - d$ **b.** $d - 4$ **c.** $d + 4$

10. Ms. Yee has $550 in her art supply budget. She plans to spend $75 per month. Which expression shows how much will be left after m months?

   a. $550 - 75 \cdot m$ **b.** $75 \cdot m - 550$ **c.** $(550 - 75) \cdot m$

11. At most 25 people at the senior center can sign up for the painting class. Which inequality shows the number of people (p) who can take the class?

   a. $p \geq 25$ **b.** $p \neq 25$ **c.** $p \leq 25$

Remembering

Use the data in the line plot to answer questions 1–7.

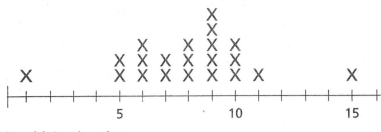

1. Identify the outlier(s) in the data: _____

2. Identify the gaps in the data: _____

3. Identify the cluster(s) in the data: _____

4. What is the mode of the data? _____   5. What is the median of the data? _____

6. What is the range of the data? _____   7. What is the mean of the data? _____

Solve.

8. At the amusement park, it takes 15 tickets to ride the largest roller coaster. On one day, the roller coaster collected 52,470 tickets. How many people rode this roller coaster?

   _____

9. It costs $22.95 for an adult and $15.95 for a child to get into the park. How much would it cost for 8 adults and 13 children?

   _____

10. The park opens at 8:30 A.M. and closes at 11:45 P.M. on weekends. How long is the park open on these days?

   _____

11. During one week in the summer, the following numbers of people visited the park:

Monday	2,496	Tuesday	3,012	Wednesday	5,381
Thursday	5,932	Friday	8,116	Saturday	10,046
Sunday	8,312				

What was the average number of visitors per day that week?

   _____

Evaluate Expressions, Equations, and Inequalities

Homework

Name _____ Date _____

Fill in the missing parts of each function table.

1.
Rule in Words	Divide by 2, then subtract 1.				
Equation					
Input (x)	2	4		8	
Output (y)			2		4

2.
Rule in Words	Multiply by 10, then add __.				
Equation					
Input (x)	1		3		5
Output (y)		25		45	

For each situation, complete the table and write an equation.
Then solve the problem.

3. Kalid has made a goal of walking 180 miles. He plans to walk 5 miles each week.

Equation					
Number of weeks (w)	1	2	3	4	5
Miles to walk (m)	175				

How many miles does Kalid have to walk after walking for 5 weeks? _____

4. Evie rents a bicycle for $20 plus $7.50 per hour.

Equation					
Number of hours (h)	1	2	3	4	5
Total cost (c)	$27.50				

How many hours can she use the bike for $50? _____

Remembering

Simplify.

1. $2^3 \times 15 =$ _____

2. $5^2 \times 19 =$ _____

3. $3^4 \times 5 =$ _____

4. $2^4 \times 4 =$ _____

5. $4^3 \times 13 =$ _____

6. $8^2 \times 7 =$ _____

Find the prime factorization of each number.

7. 52

8. 96

9. 108

_____   _____   _____

Solve.

10. One gallon of paint will cover 200 square feet of wall. The room you want to paint has walls that are 7.5 feet high. What is the greatest length of wall that can be covered by one gallon of this paint?

_____

11. The room you want to paint has two doors, each 6.5 feet tall and covering 20.8 square feet. What is the width of each door?

_____

12. Your room has two windows. Each window occupies 11.76 square feet of wall space. If the windows are each 2.8 feet wide, how tall is each window?

_____

13. One quart of paint will cover 50 square feet of wall, but it costs $10. One gallon of paint costs $32. If your room is 20.3 feet wide and 18.2 feet long, would it be cheaper to buy 3 gallons of paint or 2 gallons and some quarts? Remember that the room has two doors and two windows.

_____

_____

_____ _____

Homework

1. Draw an isosceles trapezoid. Write the ordered pairs for its vertices.

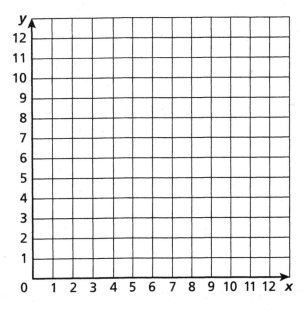

_____ _____ _____ _____

2. Now draw an isosceles triangle. Write the ordered pairs for its vertices.

_____ _____ _____

3. Draw a rectangle. Write the ordered pairs for its vertices.
Use subtraction to find the perimeter of your rectangle.

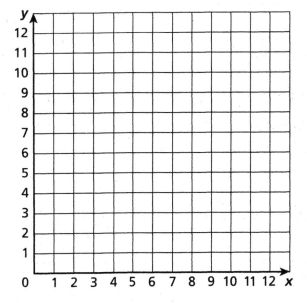

_____ _____ _____ _____

_____

Remembering

Find the perimeter and area.

1.

1 unit

6 units

4 units

2 units

5 units

$P =$ _____ units $A =$ _____ square units

2. The area of triangle *ABC* is 10 sq cm. Name a possible base measure and a possible height measure for triangle *ABC*. Explain your answer.

_____

_____

_____

3. Can one angle of a right triangle measure 100°? Explain your answer.

_____

_____

_____

_____

Multiply or divide.

4. $84 \div 6 =$ _____

5. $27 \times 10 =$ _____

6. $108 \div 12 =$ _____

7. $15 \times 100 =$ _____

8. $144 \div 24 =$ _____

9. $1{,}000 \times 3 =$ _____

10. $8.4 \div 6 =$ _____

11. $27 \times 0.1 =$ _____

12. $10.8 \div 12 =$ _____

13. $1.5 \times 0.01 =$ _____

14. $144 \div 2.4 =$ _____

15. $0.100 \times 0.3 =$ _____

Homework

1. Describe the function $y = 5x$.

_____

_____

2. Write an equation for the function described by this rule:
the value of y is 10 times greater than the value of x.

_____

3. Complete the table of ordered pairs for the function $y = x + 5$.
Plot the ordered pairs and draw a line to connect the points.

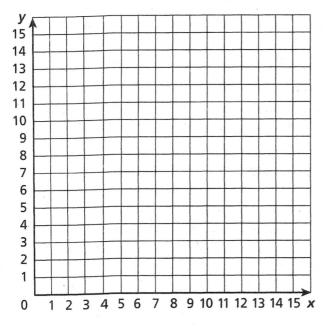

$y = x + 5$	
x	y
___	___
___	___
___	___
___	___
___	___

Write the rule in words.

_____

_____

4. For which function, $y = 2x$ or $y = x + 2$, is the value of y
always greater than the value of x? Explain your answer.

_____

_____

_____

Remembering

Circle the values for the variable that make each inequality true.

1. $5b \geq 80$

| 16 | 13 | 85 | 15 | 20 |

2. $18 + k < 53$

| 31 | 71 | 35 | 33 | 8 |

3. $m - 258 \leq 402$

| 144 | 283 | 720 | 660 | 508 |

Solve.

4. It takes Connor an average of 8 minutes to deliver 5 newspapers every morning. Complete the function table to find how long it takes him to deliver 35 newspapers.

Number of newspapers delivered	5	10	15				
Time (minutes)	8	16	24				

5. Mrs. Edwards has an appointment at 2:30 P.M. It will take her half an hour to drive to the appointment. She wants to do a load of laundry that will take 42 minutes to wash and 1 hour, 15 minutes to dry before she leaves. It is now 11:45 A.M. Does Mrs. Edwards have enough time to do the laundry?

Show your work.

6. Zack is making lasagna for his father's birthday. It takes 1 hour, 15 minutes of preparation time, 2 hours of cooling in the refrigerator, 1 hour, 10 minutes of baking time, and 10 minutes of cooling until it is ready to serve. When should Zack start preparing the lasagna so it is ready to eat when his father gets home at 6:15 P.M.?

Graph Functions

Homework

Solve. Write a multiplication equation for each problem.

Miguel swam 6 lengths of the pool. Po Lan swam 3 times as far as Miguel. Lionel swam $\frac{1}{3}$ as far as Miguel.

1. How many lengths did Po Lan swim? _____ Write the equation. _____

2. How many lengths did Lionel swim? _____ Write the equation. _____

Chris cut a length of rope that was 12 feet long. Dayna cut one that was 4 times as long as Chris's rope. Benita cut one that was $\frac{1}{4}$ as long as Chris's rope.

3. How long is Dayna's rope? _____ Write the equation.
_____

4. How long is Benita's rope? _____ Write the equation.
_____

Write two statements for each pair of treats. Use the word *times*.

5. Compare cookies and drinks.
_____
_____

6. Compare drinks and pizzas.
_____
_____

7. Compare cookies and pizzas.
_____
_____

Treat	Number
cookies	24
drink	8
pizza	2

Solve.

8. $\frac{1}{3} \times 18 =$ _____

9. $\frac{1}{4}$ of $12 =$ _____

10. $\frac{1}{8} \times 32 =$ _____

11. $\frac{1}{9}$ of $27 =$ _____

12. $\frac{1}{8} \times 56 =$ _____

13. $\frac{1}{3}$ of $15 =$ _____

14. $\frac{1}{6} \times 54 =$ _____

15. $\frac{1}{5} \times 35 =$ _____

16. $\frac{1}{10}$ of $60 =$ _____

Remembering

Multiply or divide. You may need a separate sheet of paper.

1.　38
　　× 0.69

2.　0.75
　　× 54

3. 0.8)7.76

4. 0.13)0.754

5.　42
　　× 1.6

6.　0.15
　　× 63

7. 0.4)0.168

8. 0.24)0.336

Find the prime factorization for each number.

9. 42

10. 75

11. 86

Write whether each is a measurement of length, area, or volume.

12. the amount of gravel in a dump truck

13. the distance between two houses

_____

_____

14. the amount of floor covered by a rug

15. the amount of air in a room

_____

_____

Write each measurement using a number and a symbol.

16. 32 hundredths of a centimeter _____

17. 7 tenths of a millimeter _____

18. 62 thousandths of a decimeter _____

> **Example:**
>
> 9 tenths of a decimeter = 0.9 dm

Find the number of cubes. Show your work.

19.

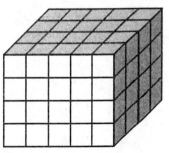

20.

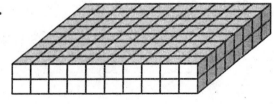

Basic Multiplication Concepts

Homework

Multiply. You may need a separate sheet of paper.

1. $\frac{2}{3} \times 15 =$ _____

2. $\frac{3}{4} \times 8 =$ _____

3. $\frac{7}{8} \times 32 =$ _____

4. $\frac{2}{9} \times 27 =$ _____

5. $\frac{3}{8} \times 56 =$ _____

6. $\frac{3}{4} \times 16 =$ _____

7. $\frac{2}{3} \times 21 =$ _____

8. $\frac{4}{5} \times 35 =$ _____

9. $\frac{5}{7} \times 28 =$ _____

10. $\frac{4}{9} \times 45 =$ _____

11. $\frac{5}{12} \times 24 =$ _____

12. $\frac{9}{10} \times 70 =$ _____

Solve.   *Show your work.*

13. Rebecca has 21 math problems to solve. She has solved $\frac{2}{7}$ of them. How many problems has she solved?

    _____

    _____

14. Tessa threw 36 free throws at basketball practice. She sank 27 of them. What fraction of her free throws did Tessa sink?

    _____

    _____

15. A carousel has 56 horses. $\frac{3}{8}$ of them are white. How many horses are not white?

    _____

    _____

16. Nathan works at a hardware store. Today he sold 48 tools. $\frac{5}{6}$ of the tools he sold were hammers. How many hammers did Nathan sell today?

    _____

    _____

Name _____ **Date** _____

Remembering

Multiply or divide.

1.   75
  × 0.15
	2. 0.62
	  × 14
		3. 1.9
		  × 1.2
			4. 0.5
			  × 0.5

5. $5\overline{)18}$ 6. $7\overline{)24.01}$ 7. $11\overline{)160.05}$ 8. $6\overline{)966}$

9. Plot these points on the coordinate grid:
   $A\,(1, 2)$ $B\,(5, 2)$ $C\,(3, 5)$

10. Join Point A, Point B, and Point C with line
    segments. Name the geometric figure this
    makes.

    _____

11. Translate the figure 4 units to the right and
    2 units up. Name the coordinates of the
    translated figure.

    A' _____ B' _____ C' _____

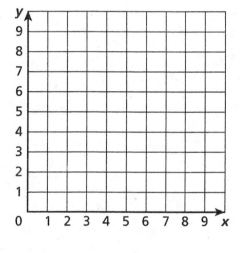

Solve.

Show your work.

12. Box A contains 20 marbles and 14 of them are red. Box
    B contains 10 marbles and 8 of them are red. You will
    choose one marble from one of the boxes. Which box
    would you prefer if you want to choose a red marble?

    _____

Multiplication with Non-Unit Fractions

Homework

The campers in each cabin at Bear Claw Camp held a contest to see who could walk the farthest in one day. Use the sign to answer the questions. Write your answers as improper fractions.

Otter Ridge 13 mi.
Silver Stream 8 mi.
Fossil Cave 9 mi.
Mammoth Mountain 25 mi.

1. The campers in Cabin A walked $\frac{1}{4}$ of the way to Otter Ridge. How many miles did they walk?

_____

2. The campers in Cabin B walked $\frac{2}{3}$ of the way to Silver Stream. How many miles did they walk?

_____

3. The campers in Cabin C walked $\frac{3}{5}$ of the way to Fossil Cave. How many miles did they walk?

_____

4. The campers in Cabin D walked $\frac{1}{6}$ of the way to Mammoth Mountain. How many miles did they walk?

_____

5. Which group of campers walked the farthest that day?

_____

6. Show $\frac{2}{3}$ of 4 on the number line.

7. Write $\frac{2}{3}$ of 4 as an improper fraction. _____

8. Write $\frac{2}{3}$ of 4 as a mixed number. _____

Write your answers as improper fractions.

9. $\frac{2}{7} \times 4 =$ _____

10. $\frac{2}{3} \times 8 =$ _____

11. $\frac{5}{6} \times 4 =$ _____

12. $\frac{2}{9} \times 20 =$ _____

13. $\frac{7}{9} \times 2 =$ _____

14. $\frac{3}{8} \times 5 =$ _____

15. $\frac{2}{3} \times 13 =$ _____

16. $\frac{5}{12} \times 18 =$ _____

17. $\frac{5}{9} \times 12 =$ _____

Remembering

Write the decimals as fractions. Simplify your answers.

1. 0.54 = _____

2. 0.6 = _____

3. 0.09 = _____

4. 0.759 = _____

5. 0.008 = _____

6. 0.67 = _____

7. 0.75 = _____

8. 0.3 = _____

9. 0.224 = _____

10. 0.492 = _____

11. 0.004 = _____

12. 0.36 = _____

Decide if each angle is *obtuse*, *right*, or *acute*.

13.

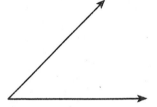

_____

14.

_____

15.

_____

16.

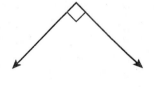

_____

17.

_____

18.

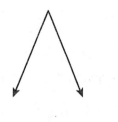

_____

Solve.

Show your work.

19. Javier has twice as many books as Emily. Emily has one third as many books as Manolo. If Manolo has 12 books, how many books does Javier have?

_____

Homework

Tanith is using a number line to find $\frac{3}{4} \times \frac{2}{5}$. This is her work so far:

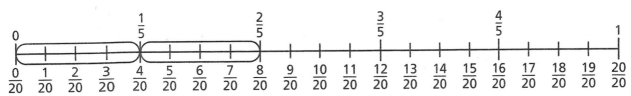

1. Explain Steps 1 and 2 to someone at home.

2. Finish Tanith's work by circling $\frac{3}{4}$ of each circled fifth.

   How many 20th's did you circle altogether? _____

   What is $\frac{3}{4} \times \frac{2}{5}$? _____

3. Use the number line to find $\frac{2}{3} \times \frac{5}{6}$.
   Label all the parts above and below. _____

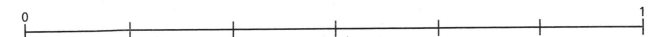

Solve.   *Show your work.*

4. Four friends at a party popped $\frac{3}{4}$ of a bag of popcorn.
   They ate half of what was popped. What fraction of the
   popcorn in the bag did they eat?

   _____

5. Ashley brought $\frac{7}{8}$ of a gallon of lemonade to the party.
   Her friends drank $\frac{2}{3}$ of it. How many gallons of
   lemonade did they drink?

   _____

Multiply. You do not need to simplify.

6. $\frac{2}{7} \times \frac{1}{3} =$ _____

7. $\frac{4}{9} \times \frac{2}{9} =$ _____

8. $\frac{1}{8} \times \frac{5}{6} =$ _____

9. $\frac{2}{7} \times 12 =$ _____

10. $\frac{4}{5} \times \frac{2}{3} =$ _____

11. $\frac{1}{7} \times \frac{3}{5} =$ _____

12. $\frac{9}{10} \times \frac{1}{2} =$ _____

13. $\frac{5}{12} \times 3 =$ _____

14. $\frac{5}{6} \times \frac{1}{6} =$ _____

Name _____ **Date** _____

Remembering

Estimate each product. Show your work.

1. $4.8 \times 47 \approx$ _____

2. $0.211 \times 8 \approx$ _____

3. $13.9 \times 11 \approx$ _____

Multiply. Compare your answer to your estimate above.

4. $\begin{array}{r} 4.8 \\ \times\ 47 \\ \hline \end{array}$

5. $\begin{array}{r} 0.211 \\ \times\ 8 \\ \hline \end{array}$

6. $\begin{array}{r} 13.9 \\ \times\ 11 \\ \hline \end{array}$

Find the unknown number in each Factor Puzzle.

7.

12	24
20	○

8.

○	12
24	18

9.

36	18
40	○

10.

7	○
28	16

11. Complete the rule, in words, for the function table.
Then write the equation.

Rule in Words: Multiply by _____, subtract _____					
Equation: _____					
Input (x)	3	5	8	13	20	31
Output (y)	2	6	12	22	36	58

Find the perimeter and area of each figure. Show your work.

12. 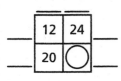 $P =$ _____

$3\frac{1}{4}$ ft $A =$ _____

4 ft

13. 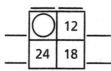 $P =$ _____

7.2 cm

$A =$ _____

5.1 cm

Multiply a Fraction by a Fraction

Homework

Multiply. Simplify first if you can.

1. $\frac{2}{5} \times \frac{6}{7} =$ _____

2. $\frac{4}{9} \times \frac{1}{8} =$ _____

3. $\frac{5}{24} \times \frac{8}{15} =$ _____

4. $\frac{2}{17} \times \frac{8}{1} =$ _____

5. $\frac{3}{4} \times \frac{12}{25} =$ _____

6. $\frac{5}{7} \times \frac{3}{8} =$ _____

7. $\frac{3}{10} \times \frac{2}{3} =$ _____

8. $\frac{5}{16} \times \frac{2}{25} =$ _____

9. $\frac{4}{35} \times \frac{7}{12} =$ _____

10. $\frac{5}{6} \times \frac{7}{1} =$ _____

11. $\frac{7}{9} \times \frac{6}{49} =$ _____

12. $\frac{7}{8} \times \frac{2}{3} =$ _____

13. Which fraction does *not* mean the same as the others?

$\frac{3}{15}$ $\frac{2}{10}$ $\frac{1}{5}$ $\frac{9}{45}$ $\frac{10}{50}$ $\frac{6}{40}$ $\frac{7}{35}$ $\frac{100}{500}$

Remembering

Solve.

Show your work.

1. Oliver has 395 books. He has 5 times as many books as Vanessa. How many books does Vanessa have?

_____

2. Armando makes clown puppets. He has 3 kinds of faces, 4 kinds of hats, and 2 kinds of clown suits. How many different puppets can Armando make?

_____

3. A farmer owns two orchards. There are 28 columns and 17 rows of trees in the apple orchard and 32 columns and 14 rows of trees in the pear orchard. Which one has more trees? How many more?

_____

4. I bought 2 bagels and a glass of juice this morning. I paid 40 cents for the juice. Altogether I paid $1.00. How much did each bagel cost?

_____

Round to the nearest tenth.

5. 0.67 _____ 6. 0.88 _____ 7. 2.14 _____ 8. 3.81 _____

Round to the nearest hundredth.

9. 0.789 _____ 10. 0.092 _____ 11. 0.818 _____ 12. 0.477 _____

Answer each question about the circle graph.

13. What fraction of the class has blonde hair?

_____

14. There are 32 students. How many have each hair color?

_____

15. How many times more students have brown hair than red hair?

_____

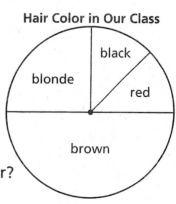

Hair Color in Our Class

Multiplication Strategies

Homework

Solve. Watch the signs. The operations are mixed.

1. $\frac{3}{4} \times \frac{1}{8} =$ _____

2. $\frac{2}{3} - \frac{1}{9} =$ _____

3. $\frac{1}{10} + \frac{1}{5} =$ _____

4. $\frac{2}{7} \times 12 =$ _____

5. $\frac{1}{5} + \frac{2}{3} =$ _____

6. $\frac{1}{4} + \frac{3}{8} =$ _____

7. $\frac{5}{7} \times \frac{5}{6} =$ _____

8. $\frac{11}{12} + 3 =$ _____

9. $\frac{4}{9} - \frac{2}{9} =$ _____

10. $\frac{1}{3} \times \frac{1}{8} =$ _____

11. $\frac{7}{8} \times \frac{3}{4} =$ _____

12. $10 - \frac{1}{9} =$ _____

Solve. Simplify before multiplying if you can.

Show your work.

13. Rodrigo's fish bowl holds $\frac{7}{8}$ of a gallon of water. It is now $\frac{1}{2}$ full. How much water is in it?

_____

14. Kenya's long jump is $7\frac{1}{6}$ feet long. Her friend Janet's is $6\frac{1}{3}$ feet long. How much longer is Kenya's jump than Janet's?

_____

15. A group of hikers walked $8\frac{7}{10}$ miles to Caribou Cave and then $5\frac{1}{5}$ miles to Silver Stream. How far did they walk altogether?

_____

16. Estevan has a recipe that calls for $\frac{3}{4}$ cup of flour. He wants to make $\frac{1}{3}$ of the recipe. How much flour will he need?

_____

17. A truck was carrying $2\frac{1}{8}$ tons of sand. When it arrived, only $1\frac{1}{2}$ tons of sand were left. How much sand was lost along the way?

_____

18. On Greenfield's Chicken Farm, $\frac{5}{6}$ of the eggs usually hatch. This year only $\frac{2}{3}$ as many hatched. What fraction of the total eggs hatched this year?

_____

Relate Fractional Operations **231**

Remembering

Multiply or divide.

1. 7.33
   × 8

2. 0.83
   × 0.5

3. 3.14
   × 72

4. 9.69
   × 6.1

5. 8)6.56

6. 6)2.88

7. 4)0.12

8. 7)46.9

Is each triangle _equilateral_, _isosceles_, or _scalene_?

9.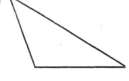

10.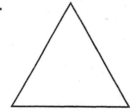

11.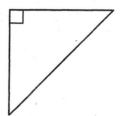

12.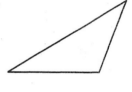

_____   _____   _____   _____

Write whether you would measure for _length_, _area_, or _volume_.

13. How much of the ground is covered by a tent?

_____

14. How far is it from the front door to the street?

_____

15. How much space is there inside a railroad car?

_____

16. How tall is an oak tree?

_____

17. How much water does an aquarium hold?

_____

Relate Fractional Operations

Write the fraction and the decimal equivalent for the shaded part.

1.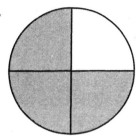

2.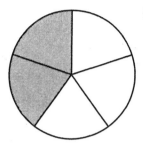

3.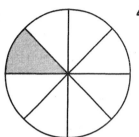

4.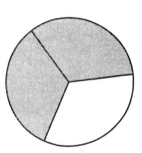

5.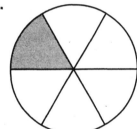

6.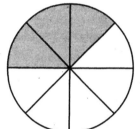

7.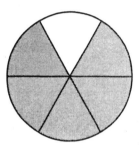

8.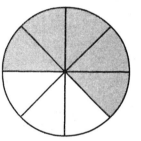

Write the fraction or decimal equivalent.

9. 0.625 = _____

10. 0.33 = _____

11. $\frac{7}{8}$ = _____

12. 0.83 = _____

13. 0.375 = _____

14. 0.250 = _____

15. 0.875 = _____

16. 0.6 = _____

17. 0.17 = _____

18. Circle the number that is *not* equal to the others.

$\frac{4}{5}$ 0.8 $\frac{16}{20}$ 0.08 $\frac{8}{10}$ 0.80

19. Label the number line with decimals above and
    fractions below.

0 |——|——|——|——|——|——|——|——|——|——| 1

Remembering

Solve.

1. Chad's wagon has a volume of 900 cu in. It is 30 in. long and 10 in. wide. How deep is the wagon?

_____

2. The McDonald family bought a new couch that is 5.4 feet long and 3.2 feet wide. How much floor space will the couch cover?

_____

3. A circular backyard swimming pool is 21 yards around the outside. About how wide is the pool at its widest point?

_____

4. A flower box is 7 feet long, 2 feet wide, and 2 feet deep. How many cubic feet of dirt will it hold?

_____

5. If dirt is sold in bags that hold 3.5 cu ft, how many bags of dirt will it take to fill the box?

_____

Subtract.

6. $7,000 - 472 =$ _____

7. $42,819 - 1,367 =$ _____

8. $689.46 - 38.2 =$ _____

9. $17.89 - 3.215 =$ _____

Solve each equation.

10. $3 + a = 15$

$a =$ _____

11. $b - 12 = 9$

$b =$ _____

12. $4c = 104$

$c =$ _____

13. $d + 125 = 362$

$d =$ _____

Homework

Divide.

1. $5 \div 6 =$ _____

2. $9 \div \frac{1}{5} =$ _____

3. $7 \div 5 =$ _____

4. $8 \div \frac{1}{6} =$ _____

5. $3 \div 10 =$ _____

6. $4 \div \frac{1}{9} =$ _____

7. $100 \div \frac{1}{6} =$ _____

8. $1 \div 65 =$ _____

9. $\frac{1}{5} \div 8 =$ _____

10. $\frac{1}{8} \div 7 =$ _____

11. $\frac{1}{2} \div 9 =$ _____

12. $\frac{1}{3} \div 5 =$ _____

Solve.

Show your work.

13. Alexander is dividing oranges into eighths. He has 5 oranges. How many eighths will he have?

_____

14. Carrie has 32 ounces of ice cream. She will divide it equally among 10 people. How much will each person get? Give your answer as an unsimplified improper fraction and as a simplified mixed number.

_____

15. Nayati wants to swim 50 miles this school year. She plans to swim $\frac{1}{4}$ mile each day. How many days will it take her to swim 50 miles?

_____

16. Eric has $\frac{1}{3}$ of a watermelon he wants to share with 3 friends. How much of the watermelon will he give to each person?

_____

17. A vegetable gardener needs to pack 16 pounds of beans into 20 bags. He wants all the bags to weigh about the same. About how much will each bag weigh? Give your answer in both unsimplified and simplest forms.

_____

When Dividing Is Also Multiplying **235**

Remembering

Write the fraction as a decimal number.

1. $\frac{1}{3}$ = _____   2. $\frac{2}{5}$ = _____   3. $\frac{1}{6}$ = _____   4. $\frac{14}{1,000}$ = _____

5. $\frac{4}{5}$ = _____   6. $\frac{9}{10}$ = _____   7. $\frac{3}{4}$ = _____   8. $\frac{3}{8}$ = _____

9. $\frac{3}{5}$ = _____   10. $\frac{2}{3}$ = _____   11. $\frac{5}{6}$ = _____   12. $\frac{12}{100}$ = _____

Write a decimal or whole number for the expression.

13. Nine tenths _____   14. Seven hundredths _____

15. Three million _____   16. Forty thousand, twenty-one _____

17. Two thousandths _____   18. Sixteen hundredths _____

Answer each question about the graph.

19. How many people are in the class? How do you know?

    _____

    _____

20. How many birthdays in the class are in the autumn? What fraction of the whole class is that?

    _____

21. How many more birthdays are in the winter than are in the spring?

    _____

22. How many birthdays are in the summer? In the summer and spring?

    _____

23. Write your own question about the graph.

    _____

    _____

Class Birthdays by Season

Number of Birthdays
12
10
8
6
4
2
0

Summer   Winter   Spring   Autumn

Season

Homework

Complete each fraction box.

1.

$\frac{7}{8}$ and $\frac{3}{4}$	
>	$\frac{7}{8} > \frac{3}{4}$ or $\frac{7}{8} > \frac{6}{8}$
+	
−	
×	

2.

$\frac{1}{2}$ and $\frac{3}{5}$	
>	
+	
−	
×	

Solve.

Show your work.

3. The Eagle Trucking Company must deliver $\frac{7}{8}$ of a ton of cement blocks and $\frac{5}{8}$ of a ton of bricks to one place. How much will this load weigh?

_____

4. A truck carried $3\frac{1}{3}$ tons of sand, but lost $\frac{1}{4}$ of a ton along the way. How many tons of sand were delivered?

_____

5. The trucking company also needs to deliver $1\frac{2}{3}$ tons of oak logs and $1\frac{7}{12}$ tons of maple logs. Which load weighs more?

_____

6. In a load of $\frac{3}{4}$ ton of steel rods, $\frac{1}{8}$ of them are bent. How many tons of steel rods are bent?

_____

7. The truck driver has to deliver $\frac{3}{5}$ ton of boards to a lumberyard. Circle the correct crate.

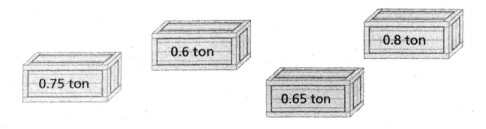

Name _____ **Date** _____

Remembering

Find the perimeter and area of each figure. Show your work.

1.

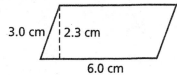

3.0 cm   2.3 cm

6.0 cm

P = _____

A = _____

2.

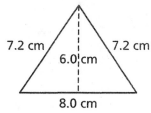

7.2 cm   6.0 cm   7.2 cm

8.0 cm

P = _____

A = _____

3.

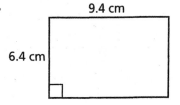

9.4 cm

6.4 cm

P = _____

A = _____

4.

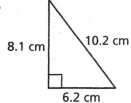

8.1 cm   10.2 cm

6.2 cm

P = _____

A = _____

Multiply or divide.

5. $0.05 \times 1.2 =$ _____

6. $8.25 \div 10 =$ _____

7. $11\overline{)7.81}$

8. $0.4 \times 6 =$ _____

9. $7.8 \div 6 =$ _____

10. $0.01 \times 0.9 =$ _____

11. $0.001 \times 8 =$ _____

12. $7\overline{)5.11}$

13. $16 \times 9.5 =$ _____

14. $1.44 \div 8 =$ _____

15. $12 \times 0.55 =$ _____

16. $\$2.48 \div 4 =$ _____

Mixed Practice with Fractions

Name _____ **Date** _____

Homework

Solve.

1. The Hot Chocolate Problem

Marco has $\frac{3}{4}$ pint of hot chocolate.
He is pouring it into cups that each hold
$\frac{3}{8}$ pint. How many cups can he fill?

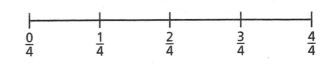

Think: How many _____ s are in _____?

Write the division equation. _____

Check your answer by writing the multiplication equation.

_____

2. The Honeybee Problem

A honeybee gathered nectar for $\frac{3}{4}$ of
an hour. It returned to the hive every
$\frac{1}{12}$ hour. How many trips did the bee make?

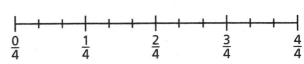

Think: How many _____ s are in _____?

Write the division equation. _____

Check your answer by writing the multiplication equation.

_____

Find the unknown factor. Rewrite the equation as a division equation.

<u>Division Equation</u>

3. $\frac{2}{3} \times$ _____ $= \frac{10}{18}$ $\frac{10}{18} \div \frac{2}{3} =$ _____

4. $\frac{4}{9} \times$ _____ $= \frac{36}{72}$ _____

5. $\frac{5}{6} \times$ _____ $= \frac{60}{150}$ _____

6. $\frac{2}{7} \times$ _____ $= \frac{42}{28}$ _____

7. $\frac{3}{10} \times$ _____ $= \frac{6}{30}$ _____

Explore Fractional Division **239**

Remembering

Multiply.

1. $\begin{array}{r} 52 \\ \times\ 75 \\ \hline \end{array}$

2. $\begin{array}{r} 263 \\ \times\ 38 \\ \hline \end{array}$

3. $\begin{array}{r} 396 \\ \times\ 27 \\ \hline \end{array}$

4. $\begin{array}{r} 945 \\ \times\ 78 \\ \hline \end{array}$

5. $\begin{array}{r} 96 \\ \times\ 8.7 \\ \hline \end{array}$

6. $\begin{array}{r} 0.63 \\ \times\ 54 \\ \hline \end{array}$

7. $\begin{array}{r} 0.75 \\ \times\ 0.08 \\ \hline \end{array}$

8. $\begin{array}{r} 0.049 \\ \times\ 0.18 \\ \hline \end{array}$

Divide.

9. $15\overline{)225}$

10. $23\overline{)253}$

11. $9.3\overline{)93}$

12. $7.4\overline{)111}$

Circle each value for the variable that makes the inequality true.

13. $s + 13 > 22$

   4   7   8   12   16

14. $t - 51 \geq 87$

   36   138   141   106   157

Solve each division problem. Try to do them in your head.

15. $7 \div 9 =$ _____

16. $8 \div \frac{1}{5} =$ _____

17. $5 \div 4 =$ _____

18. $12 \div \frac{1}{4} =$ _____

19. $1 \div 16 =$ _____

20. $10 \div \frac{1}{7} =$ _____

21. $9 \div \frac{1}{6} =$ _____

22. $3 \div 16 =$ _____

23. $1,000 \div \frac{1}{3} =$ _____

Explore Fractional Division

Homework

Solve. You may need a separate sheet of paper.

1. $\frac{9}{20} \div \frac{3}{5} =$ _____

2. $\frac{6}{7} \div \frac{2}{7} =$ _____

3. $\frac{21}{50} \div \frac{7}{10} =$ _____

4. $\frac{8}{9} \div \frac{2}{3} =$ _____

5. $\frac{27}{28} \div \frac{9}{7} =$ _____

6. $\frac{4}{9} \div 2 =$ _____

7. $\frac{7}{20} \div \frac{7}{5} =$ _____

8. $6\frac{3}{10} \div \frac{9}{5} =$ _____

Solve.   *Show your work.*

9. The Hwang family has a grove of sugar maple trees. They make maple syrup every year to give as gifts. Yesterday they made $2\frac{1}{4}$ quarts of syrup. They poured it into bottles that each held $\frac{3}{4}$ quart. How many bottles did they fill?

   _____

10. Last weekend the Hwangs made $2\frac{2}{3}$ quarts of maple syrup. They poured it into bottles that each held $\frac{1}{3}$ quart. How many bottles did the Hwangs fill?

    _____

11. On Monday the Hwangs made $1\frac{7}{8}$ quarts of syrup. They poured it into bottles that each held $\frac{3}{4}$ quart. How many full bottles are there? What fraction of the last bottle will be filled?

    _____

12. Today the Hwangs only made $\frac{7}{10}$ of a quart of syrup. They will pour it into bottles that each hold $\frac{1}{2}$ quart. How many full bottles are there? What fraction of the last bottle will be filled?

    _____

Remembering

Add or subtract.

1. $\frac{1}{2} + \frac{1}{3} =$ _____

2. $\frac{7}{9} - \frac{2}{3} =$ _____

3. $\frac{4}{7} + \frac{3}{4} =$ _____

4. $\frac{7}{10} - \frac{2}{5} =$ _____

5. $\frac{3}{8} + \frac{1}{4} =$ _____

6. $\frac{11}{12} - \frac{5}{6} =$ _____

7. $\frac{2}{11} + \frac{1}{2} =$ _____

8. $\frac{5}{6} - \frac{2}{3} =$ _____

9. $\frac{3}{4} + \frac{1}{3} =$ _____

10. $\frac{1}{5} - \frac{1}{6} =$ _____

11. $\frac{2}{5} + \frac{1}{3} =$ _____

12. $\frac{5}{9} - \frac{1}{4} =$ _____

Write the measure of the unknown angle.

13.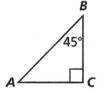

Angle $A =$ _____

14.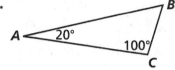

Angle $B =$ _____

15.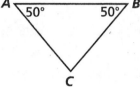

Angle $C =$ _____

Find the area.

16.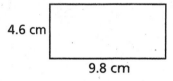

$A =$ _____

17.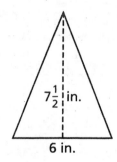

$A =$ _____

Solve.   *Show your work.*

18. Each day Kim walks for $\frac{1}{4}$ hour and runs for $\frac{2}{3}$ hour. How much more time does she spend running than walking each day?

_____

19. Ella has $\frac{1}{2}$ of a bag of marbles. Tyler has $\frac{1}{4}$ of the same-sized bag of marbles. If they combine their marbles together in one bag, how full is the bag?

_____

Division as Reverse Multiplication

Homework

Name _____ **Date** _____

Solve. You may need a separate sheet of paper.

1. $\frac{7}{8} \div \frac{3}{4} =$ _____

2. $\frac{9}{16} \div \frac{3}{4} =$ _____

3. $\frac{3}{20} \div \frac{3}{5} =$ _____

4. $\frac{3}{4} \div \frac{5}{9} =$ _____

5. $\frac{2}{9} \div \frac{3}{8} =$ _____

6. $\frac{8}{9} \div 4 =$ _____

7. $\frac{3}{7} \div \frac{9}{10} =$ _____

8. $1\frac{3}{7} \div \frac{1}{2} =$ _____

9. $\frac{2}{3} \div \frac{5}{6} =$ _____

10. $2\frac{3}{4} \div \frac{2}{3} =$ _____

11. Which one does *not* mean the same as the others?

$\frac{1}{2} \div \frac{1}{3}$ $3 \times \frac{1}{2}$ $\frac{1}{3} \div \frac{1}{2}$ $\frac{1}{2} \times 3$ $\frac{3}{2}$

Solve.

12. Containers of Annie's Apple Cider come in 2 sizes. The large bottle holds $2\frac{1}{4}$ gallons. The small bottle holds $\frac{3}{4}$ of a gallon. How many small bottles does it take to fill a large bottle?

_____

13. Annie is planning to sell apple cider in small drink boxes. Each box will hold $\frac{1}{16}$ of a gallon. How many boxes fill a $\frac{3}{4}$ gallon bottle?

_____

14. How many boxes fill a $2\frac{1}{4}$ gallon bottle?

_____

15. Three mugs of apple cider hold $\frac{1}{4}$ of a gallon. How much does each mug hold?

_____

Remembering

Solve. Use mental math.

1. $90,000 - 10,000 =$ _____

2. $0.004 + 40 =$ _____

3. $8,000 - 500 =$ _____

4. $0.030 + 0.007 =$ _____

5. Graph 8 points for the equation $y = x + 3$.

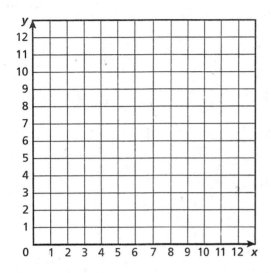

6. Complete the function table for the equation $y = 2x$. Then plot the points on the graph.

x	y
0	
1	
2	
3	
4	
5	

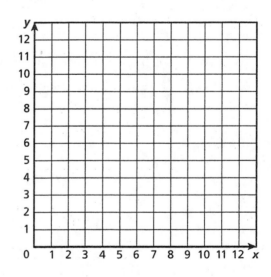

Write a verbal rule for the equation.

7. $y = \frac{1}{2}x$

_____

8. $y = x + \frac{1}{2}$

_____

Homework

Name _____   **Date** _____

Solve. Watch the signs! Give your answer in the simplest form.

1. $\frac{5}{12} \div \frac{3}{4} =$ _____

2. $\frac{11}{15} \div \frac{2}{5} =$ _____

3. $\frac{10}{21} \div \frac{2}{3} =$ _____

4. $\frac{2}{3} \times \frac{3}{8} =$ _____

5. $\frac{5}{9} \times \frac{3}{5} =$ _____

6. $\frac{4}{5} \times \frac{3}{8} =$ _____

7. $\frac{8}{9} \div 3 =$ _____

8. $\frac{1}{12} \div \frac{3}{4} =$ _____

9. $\frac{3}{7} \times \frac{2}{3} =$ _____

10. $\frac{5}{6} \times \frac{4}{7} =$ _____

11. $\frac{7}{11} \times \frac{5}{7} =$ _____

12. $\frac{5}{7} \div \frac{2}{3} =$ _____

13. Which one does *not* mean the same as the others?

$\frac{4}{5}$ $\frac{1}{5} \times 4$ $\frac{1}{5} \div \frac{1}{4}$ $\frac{1}{4} \div \frac{1}{5}$ $4 \times \frac{1}{5}$

Solve.

14. Harvest Cereal comes in boxes of different sizes. The regular box holds $\frac{7}{8}$ pound. The small box holds $\frac{2}{3}$ as much. How much cereal does the small box hold?

_____

15. The company will soon introduce a new giant size box. It will be $1\frac{1}{2}$ times as big as the regular box, which holds $\frac{7}{8}$ pound of cereal. How much cereal will the giant box hold?

_____

16. A six-pack of Harvest Cereal holds $1\frac{1}{8}$ pounds. How much does each little box hold?

_____

17. If a bowl of cereal holds $\frac{1}{8}$ pound, how many bowls can you get from a regular box of Harvest Cereal, which holds $\frac{7}{8}$ pound?

_____

Name _____ **Date** _____

Remembering

Round to the nearest tenth.

1. 14.57 = _____   2. 52.34 = _____   3. 1.90 = _____

Round to the nearest hundredth.

4. 140.517 = _____   5. 9.432 = _____   6. 74.366 = _____

7. A classroom survey asks how many pets each student has at home. The results are shown in the chart below. Draw and label a circle graph to represent the survey data.

Number of Pets	Number of Students
0	8
1	6
2	4
more than 2	6

Calculate the circumference of each circle. Use 3.14 for π.

8.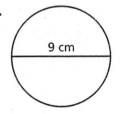

9 cm

circumference = _____

9.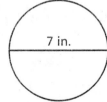

7 in.

circumference = _____

10. Make a graph of the data in the function table.

Equation: $y = 2x - 1$						
Input (x)	1	2	3	4	5	6
Output (y)	1	3	5	7	9	11

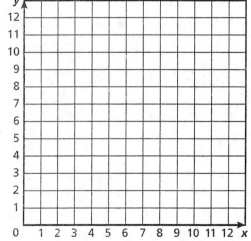

Distinguish Multiplication from Division

Name _____   **Date** _____

Solve.   *Show your work.*

1. Dan's Ice Cream comes in cartons of two sizes. The large carton holds $4\frac{1}{2}$ pounds. The small carton holds $1\frac{3}{4}$ pounds less. How much ice cream does the small carton hold?

   _____

2. Mac picked seven baskets of blueberries. The weights of the berries are given, in pounds, below. Find the mean of the weights of the berries.

   $\frac{5}{4}$ $\frac{9}{10}$ $\frac{11}{20}$ $\frac{4}{5}$ $\frac{6}{5}$ $\frac{11}{10}$ $\frac{13}{20}$

   _____

3. Four cones of Dan's Ice Cream hold $\frac{5}{8}$ pound. How much does each cone hold?

   _____

4. If a dish of ice cream holds $\frac{1}{4}$ pound, how many dishes can you get from a large carton of Dan's Ice Cream?

   _____

Solve. Give your answer in simplest form.

5. $\frac{3}{10} \div \frac{1}{5} =$ _____

6. $\frac{3}{4} \div \frac{11}{16} =$ _____

7. $\frac{9}{14} \div \frac{3}{7} =$ _____

8. $\frac{3}{5} \div 6 =$ _____

9. $\frac{1}{3} + \frac{3}{5} =$ _____

10. $\frac{5}{6} + \frac{1}{9} =$ _____

11. $\frac{3}{8} \div 4 =$ _____

12. $\frac{2}{5} - \frac{1}{10} =$ _____

13. $\frac{5}{7} - \frac{1}{2} =$ _____

14. $\frac{7}{8} \times \frac{2}{7} =$ _____

15. $\frac{5}{9} \times \frac{2}{3} =$ _____

16. $2 - \frac{3}{5} =$ _____

Name _____ **Date** _____

Remembering

Solve.

1. $8\overline{)6.08}$
2. $0.9\overline{)7.2}$
3. $0.04\overline{)3.72}$
4. $0.21\overline{)1.827}$

5. $0.19\overline{)13.3}$
6. $0.8\overline{)5.76}$
7. $0.06\overline{)27.6}$
8. $0.32\overline{)1.472}$

9. $\frac{1}{6} + \frac{2}{9} =$ _____

10. $\frac{4}{5} - \frac{1}{10} =$ _____

11. $\frac{5}{8} \times \frac{2}{5} =$ _____

12. $1 - \frac{4}{5} =$ _____

Draw the lines of symmetry.

13.

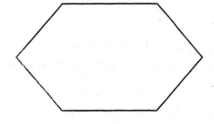

14.

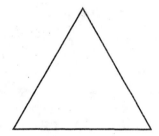

Solve.

Show your work.

15. The Singhs drove $50\frac{3}{4}$ miles in one hour. How far will they drive in $1\frac{1}{2}$ hours at the same speed?

_____

16. Julia has $4\frac{1}{2}$ cups of sugar. A cookie recipe calls for $\frac{3}{4}$ of a cup of sugar. How many batches of cookies can she make?

_____

Review Operations with Fractions

1. Connections

A recipe for 8 servings of crab cakes requires $\frac{1}{3}$ cup chopped scallions, $\frac{1}{4}$ cup diced onions, and $\frac{1}{2}$ cup chopped green peppers. If the cook has 1 cup chopped scallions, $\frac{1}{2}$ cup diced onions, and $1\frac{1}{4}$ cup green peppers, what is the greatest number of servings he can prepare?

_____

2. Reasoning and Proof

Sophia is 5 years too young to drive a car in her state. Dina is older than Sophia. Jose is 6 years older than Dina. The driving age is 16. Is Jose old enough to drive a car? Explain your reasoning.

_____

_____

_____

_____

3. Communication

Write a number between 1,000 and 2,000 that is divisible by 3, 6, and 9. Explain.

_____

_____

_____

_____

4. Representation

Dante had some baseball cards. He gave away 8 duplicates, and then bought 14 new cards. Yesterday he discovered that his puppy destroyed half of his cards. He has 24 cards left. How many cards did he have to start? Write an equation to represent the problem. Then solve it.

_____

_____

_____

_____

Remembering

Unsimplify the product to complete each division. Show your work.

1. $\frac{5}{8} \div \frac{3}{7} =$ _____

2. $\frac{9}{10} \div \frac{5}{8} =$ _____

3. $\frac{7}{16} \div \frac{1}{5} =$ _____

4. $\frac{2}{3} \div \frac{5}{12} =$ _____

Solve. Check your work.

5. $\frac{5}{8} \div \frac{2}{3} =$ _____

6. $\frac{7}{10} \div \frac{3}{16} =$ _____

7. $\frac{4}{5} \div \frac{7}{9} =$ _____

8. $\frac{1}{8} \div \frac{5}{16} =$ _____

9. $\frac{7}{12} \div \frac{1}{9} =$ _____

10. $\frac{1}{5} \div \frac{3}{10} =$ _____

**Decide whether you need to multiply or divide.
Then solve each problem.**

11. Mr. Jake's thermos holds $\frac{2}{5}$ gallon of coffee. The cap
    of the thermos can be used as a cup and holds $\frac{1}{32}$
    gallon. How many capfuls of coffee does the
    thermos hold?

    Show your work.

    _____

12. Dave is in charge of cutting small pieces of wood to
    cover the screws that are used to make furniture.
    These pieces are cut into pieces $\frac{1}{32}$ inch long from a
    wooden rod $8\frac{1}{2}$ inches long. How many screw covers can
    be cut from each rod?

    _____

Homework

Use the pattern below to solve exercises 1–2.

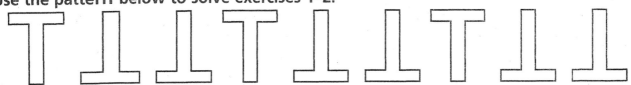

1. Draw the repeating terms of the pattern.

2. How many times does the pattern repeat?

_____

Use the pattern below to solve exercises 3–4.

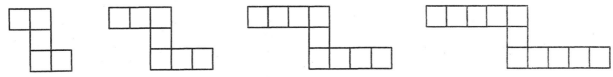

3. How does each figure in the pattern change from one term to the next?

_____

_____

_____

4. Draw the next figure in the pattern.

Use the pattern below to solve exercises 5–6.

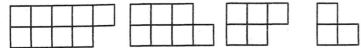

5. What rule describes the pattern?

_____

6. How many squares would be in the fifth figure in the pattern?

_____

Remembering

Solve each equation by unsimplifying the factor. Show your work.
Simplify your answers.

1. $\frac{5}{8} \div \frac{2}{3} =$ _____

2. $\frac{3}{7} \div \frac{1}{2} =$ _____

3. $\frac{3}{4} \div \frac{1}{5} =$ _____

4. $\frac{9}{10} \div \frac{4}{5} =$ _____

5. $\frac{7}{12} \div \frac{3}{8} =$ _____

6. $\frac{5}{16} \div \frac{3}{4} =$ _____

Solve each equation by inversion. Show your work. Simplify your answers.

7. $\frac{1}{3} \div \frac{4}{9} =$ _____

8. $\frac{15}{16} \div \frac{5}{8} =$ _____

9. $\frac{5}{12} \div \frac{1}{4} =$ _____

10. $\frac{1}{9} \div \frac{7}{10} =$ _____

11. $\frac{6}{7} \div \frac{1}{5} =$ _____

12. $\frac{7}{8} \div \frac{2}{3} =$ _____

Solve.

13. Kara is making a fancy collar for her cat. The collar will be $8\frac{2}{5}$ inches long. Kara plans to sew beads all along the length of the collar. If each bead is $\frac{2}{5}$ inch long, how many beads will she need to complete the collar?

_____

14. Cooper's father put a shelf in his room to hold CDs. The shelf is $38\frac{1}{2}$ inches long. A CD holder is $\frac{7}{32}$ inch wide. How many CDs will fit on the shelf?

_____

15. Mrs. Albertson bought $1\frac{1}{2}$ pounds of grapes. If each grape weighs $\frac{1}{4}$ of an ounce, how many grapes did she buy?

_____

Geometric Patterns

Homework

Study the pattern. Then answer the questions.

1. 70, 90, 90, 70, 90, 90, 70, 90, 90, 70, 90, …

    a. What are the repeating terms in the pattern? _____

    b. What is the next term in the pattern? _____

Show two different ways to extend each pattern.

2. 12, 10, 12, …

_____

_____

3. 5, 8, 8, 5, …

_____

_____

Write an equation to represent the function. Then complete the table.

4.

b	1	2	3	4	5
c	8	16	24	32	

_____

5.

s	1	2	3	4	5
t	7	9	11	13	

_____

6.

p	30	24	18	12	6
q	5	4	3	2	

_____

7.

x	36	33	30	27	24
y	10	9	8	7	

_____

Make a drawing to solve.

8. Jay saves $2 in June, $4 in July, $6 in August, and $8 in September. If the pattern continues for 3 more months, how much money will Jay save in all?

_____

Remembering

**Complete the fractional division using any method. Show your work.
Simplify your answers.**

1. $\frac{1}{2} \div \frac{5}{8} =$ _____

2. $\frac{1}{10} \div \frac{5}{16} =$ _____

3. $\frac{11}{12} \div \frac{2}{5} =$ _____

4. $\frac{9}{10} \div \frac{3}{4} =$ _____

5. $\frac{1}{3} \div \frac{5}{8} =$ _____

6. $\frac{2}{7} \div \frac{3}{10} =$ _____

Divide. Simplify your answers.

7. $\frac{1}{5} \div \frac{3}{8} =$ _____

8. $\frac{5}{6} \div \frac{7}{10} =$ _____

9. $\frac{5}{16} \div \frac{2}{3} =$ _____

10. $\frac{11}{12} \div \frac{1}{6} =$ _____

11. $\frac{3}{5} \div \frac{3}{5} =$ _____

12. $\frac{5}{8} \div \frac{11}{12} =$ _____

Decide if you need to multiply or divide. Then solve each problem.

13. One brand of trail mix is $\frac{1}{12}$ cashew nuts. How many pound of cashews would be found in $8\frac{1}{2}$ pounds of the trail mix?

_____

14. The company packs its trail mix in $\frac{1}{8}$-pound packets. How many packets can be filled using $7\frac{3}{4}$ pounds of the trail mix?

_____

15. The company adds a honey mixture to the trail mix and manufactures health bars that each weigh $\frac{3}{8}$ pound. How many whole bars can be made from $12\frac{1}{2}$ pounds of the honey and nuts mixture?

_____

Homework

Draw each transformation.

1. a translation along the line

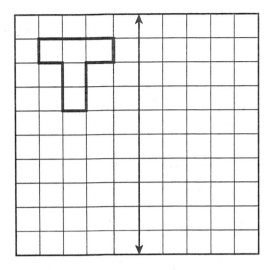

2. a reflection across the line

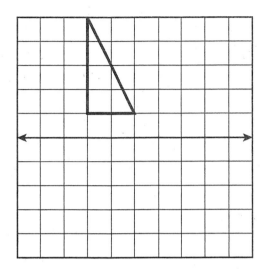

3. a 90° clockwise rotation about point *Z*

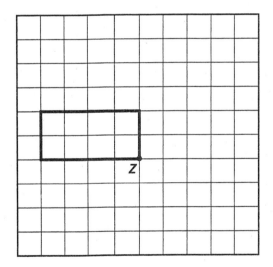

4. a reflection across the line

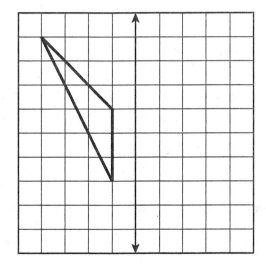

5. Are all transformed figures congruent to the original figures? Explain.

_____

_____

_____

Remembering

Divide. Simplify your answers.

1. $\frac{7}{10} \div \frac{3}{8} = $ _____

2. $\frac{1}{5} \div \frac{3}{4} = $ _____

3. $\frac{11}{12} \div \frac{5}{9} = $ _____

4. $\frac{2}{3} \div \frac{5}{8} = $ _____

5. $\frac{3}{16} \div \frac{1}{12} = $ _____

6. $\frac{1}{2} \div \frac{7}{8} = $ _____

7. $\frac{7}{9} \div \frac{2}{5} = $ _____

8. $\frac{5}{8} \div \frac{2}{7} = $ _____

9. $\frac{1}{3} \div \frac{5}{16} = $ _____

Decide if you need to multiply or divide. Then solve each problem.

10. A flat-screen television is $2\frac{1}{8}$ feet high, $3\frac{3}{12}$ feet wide, and $\frac{1}{3}$ foot deep. What is the volume of this rectangular prism?

_____

11. The area of a rectangular patio is $196\frac{1}{2}$ square feet. One side of the patio measures $12\frac{1}{2}$ feet. How wide is the patio?

_____

12. A recipe for baked beans calls for $\frac{2}{3}$ pound of dried pinto beans. How many complete recipes can be made from $6\frac{3}{8}$ pounds of pinto beans?

_____

13. If $\frac{1}{16}$ ounce of pure gold is used to make a bead for a necklace, how many ounces of gold would be needed to make 32 beads?

_____

14. Explain: a is greater than 1 and $\frac{n}{d}$ is a fraction less than 1. If $a \div \frac{n}{d} = c$, what do you know about c in relation to a?

_____

_____

Explore Transformations

Homework

Complete.

1. Draw the reflection of the trapezoid across the given line. Write the coordinates of the vertices.

2. Draw a translation of the rectangle 4 units to the left. Write the coordinates of the vertices.

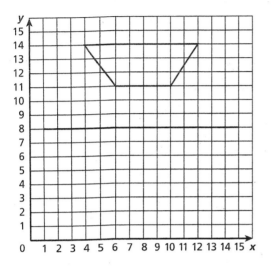

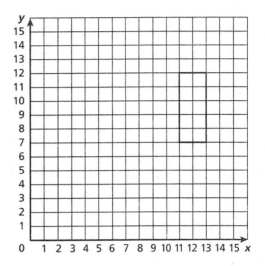

_____   _____

3. Draw a line through points (8, 1) and (8, 14). Draw a parallelogram with vertices (1, 1), (2, 5), (6, 1), and (7, 5). Reflect the parallelogram over the line. Write the coordinates of the vertices.

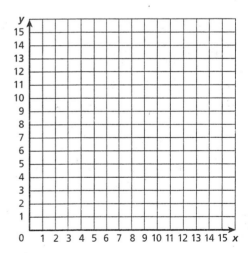

_____

4. On a separate sheet of grid paper, use transformations to make a shape pattern. Explain the transformations you used to create your pattern.

Remembering

Circle the greater answer. Do not try to calculate the answer.

1. $452 \times \frac{2}{3}$

   $452 \div \frac{2}{3}$

2. $\frac{9}{10} \times \frac{3}{4}$

   $\frac{9}{10} \div \frac{3}{4}$

3. $\frac{1}{3} \times \frac{3}{10}$

   $\frac{1}{3} \div \frac{3}{10}$

4. $4\frac{2}{3} \times 7\frac{1}{5}$

   $4\frac{2}{3} \div 7\frac{1}{5}$

Decide what operation to use. Then solve. Simplify your answers.

5. A U.S. penny weighs about $\frac{11}{25}$ ounce and is made of copper and zinc. How many complete pennies could be made from $4\frac{1}{2}$ pounds of the copper and zinc mixture? (Hint: Remember that 1 pound = 16 ounces.)

   _____

6. A U.S. nickel is made from copper and nickel and weighs about $\frac{22}{125}$ ounce. How much would 275 nickels weigh?

   _____

7. A U.S. dime weighs about $\frac{2}{25}$ ounce and is also made of copper and nickel. How much would one dime, one nickel, and one penny weigh altogether?

   _____

8. A U.S. quarter weighs about $\frac{1}{5}$ ounce and is also made of copper and nickel. Serena saves only quarters. Her quarter collection weighs $64\frac{2}{5}$ ounces. How many quarters does she have?

   _____

9. A U.S. half-dollar is made from the same copper-nickel metal as the dime and quarter and weighs about $\frac{2}{5}$ ounce. How much more does a half-dollar weigh than a nickel?

   _____

Transformations in the Coordinate Plane

Homework

Complete this story about Noreen's older brother, Tim.
Tim saved $5 every day. He and Noreen started to save
on the same day. Draw pictures of Tim's bank each day
if that helps you decide how much he has saved.

On Day 0 Tim did not put money into his bear bank.
On Day 0 Tim's bear bank was empty. He had $0 in his bank.

1. On Day 1 Tim put $5 into his bear bank.
On Day 1 Tim had _____ in his bank.

2. On Day 2 Tim put $5 into his bear bank.
On Day 2 Tim had _____ in his bank.

3. On Day 3 Tim put $5 into his bear bank.
On Day 3 Tim had _____ in his bank.

4. On Day 4 Tim put $5 into his bear bank.
On Day 4 Tim had _____ in his bank.

5. On Day 5 Tim put $5 into his bear bank.
On Day 5 Tim had _____ in his bank.

6. On Day 6 Tim put $5 into his bear bank.
On Day 6 Tim had _____ in his bank.

7. On Day 7 Tim put $5 into his bear bank.
On Day 7 Tim had _____ in his bank.

8. On Day 8 Tim put $5 into his bear bank.
On Day 8 Tim had _____ in his bank.

9. Complete the Multiplication Column
Table to show Tim's savings.

Days	Dollars
0	0
1	
2	
3	
4	
5	
6	
7	
8	

+ _____
+ _____
+ _____
+ _____
+ _____
+ _____
+ _____
+ _____

Name _____ **Date** _____

Remembering

Which is greater? How much greater?

1. 32 × 16 or 36 × 12

_____

2. 8 × 5 or 9 × 4

_____

3. 20 × 0.3 or 0.2 × 300

_____

4. 171 × 28 or 281 × 17

_____

5. Plot these points on a coordinate grid and join them to make a figure. What figure did you make?

A (6, 12)

B (11, 12)

C (2, 3)

D (13, 3)

_____

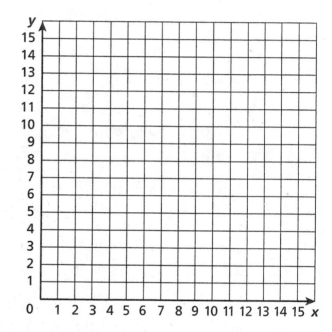

Solve.

6. Justin buys a card for his cousin for $3.29 and a card for his aunt for $4.25. He pays with a $10 bill. How much change should Justin receive?

_____

7. Cheese costs $5.79 per pound. How much will $\frac{1}{3}$ pound of cheese cost?

_____

8. Tell whether this is a growing pattern or a shrinking pattern and why you think so. Then draw the next figure in the pattern.

_____

Multiplication Patterns

Homework

Grandma Jackson has 8 tomato plants in each row in her garden.

1. Write this story using the word *per*.

_____

2. Make a Multiplication Column
Table to describe Grandma
Jackson's tomato plants.

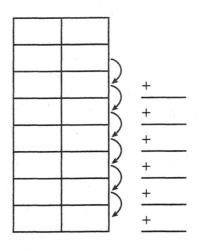

**Decide whether each story is a multiplication column story. If it
is, rewrite it using the words *per* and *each*.**

3. The balloon man at the fair gave away 6 balloons in the
morning, 15 in the afternoon, and 11 in the evening.

_____

4. A large bag of potatoes costs $8 at Season's Produce Store.

_____

5. Write a story for this multiplication
column table. Label the columns
to show your story.

0	0
1	7
2	14
3	21
4	28
5	35
6	42

+ 7
+ 7
+ 7
+ 7
+ 7
+ 7

_____

_____

Name _____ **Date** _____

Remembering

Add or subtract.

1. 23,165.1
    + 13,223.7

2. 24,722.30
    + 28,149.61

3.   4,598.75
    + 133,236.13

4. 410,410.41
    − 301,229.60

5. 782,312.5
    −   63.4

6. 97,287.811
    − 3,719.552

Use a protractor to find each unknown angle measure.

7.

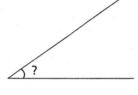

?

_____

8.

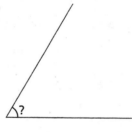

?

_____

9.

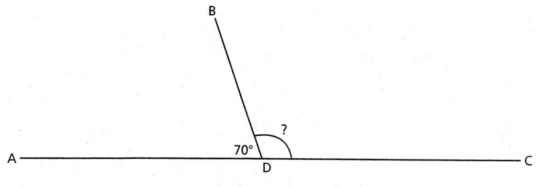

_____

Solve.   *Show your work.*

10. The Lucases made $14\frac{1}{2}$ pints of jam. They have empty
    $\frac{1}{4}$-pint jars to pour the jam into. How many jars will
    they need?

_____

Unit Rate

Homework

Decide if each situation is a Multiplication Column Situation.
Make a Multiplication Column Table for situation 5.

1. Every week, Noreen eats half a dozen oranges.

   _____

2. In the spring, David plants 8 carrots in each row of his garden.

   _____

3. On the first 4 days of the week, Jeff takes Cooper the dog
   for 2-mile walks. On the last 3 days, they walk 3 miles each
   day.

   _____

4. José read 5 books this week, but read 6 books last week.

   _____

5. Jason saves $4 every day so he can buy a basketball hoop.

   _____

6. Carole feeds her tropical fish 6 pinches of fish food every day.

   _____

Decide whether each table is a Multiplication Column Table.
Explain why or why not.

7.

0	0
1	6
2	12
3	18
4	24
5	30

8.

0	0
1	2
2	6
3	7
4	10
5	12

9.

0	0
1	4
2	8
3	9
4	12
5	17

10.

0	0
1	9
2	18
3	27
4	36
5	45

_____ _____ _____ _____

_____ _____ _____ _____

Remembering

Multiply.

1. $\frac{1}{6} \times 42 =$ _____

2. $\frac{2}{3} \times 63 =$ _____

3. $\frac{3}{5} \times 28 =$ _____

4. $\frac{1}{5} \times \frac{1}{2} =$ _____

5. $\frac{2}{3} \times \frac{1}{2} =$ _____

6. $\frac{1}{4} \times \frac{9}{10} =$ _____

7. $\frac{3}{4} \times \frac{2}{9} =$ _____

8. $\frac{8}{15} \times \frac{5}{20} =$ _____

9. $\frac{22}{25} \times \frac{5}{6} =$ _____

Identify the next three elements in each pattern.

10.

11. $0, \frac{2}{3}, 1\frac{1}{3}, 2, 2\frac{2}{3},$ _____, _____, _____

12. $2, 6, 18, 54,$ _____, _____, _____

Justine wants to show how her school's population has changed. She has data from 1990, 1995, 2000, and 2005.

Year	Number of Students
1990	450
1995	525
2000	910
2005	820

13. Make a graph that will help Justine show the trend in population. Label your graph.

What Is a Multiplication Column Situation?

Homework

Make a Ratio Table for each situation. Be sure to label the tables.

1. Two bands marched onto the football field. One marches on in rows of 15, and the other marches on in rows of 7.

2. John can plant 7 tomato vines in the time it takes Joanna to plant 4 tomato vines.

3. The twins Diana and Walter make fruit salad. Their recipe is 6 bananas and 4 oranges.

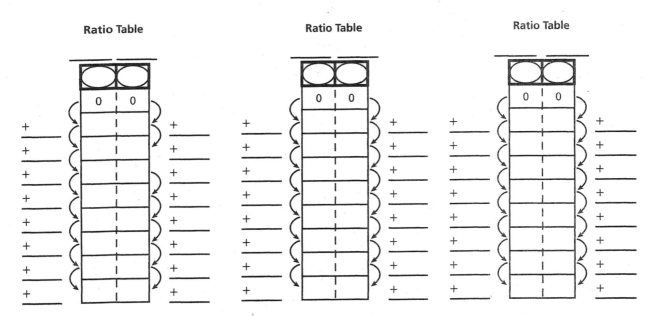

4. Circle each Ratio Table below. Write numbers to show the two multiplication columns that are in each Ratio Table.

A.			B.			C.			D.	
0	0		0	0		0	0		0	0
7	3		2	3		7	4		0	1
14	6		4	5		14	8		0	2
21	9		6	8		21	12		0	3
28	12		8	10		28	16		0	4
35	15		10	13		35	20		0	5
42	18		12	15		42	24		0	6

Remembering

Circle the greater fraction in each pair.

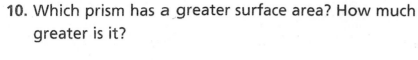

1. $\frac{3}{5}$ or $\frac{3}{6}$

2. $\frac{3}{6}$ or $\frac{9}{12}$

3. $\frac{3}{7}$ or $\frac{4}{9}$

4. $\frac{1}{15}$ or $\frac{3}{42}$

5. $\frac{3}{8}$ or $\frac{8}{20}$

6. $\frac{7}{20}$ or $\frac{4}{12}$

7. $\frac{12}{5}$ or $2\frac{1}{5}$

8. $4\frac{8}{12}$ or $\frac{58}{12}$

9. $3\frac{2}{7}$ or $\frac{10}{3}$

10. Which prism has a greater surface area? How much greater is it?

Show your work.

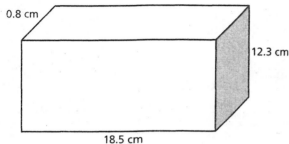

0.8 cm

12.3 cm

18.5 cm

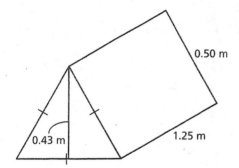

0.50 m

0.43 m

1.25 m

Solve.

11. The figure skating club has 20 yards of fabric to make costumes. They need 12 costumes. How many yards of fabric can be used for each costume?

_____

12. Tell what transformation(s) was used to create this pattern. Then draw the next 3 terms of the pattern.

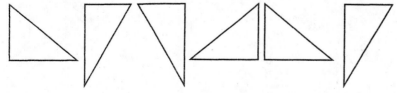

_____

Linked Stories Are Ratios

Homework

Explain why each table is or is not a Ratio Table. For the Ratio Tables, tell the Multiplication Columns and the basic ratio.

1.

0	0
2	3
4	6
6	9
9	12
11	15

2.

0	0
6	8
12	16
18	24
24	32
30	40

3.

0	0
1	0
2	0
3	0
4	1
5	2

1. _____

_____

_____

2. _____

_____

_____

3. _____

_____

Solve each Factor Puzzle.

4. Central School has 6 printers and 14 computers. If East School has 28 computers, how many printers does it have?

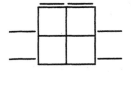

_____

5. Sally saved $10, and Luke saved $40. When Luke saved $32, how much had Sally saved?

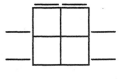

_____

Remembering

Multiply.

1. $3 \times 0.11 =$ _____
2. $0.5 \times 7 =$ _____
3. $0.12 \times 0.6 =$ _____

4. $0.04 \times 0.8 =$ _____
5. $0.2 \times 0.9 =$ _____
6. $0.01 \times 1.2 =$ _____

7. $0 \times 0.8 =$ _____
8. $1.1 \times 1.2 =$ _____
9. $0.13 \times .04 =$ _____

10. $1.4 \times 0.1 =$ _____
11. $0.8 \times 0.2 =$ _____
12. $3 \times 0.5 =$ _____

The bar graph shows favorite kinds of muffins for a grade 5 class.

Favorite Kind of Muffin

Answer each question about the bar graph.

13. Which kind of muffin is the favorite? _____

14. Which kind of muffin is the least favorite? _____

15. Which kind of muffin is about half as popular as the oatmeal muffin? _____

16. Which kind of muffin is three times as popular as the banana muffin? _____

Complete.

17. 50 mm = _____ cm
18. 100 m = _____ cm

19. 4,000 mg = _____ g
20. 3 kg = _____ g

21. 2,000 mL = _____ L
22. 6 L = _____ mL

What Are Proportion Situations?

Homework

Solve.

1. Dana and Sue work in the same office. They leave for work at the same time. It takes Dana 25 minutes to get to work, and Sue 30 minutes to get to work. If it takes Dana 35 minutes to get home, how long does it take Sue to get home?

   _____

2. One day Dana got to work sooner than usual because there was very little traffic. It took her only 15 minutes. How long did it take Sue to get to work that day?

   _____

3. Maggie is buying vegetables at the farmers' market to make vegetable soup. The recipe for this soup calls for 6 tomatoes and 9 heads of broccoli. But Maggie wants to make a lot of soup, so she buys 8 tomatoes. How many broccoli heads should she buy?

   _____

4. Six of Susan's cookies weigh the same as 5 of Tara's cookies. How many of Susan's cookies weigh the same as 15 of Tara's cookies?

   _____

Tell which table belongs to each story above. Then write the basic ratio for each table in the circles.

5. ◯ : ◯
0 : 0
2 : 3
4 : 6
6 : 9
8 : 12
10 : 15
12 : 18
14 : 21

6. ◯ : ◯
0 : 0
5 : 6
10 : 12
15 : 18
20 : 24
25 : 30
30 : 36
35 : 42

7. ◯ : ◯
0 : 0
6 : 5
12 : 10
18 : 15
24 : 20
30 : 25
36 : 30
42 : 35

8. ◯ : ◯
0 : 0
9 : 2
18 : 4
27 : 6
36 : 8
45 : 10
54 : 12
63 : 14

_____   _____   _____   _____

_____   _____   _____   _____

Name _____ **Date** _____

Remembering

Divide.

1. $5\overline{)60}$ 2. $4\overline{)24}$ 3. $9\overline{)36}$ 4. $3\overline{)39}$

5. Write an equation for the function tables.

x	y
1	2
2	4
3	6
4	8
5	10

_____

x	y
2	1
4	2
6	3
8	4
10	5

_____

x	y
0	3
1	4
2	5
3	6
4	7

_____

Find each unknown angle.

6.
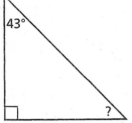

_____

7.
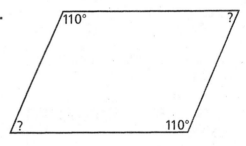

_____

Solve.

8. Thomas has 100 stamps. Ten are from Mexico. The rest are from the United States and Canada. He has twice as many U.S. stamps as Canadian. How many U.S. stamps does Thomas have?

_____

9. There are cows and chickens in a farmyard. There are 63 animals and 148 legs. How many cows are there in the farmyard?

_____

Solve Proportion Problems

Name _____ **Date** _____

Homework

Solve the numeric proportion problems using Factor Puzzles.
Use a separate sheet of paper.

1. _____ : 21 = 32 : 56

2. 24 : _____ = 18 : 30

3. 6 : 15 = _____ : 35

4. 56 : 72 = 35 : _____

Tell which are proportion problems and which are not. Solve
each proportion problem and write the basic ratio.

5. The law in Sunny Land City says that every 3-story building must have 21 windows. How many windows must an 18-story building have?

_____

_____

_____

6. Josh runs 7 mi for every 8 mi run by Sally. If Sally runs 16 mi, how far does Josh run?

_____

_____

_____

7. In one town, every family has 2 dogs and 5 cats. If 16 dogs live in the town, how many cats live there?

_____

_____

_____

8. Mark drives 28 miles in 40 minutes. How long does it take him to drive 35 miles at the same rate?

_____

_____

_____

9. Andrew and Barbara collect stamps. Every week Andrew adds 5 stamps to his collection, and Barbara adds 7 to hers. When Andrew has collected 30 stamps, how many will Barbara have collected?

_____

_____

_____

10. The daffodils in my garden appeared in April, and the tulips appeared in May. Both the daffodils and the tulips grew 2 in. every week. How tall were the daffodils when the tulips were 10 in. tall? Explain your answer.

_____

_____

_____

11. On the separate sheet of paper, write one proportion problem and one non-proportion problem. Each problem should have 3 numbers and should ask a question.

Solve Proportions as Factor Puzzles **271**

Name _____ **Date** _____

Remembering

Evaluate each expression.

1. $(110 - 50) + 9 =$ _____

2. $3 \times (4 - 1) =$ _____

3. $14 \div (5 + 2) =$ _____

4. $(10 + 10) - 4 =$ _____

5. $(36 \div 9) + 14 =$ _____

6. $(6 \times 7) \div 21 =$ _____

7. $16 \times (0 \div 2) =$ _____

8. $81 - (4 \times 5) =$ _____

The line graph shows the average temperature each month in
San Francisco.

Answer each question about the line graph.

9. Which month has the lowest average temperature?

_____

10. What is the greatest average temperature?

_____

11. Does the average temperature increase or
decrease from January to August?

_____

12. Does the average temperature increase or decrease
from September to December?

_____

**Average Temperature
in San Francisco**

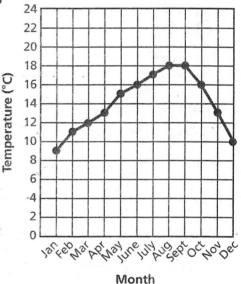

13. Reflect the parallelogram over the line. Write the
coordinates of the reflected parallelogram.

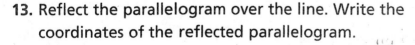

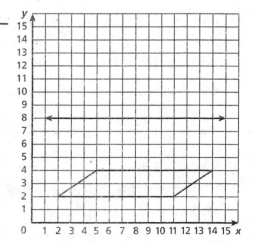

Solve Proportions as Factor Puzzles

Name _____ **Date** _____

Solve each proportion.

1. $32 : 50 = a : 75$ _____

2. $32 : b = 96 : 12$ _____

Solve each proportion problem or tell why it is not a proportion problem. For each proportion problem tell your assumptions.

3. Two express elevators leave the ground floor of a skyscraper on their way to the 100th floor and make no stops. They both move at the same speed, but elevator A left before elevator B because its doors close faster. When elevator A passes the 15th floor, elevator B passes the 10th floor. When elevator A gets to the top, where will elevator B be? Explain your answer.

_____

_____

_____

4. Jean used 25 small cans of paint to paint 30 tables. How many tables did she paint with 15 small cans of paint?

_____

_____

5. The Foster Publishers' printing press can print 5 dictionaries in 8 minutes. How many dictionaries can it print in 32 minutes?

_____

_____

6. Every week Farmer Percy fed 12 buckets of oats to his 3 horses. Then he bought some more horses. Now he feeds his horses 40 buckets of oats. How many horses does Farmer Percy have now?

_____

_____

7. On a separate sheet of paper, write a proportion word problem and a non-proportion problem. Each problem should have 3 numbers and ask a question.

Name _____ **Date** _____

Remembering

Multiply or divide.

1. $0.4 \times 0.3 =$ _____

2. $5.6 \div 0.8 =$ _____

3. $0.35 \times 1.21 =$ _____

4. $1.44 \div 0.12 =$ _____

5. $3.4 \times 2.7 =$ _____

6. $36.0 \div 1.6 =$ _____

7. $9.1 \times 0.6 =$ _____

8. $8.1 \div 0.9 =$ _____

Multiply or divide. Simplify your answers.

9. $\frac{3}{8} \times 14 =$ _____

10. $\frac{9}{6} \div 6 =$ _____

11. $\frac{5}{6} \times \frac{3}{4} =$ _____

12. $\frac{5}{12} \div \frac{3}{4} =$ _____

Find the area of each figure.

13.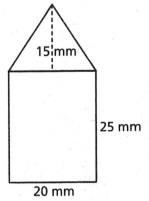

$A =$ _____

14.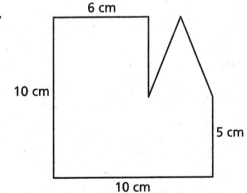

$A =$ _____

Basic Ratios

Homework

Make up a proportion problem for the proportion. Then solve the problem.

1. $a : 35 = 32 : 40$

_____

_____

_____

_____

_____

_____

_____

_____

_____

_____

_____

_____

Solve each proportion.

2. $18 : 54 = c : 42$

$c = $ _____

3. $32 : 50 = a : 75$

$a = $ _____

4. $32 : b = 56 : 35$

$b = $ _____

5. $40 : t = 45 : 54$

$t = $ _____

6. $c : 24 :: 30 : 36$

$c = $ _____

7. $27 : 63 = 12 : q$

$q = $ _____

Remembering

Add or subtract.

1. $4.1 + 3.2 =$ _____

2. $7.9 - 5.3 =$ _____

3. $3.16 + 0.25 =$ _____

4. $1.02 - 0.63 =$ _____

5. $9.63 + 0.07 =$ _____

6. $13.42 - 3.42 =$ _____

7. $10.50 + 2.43 =$ _____

8. $5.01 - 0.02 =$ _____

Solve.   *Show your work.*

9. Isabel has 27 white balls and 49 black balls in each bucket. She has 19 buckets of balls. How many balls does Isabel have altogether?

_____

10. Tyler has 350 baseball cards. He gives $\frac{1}{5}$ of them to his friend. Then he gives $\frac{1}{4}$ of the rest to his brother. What fraction of his 350 baseball cards does Tyler have left?

_____

Draw all lines of symmetry for each figure.

11.

12.

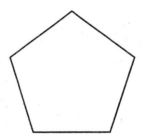

13.

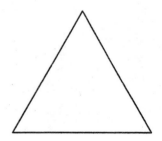

Find the unknown.

14. $5d + 3 = 28$

$d =$ _____

15. $\frac{1}{8}r = 8$

$r =$ _____

16. $32 + f = 40$

$f =$ _____

17. $9(x + 6) = 81$

$x =$ _____

18. $7y - 3 = 25$

$y =$ _____

19. $49 \div s = 7$

$s =$ _____

Circle each percent on the 100-millimeter line.

1. 15%

2. 48%

3. 85%

Fill in the missing percents, decimals, and fractions.

4.

Percent, Decimal, and Fraction Equivalencies					
Cents	Percent of a dollar	Dollars	Decimal	Fraction of 100	Simplest fraction
25 ¢	25%	$0.25	0.25	$\frac{25}{100}$	$\frac{1}{4}$
20 ¢					
		$0.75			
					$\frac{1}{2}$
				$\frac{90}{100}$	
			0.1		
	100%				
					$\frac{4}{5}$
				$\frac{70}{100}$	
		$0.40			
	30%				
			0.6		

Remembering

Simplify each fraction.

1. $\frac{6}{10} =$ _____

2. $\frac{12}{48} =$ _____

3. $\frac{35}{42} =$ _____

4. $\frac{9}{81} =$ _____

5. $\frac{10}{80} =$ _____

6. $\frac{3}{6} =$ _____

7. $\frac{9}{12} =$ _____

8. $\frac{16}{48} =$ _____

The circle graph shows favorite kinds of television programs for a grade 5 class.

Answer each question about the circle graph.

Preferred Programs

9. What fraction of the class likes drama programs the best?

_____

10. What is the most popular kind of television program?

_____

11. What fraction of the class likes sports or documentary programs the best?

_____

12. Find the perimeter of the triangle.

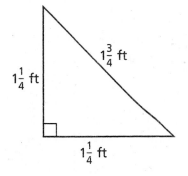

$P =$ _____

13. Translate the trapezoid 4 units up and 3 units to the right. Write the coordinates of the translated trapezoid.

_____

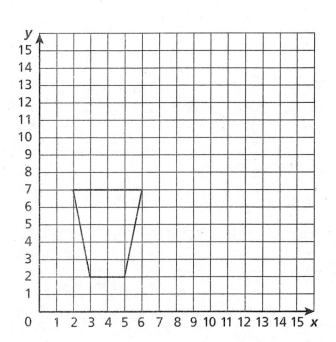

   The Meaning of Percent

Name _____ **Date** _____

Homework

This is half of a shape.

1. Draw 100% of the shape.

2. Draw 200% of the shape.

This is 80% of a group. ☐☐☐☐

3. Draw 20% of the group.

4. Draw 120% of the group.

Set up a proportion and solve by simplifying and finding an equivalent fraction.

5. 24 out of 60 is _____ %.

6. What percent of 56 is 14? _____

7. 120% of 25 is _____.

8. 42 is 75% of _____.

9. 15 is 30% of _____.

10. 75% of 96 is _____.

Solve each percent problem using any method.

11. Simon keeps 250 pet spiders in his living room. 70 of these love spinach. What percent of Simon's pet spiders love spinach?

_____

12. John eats 18 raisins. That is 20% of the number of raisins Sam eats. How many raisins does Sam eat?

_____

13. Annie's age is 85% of her brother's age. If her brother is 20, how old is Annie?

_____

14. Six blocks spilled out of a can of blocks. That was 25% of the total number of blocks in the can. How many blocks were in the can to begin with?

_____

Name _____ **Date** _____

Remembering

Add or subtract.

1. $\frac{1}{2} + \frac{3}{4} =$ _____

2. $\frac{5}{12} - \frac{1}{6} =$ _____

3. $\frac{7}{9} + \frac{3}{18} =$ _____

4. $\frac{17}{20} - \frac{3}{10} =$ _____

5. $\frac{2}{3} + \frac{1}{12} =$ _____

6. $\frac{18}{24} - \frac{3}{12} =$ _____

7. $\frac{2}{7} + \frac{9}{21} =$ _____

8. $\frac{9}{10} - \frac{1}{5} =$ _____

Solve. Make a Factor Puzzle for each problem.

9. Jasmine sold 12 baskets of peppers and Selina sold 18. How many baskets of peppers had Jasmine sold when Selina sold 12?

10. Maria peels 5 apples in the time it takes Brian to peel 3 apples. How many apples will Brian have peeled when Maria has peeled 20 apples?

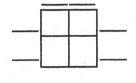

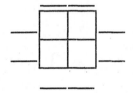

11. $r : 27 = 35 : 45$

$r =$ _____

12. $25 : 50 :: t : 30$

$t =$ _____

13. $15 : 40 = 18 : p$

$p =$ _____

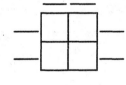

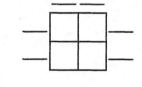

Find the area of each rectangle.

14.

$1\frac{1}{2}$ in.

$2\frac{1}{4}$ in.

$A =$ _____

15.

$1\frac{3}{4}$ ft

$3\frac{1}{3}$ ft

$A =$ _____

Solving Problems Using Percents

Solve each problem using any method.

1. A box of ballpoint pens contains 54 pens with black ink, 36 with blue ink, and 30 with red ink. If you took 20 pens from the box, how many would you expect to have black ink? Blue ink? Red ink?

   _____

   _____

2. 20 boxes of shirts arrived at the Men's Shop. 15 of the boxes contained blue shirts and the rest contained white shirts. What are the chances that the first box the owner opens will contain white shirts? Express your answer as a percent.

   _____

3. What are your chances of the spinner landing on a white space? Express your answer as a percent.

   _____

4. Andy has a drawer full of 24 pairs of socks. Some are black and some are blue. He pulled out 3 pairs. 2 pairs were black and 1 pair was blue. How many pairs of black socks and how many pairs of blue socks do you think Andy has?

   _____

   _____

5. The town parking lot can hold 200 vehicles. If 600 people in town own SUVs and 900 own cars, how many of each kind of vehicle would you expect to see in the lot when it is full?

   _____

   _____

6. On average, David throws 8 strikes out of every 10 pitches. If he pitches the ball 15 times, how many strikes would you expect him to throw?

   _____

Name _____ **Date** _____

Remembering

Multiply or divide.

1. $\frac{5}{8} \times \frac{2}{3} =$ _____

2. $\frac{2}{5} \div \frac{1}{3} =$ _____

3. $\frac{7}{10} \times \frac{1}{2} =$ _____

4. $\frac{11}{12} \div \frac{3}{4} =$ _____

5. $\frac{4}{5} \times \frac{8}{9} =$ _____

6. $\frac{6}{8} \div \frac{2}{7} =$ _____

7. $\frac{10}{11} \times \frac{7}{11} =$ _____

8. $\frac{9}{12} \div \frac{3}{12} =$ _____

Solve. Make a Factor Puzzle for each problem.

9. Coleen did 32 jumping jacks when Nathan did 44 jumping jacks. Earlier, when Coleen did 24 jumping jacks, how many did Nathan do?

10. Sheila saved $16 when Jonathan saved $28. When Sheila saves $40, how much will Jonathan have saved?

11. $30 : c = 35 : 56$

    $c =$ _____

12. $27 : 24 :: d : 40$

    $d =$ _____

13. $a : 81 = 42 : 63$

    $a =$ _____

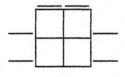

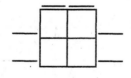

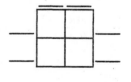

14. Which net will make a cube? _____

   A.

   B.

   C.

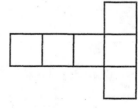

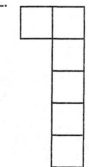

Probability Using Percents and Decimals

Homework

For each figure, write a ratio that compares the base to the
height. Then draw a similar figure that is not congruent.

1.
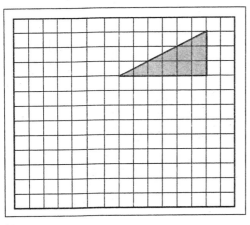

_____

2.
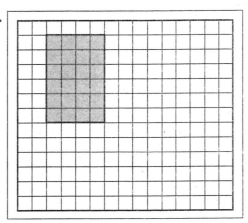

_____

The two figures are similar. Find the unknown measurement.
Show your work.

3.
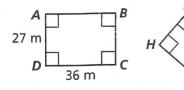

EF = _____

_____

_____

4.
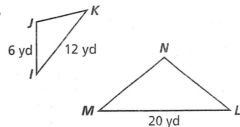

MN = _____

_____

_____

5.
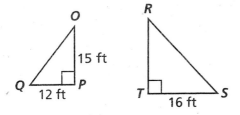

TR = _____

_____

_____

6.
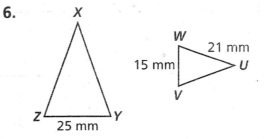

XY = _____

_____

_____

Name _____

Date _____

Remembering

Add or subtract. Write the answer in simplest form.

1. $\frac{7}{8} - \frac{1}{2} =$ _____

2. $\frac{7}{10} - \frac{1}{5} =$ _____

3. $\frac{4}{9} + \frac{2}{9} =$ _____

4. $\frac{3}{10} + \frac{2}{5} =$ _____

5. $\frac{2}{5} - \frac{3}{10} =$ _____

6. $\frac{1}{2} - \frac{2}{5} =$ _____

7. $2\frac{7}{8} - 1\frac{1}{2} =$ _____

8. $2 + 1\frac{4}{6} =$ _____

9. $5\frac{3}{8} - 1\frac{1}{4} =$ _____

10. $\frac{7}{8} + \frac{1}{2} =$ _____

11. $\frac{2}{3} + \frac{2}{9} =$ _____

12. $4\frac{1}{5} + 3\frac{1}{2} =$ _____

What figure will each net make?

13.

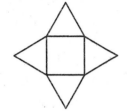

_____

14.

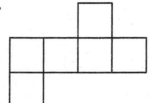

_____

15.

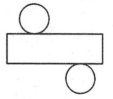

_____

16. Translate the parallelogram up 3 units.
Then reflect it over the line. Write the
coordinates of the transformed parallelogram.

_____

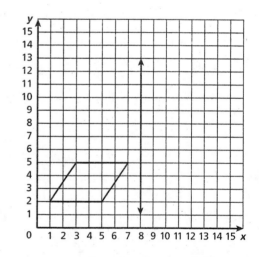

Solve.

Show your work.

17. Meg has $15. She wants to buy a DVD that usually costs
$18. The DVD is on sale for 25% off. Does Meg have
enough money?

_____

18. Last year about 15,000 people went to the fall fair.
Attendance this year increased by 15%. About how
many people went to the fair this year?

_____

Similar Figures

Use the map and an inch ruler to answer each question below.

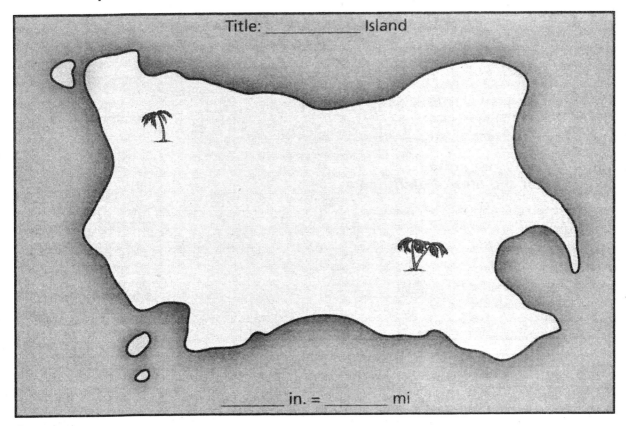

Title: _____ Island

_____ in. = _____ mi

1. In the blank spaces on the map, write a name for the island and a scale for the map.

2. List six features you might see on your island. Mark them on the map.

   _____   _____

   _____   _____

   _____   _____

3. Plan a route that allows you to visit all of the features listed above. The route should begin and end at the same feature. Name the features in the order you will visit them.

   _____

   _____

4. Use the map scale and an inch ruler to estimate the total distance you will travel on your route.

   _____

Remembering

Multiply or divide. Write each answer in simplest form.

1. $\frac{2}{5} \times \frac{5}{6} =$ _____

2. $\frac{4}{5} \div 8 =$ _____

3. $\frac{1}{2} \times \frac{4}{7} =$ _____

4. $\frac{1}{3} \div 6 =$ _____

5. $5 \times \frac{3}{4} =$ _____

6. $\frac{2}{3} \div \frac{5}{6} =$ _____

7. $1\frac{4}{5} \times 1\frac{1}{2} =$ _____

8. $3 \times 6\frac{2}{3} =$ _____

9. $\frac{7}{8} \div \frac{3}{4} =$ _____

10. $5 \div 8 =$ _____

11. $3\frac{1}{3} \times \frac{5}{6} =$ _____

12. $\frac{2}{3} \div 1\frac{1}{2} =$ _____

Find the perimeter and area of each figure.

13.

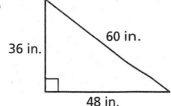

36 in.   60 in.   48 in.

P = _____

A = _____

14.

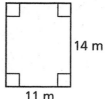

14 m   11 m

P = _____

A = _____

15.

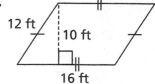

12 ft   10 ft   16 ft

P = _____

A = _____

Solve.   *Show your work.*

16. The new park will take up 3.5 acres. Four tenths of the park will remain natural forest. How large is the area that will remain natural forest?

_____

17. Cecilia walks 1.2 miles to get to the corner store. She stops to tie her shoe when she is $\frac{2}{3}$ of the way there. How far does she have left to walk to reach the store?

_____

18. Emily worked 4.25 hours on Saturday and 6.75 hours on Sunday. If she earned $8.60 per hour, how much did she earn on the weekend?

_____

Homework

1. The scale drawing shows that the distance from Lexington to Lincoln is 100 km. What is the distance from Lexington to Manchester?

Lexington   Lincoln   Manchester

_____

Make a scale drawing of each object. Include a key.

2. a rug that measures 6 feet by 12 feet

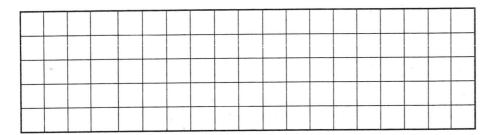

3. a desktop that is 36 cm wide and 72 cm long

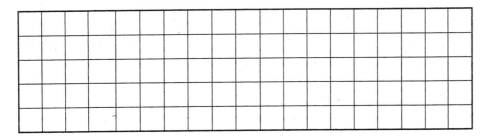

4. a swimming pool that is 32 feet long and 16 feet wide

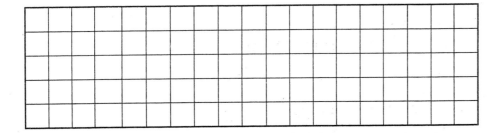

Name _____ **Date** _____

Remembering

Order each set from least to greatest.

1. $\frac{3}{5}$ 0.25 35%

_____

2. $\frac{9}{10}$ 0.65 85%

_____

3. $\frac{3}{75}$ 0.4 62%

_____

4. $\frac{13}{20}$ 0.75 49%

_____

5. $\frac{1}{3}$ 0.5 35%

_____

6. $\frac{3}{8}$ 0.23 35%

_____

7. $\frac{19}{25}$ 0.25 89%

_____

8. $\frac{12}{20}$ 0.3 50%

_____

9. $\frac{4}{5}$ 0.81 79%

_____

Write a number to make each number sentence true.

10. 44% < _____ < 0.77

11. $\frac{2}{3}$ < _____ < 69%

12. $\frac{1}{16}$ < _____ < 35%

13. 0.2 < _____ < 23%

14. $\frac{3}{5}$ < _____ < 95%

15. $\frac{3}{8}$ < _____ < 0.45

Find the surface area of each solid. Show your work.

16.

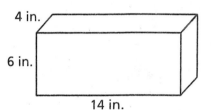

4 in.
6 in.
14 in.

_____

_____

_____

_____

17.

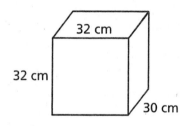

32 cm
32 cm
30 cm

_____

_____

_____

_____

Solve.

18. Three eighths of Ms. Nester's class of twenty-four students are on the track team. Three fifths of Mr. Boyko's class of twenty-five students are not on the track team. In which class are more students on the track team?

_____

19. Ali has seven coins in his pocket that total 81¢. What coins does he have? _____

Explore Scale Drawings

Homework

Use the scale to solve for _n_. Show your work.

1. 1 in. = 6 ft

3 in. = _n_ ft

_____

_____

_____

2. $\frac{1}{4}$ in. = 1 yd

$2\frac{1}{2}$ in. = _n_ yd

_____

_____

_____

3. $\frac{1}{8}$ in. = 1 ft

_n_ in. = 4.5 ft

_____

_____

_____

4. Make a floor plan of a room using the scale $\frac{1}{4}$ inch = 1 foot. Include the items listed in the box and two others of your choice.

room size: _____

item 1: _____

item 2: _____

Actual Dimensions
rug: 6 feet by 9 feet
chair: 3 feet by 4 feet
table: 2 feet by 3 feet
sofa: 3 feet by 8 feet

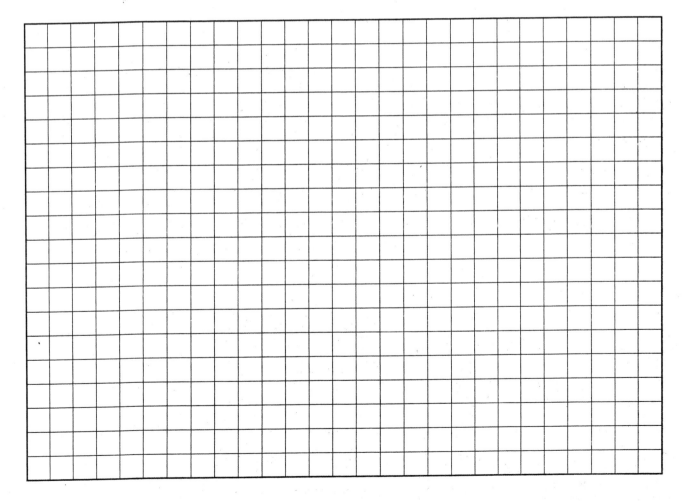

Name _____ **Date** _____

Remembering

Find 10% of each number. Then find 20% of each number.

1. 88 _____ _____   2. 420 _____ _____   3. 3,410 _____ _____

4. 6 _____ _____   5. 720.25 _____ _____   6. 2.1305 _____ _____

Solve using any method.

7. _____% of 80 = 24   8. 75% of _____ = 45   9. _____% of 850 = 85

10. 23% of 60 = _____   11. 10% of _____ = 30   12. 8% of 56 = _____

13. 50% of _____ = 36   14. 45% of 800 = _____   15. _____% of 84 = 21

Draw the top, side, and front views.

16.

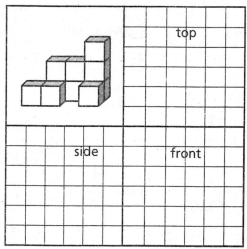

17.

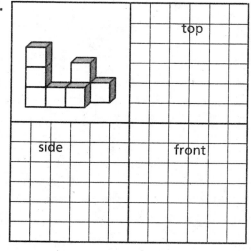

18. Describe how the triangle *ABC* was transformed to the triangle *A'B'C'*.

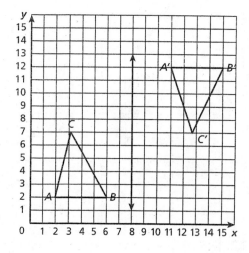

Use Scale Drawings

Name _____   Date _____

1. Communication

Estimate the quotient 6,256 ÷ 68.
Then explain how you used mental
math to do so.

_____

_____

_____

_____

2. Representation

If a 10 × 10 grid represents 100%,
how would you represent 139%?
Draw and explain your answer.

_____

_____

3. Connections

The height to width ratio of the British
flag is 1 : 2. The height to width ratio
of the American flag is 10 : 19. The
height of a British flag is 65 inches.
What is its width? Find the width of
an American flag having the same
height.

_____

4. Reasoning and Proof

Mikey's baseball caps are mixed up in
a box. If he reaches in at random and
selects one hat, the probability that he
selects a red hat is $\frac{7}{12}$; the probability
of selecting a blue hat is $\frac{1}{4}$, and the
probability of selecting a green hat
is $\frac{1}{6}$. There are no other colors Mikey
can pick. What is the least number
of hats there can be in the box and
how many of them are of each color?
Explain your reasoning.

_____

_____

_____

_____

Remembering

Solve each problem using any method. Express your answers as a percent and as a decimal.

1. A package of 50 balloons contains 18 blue balloons, 15 red balloons, 12 yellow balloons, and 5 green balloons. If you select one balloon at random, what is the probability you will choose a blue balloon? a red balloon? a yellow balloon? a green balloon?

   _____

2. A game at the fair promises a prize behind every target. There are 200 targets. Behind one target is the Grand Prize, behind 20 targets are free ride tickets, behind 50 targets are free food tickets, and behind the remaining targets are small stuffed animals. What is the probability that you will win the Grand Prize? a free ride ticket? a free food ticket? a stuffed animal?

   _____

   _____

The two figures are similar. Find the unknown measurement.

3.

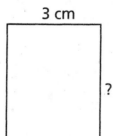
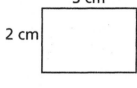

4.

_____   _____

5. This scale drawing shows the distance from Greensburg to Johnstown is 32 miles. Use a ruler to find the distance from Greensburg to Monroeville in miles.

_____

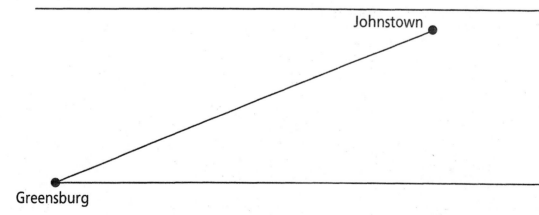

Johnstown

Greensburg   Monroeville

Use Mathematical Processes

Homework

Name the prism for each base.

1.

2.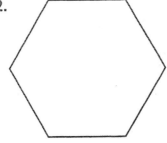

3.

_____   _____   _____

Find the surface area of each prism.

Remember: a small perpendicular mark (–) means that the edges are congruent.

4.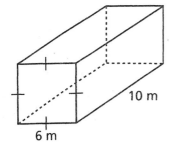

10 m

6 m

5.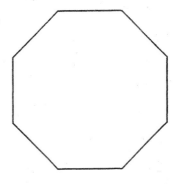

13 cm

15 cm

12 cm

10 cm

_____   _____

A cube has a surface area of 24 square centimeters.

6. What is the area of each face? _____

7. What is the length of each edge? _____

Name the solid that can be made from each net.

8.

9.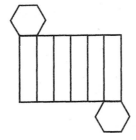

_____   _____

Name _____ **Date** _____

Remembering

Write a decimal equivalent for each fraction.

1. $\frac{1}{2} =$ _____

2. $\frac{3}{4} =$ _____

3. $\frac{1}{8} =$ _____

4. $\frac{5}{8} =$ _____

5. $\frac{3}{8} =$ _____

6. $\frac{7}{8} =$ _____

Write each mixed number as an improper fraction.

7. $2\frac{1}{2} =$ _____

8. $3\frac{5}{6} =$ _____

9. $2\frac{1}{10} =$ _____

10. $5\frac{5}{8} =$ _____

11. $8\frac{3}{5} =$ _____

12. $1\frac{7}{8} =$ _____

13. Find the perimeter and area of this figure.

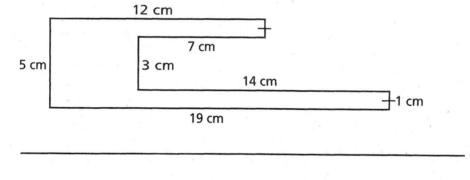

_____

_____

14. Sketch and label a figure that has an area of 47 sq cm.

15. Show two different ways to extend the pattern.

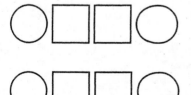

Prisms and Cylinders

Homework

These nets form pyramids.

Name the shape of the base and use it to name the pyramid.

1.

Base: _____

Name: _____

_____

2.

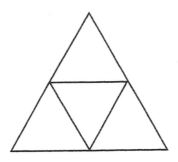

Base: _____

Name: _____

_____

3.

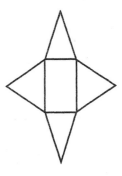

Base: _____

Name: _____

_____

4.

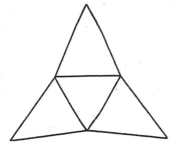

Base: _____

Name: _____

_____

5.

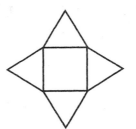

Base: _____

Name: _____

_____

6.

Base: _____

Name: _____

_____

Find the total surface area of each pyramid.

7.

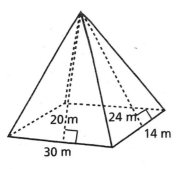

20 m 24 m 14 m 30 m

_____

8.

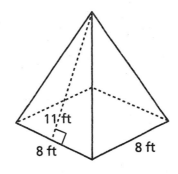

11 ft 8 ft 8 ft

_____

Remembering

Compare. Write < or >.

1. $\frac{3}{4}$ ◯ $\frac{1}{4}$

2. $\frac{5}{8}$ ◯ $\frac{7}{8}$

3. $\frac{7}{12}$ ◯ $\frac{11}{12}$

4. $\frac{1}{2}$ ◯ $\frac{1}{3}$

5. $\frac{1}{8}$ ◯ $\frac{1}{4}$

6. $\frac{1}{12}$ ◯ $\frac{1}{10}$

Write each fraction in simplest form.

7. $\frac{2}{6} =$ _____

8. $\frac{5}{10} =$ _____

9. $\frac{8}{12} =$ _____

10. $\frac{6}{8} =$ _____

11. $\frac{6}{9} =$ _____

12. $\frac{12}{20} =$ _____

Describe each figure using the language of geometry.

13.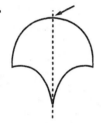

_____

14.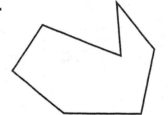

_____

15.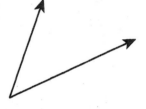

_____

16.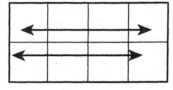

_____

17.

_____

18.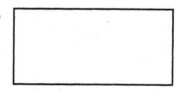

_____

19.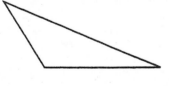

_____

20.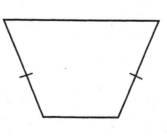

_____

21.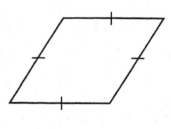

_____

Homework

Date

1. Draw the front, side, and top views of this solid. Name the solid.

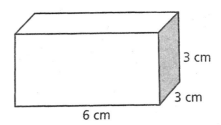

3 cm

3 cm

6 cm

Front View	Side View	Top View

Name of Solid: _____

2. Make a drawing to match the views.

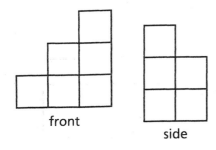

front

side

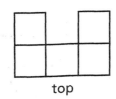

top

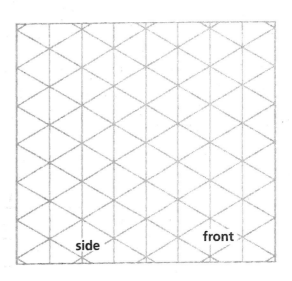

side   front

3. Find the number of faces, edges, and vertices for this solid.

Faces: _____   Edges: _____   Vertices: _____

4. A pyramid has 8 edges. How many sides does the base of the pyramid have?

_____

Compare and Contrast Geometric Solids **297**

Remembering

Multiply or divide.

1. $\frac{3}{4} \times \frac{1}{4} =$ _____

2. $\frac{5}{8} \times \frac{2}{5} =$ _____

3. $\frac{7}{12} \times \frac{2}{3} =$ _____

4. $\frac{1}{2} \div \frac{1}{3} =$ _____

5. $\frac{3}{5} \div \frac{1}{4} =$ _____

6. $\frac{5}{12} \div \frac{3}{8} =$ _____

7. $\frac{5}{6} \times \frac{9}{10} =$ _____

8. $\frac{7}{10} \div \frac{4}{5} =$ _____

9. $\frac{7}{9} \times \frac{3}{4} =$ _____

10. $\frac{3}{7} \div \frac{2}{7} =$ _____

11. $\frac{2}{3} \times \frac{6}{7} =$ _____

12. $\frac{4}{5} \div \frac{8}{15} =$ _____

Find the area.

13.

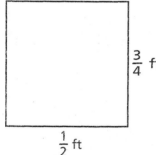

$A =$ _____

14.

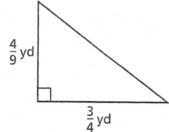

$A =$ _____

15.

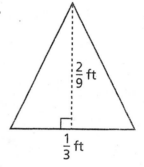

$A =$ _____

Solve.

Show your work.

16. A bottle contains $\frac{3}{4}$ quart of milk. Jan drank $\frac{1}{2}$ of the milk. What amount of milk did Jan drink?

_____

17. Rob traveled $\frac{11}{12}$ of a mile on foot. He ran $\frac{1}{4}$ of that distance. What distance did he walk?

_____

Compare and Contrast Geometric Solids

Homework

The cube is rotated about the axis of rotation.
What number is on top after each rotation? Use the cube you made in class.

1. $\frac{1}{4}$ rotation clockwise

2. $\frac{1}{4}$ rotation counterclockwise

3. $\frac{1}{2}$ rotation

4. $\frac{3}{4}$ rotation clockwise

Use these figures for exercises 5–10.

Figure A	**Figure B**	**Figure C**
base: square	base: trapezoid	base: regular hexagon

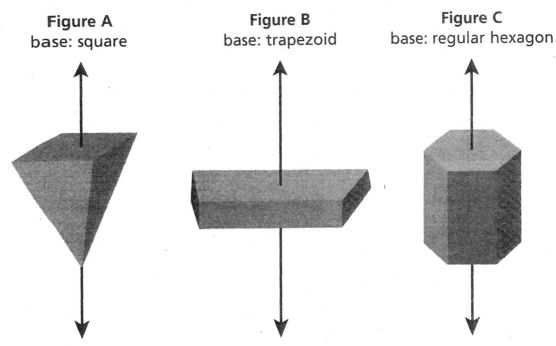

After what fraction of a rotation does each figure look the same?

5. Figure A   6. Figure B   7. Figure C

Write the letters of the figures with each type of symmetry.

8. 90° rotational symmetry   9. 180° rotational symmetry

10. How do you know that a figure does not have rotational symmetry? Explain your answer using the figures above.

_____

_____

Name _____ **Date** _____

Remembering

Write the equivalent decimal and fraction for each percent.
Write fractions in simplest terms.

1. 20% _____   2. 35% _____

3. 70% _____   4. 37.5% _____

5. 55% _____   6. 87.5% _____

Find the percent of each number.

7. 15% of 130 _____   8. 22% of 298 _____

9. 38% of 92 _____   10. 87% of 619 _____

11. 6% of 429 _____   12. 70% of 813 _____

Solve.

13. Mrs. Cahill shopped at the Bargain Bin, where everything
is sold in large quantities. The Bargain Bin sold a bag of
96 oranges, but Mrs. Cahill wanted only $\frac{1}{8}$ that many
oranges. How many oranges did she want?

_____

14. Bargain Bin sold cases of 48 boxes of oatmeal, but Mrs. Cahill
wanted only $\frac{3}{16}$ that many boxes. How many boxes did
she want?

_____

15. Bargain Bin sold 150 pounds of steak, but Mrs. Cahill
wanted only $\frac{3}{25}$ that many pounds. How many pounds of
steak did she want?

_____

16. Bargain Bin sold cartons of 324 brussel sprouts, but Mrs. Cahill
wanted only $\frac{1}{162}$ of a carton. How many brussel sprouts did she want?

_____

Three-Dimensional Rotational Symmetry

Name _____ Date _____

Compare the following numbers on a number line.
Write >, <, or =.

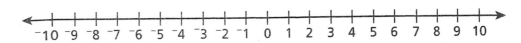

1. 5 ◯ ⁻5   2. 0 ◯ ⁻2   3. ⁻3 ◯ 10   4. ⁻1 ◯ ⁻6

5. 7 ◯ ⁻9   6. ⁻8 ◯ ⁻4   7. ⁻2 ◯ ⁻2   8. 9 ◯ ⁻10

Write the numbers in order from least to greatest.

9. ⁻6, 5, 0, ⁻1 _____

10. 9, ⁻7, ⁻10, 4 _____

11. 3, ⁻3, ⁻2, 8 _____

Use the number line above to find the distance from one number to the other.

12. 9, ⁻8   13. ⁻4, 2   14. 0, ⁻7

_____ units   _____ units   _____ units

15. 7, ⁻7   16. ⁻3, ⁻3   17. 1, ⁻6

_____ units   _____ units   _____ units

18. **On the Back** Think about a real-world career that involves negative numbers. Describe the career, and explain how negative numbers are used.

Homework

Homework

Add. Use +/− models or make a sketch if you need to.

1. $^-7 + {}^+8 =$ _____

2. $^+9 + {}^+9 =$ _____

3. $^+6 + {}^-3 =$ _____

4. $^-5 + {}^-9 =$ _____

5. $^-4 + {}^+3 =$ _____

6. $^+8 + {}^-9 =$ _____

7. $^+2 + {}^+7 =$ _____

8. $^-2 + {}^+7 =$ _____

9. $^-6 + {}^+1 =$ _____

10. $^+10 + {}^+8 =$ _____

11. $^+9 + {}^-15 =$ _____

12. $^-12 + {}^+4 =$ _____

13. $^-12 + {}^+12 =$ _____

14. $^-7 + {}^+14 =$ _____

15. $^-13 + {}^-6 =$ _____

16. $^+21 + {}^-5 =$ _____

17. $^-14 + {}^-9 =$ _____

18. $^+49 + {}^+7 =$ _____

19. $^-37 + {}^+9 =$ _____

20. $^+3 + {}^-38 =$ _____

21. $^-6 + {}^+25 =$ _____

22. $^+20 + {}^+20 =$ _____

23. $^-25 + {}^+15 =$ _____

24. $^-30 + {}^-10 =$ _____

25. $^-13 + {}^+44 =$ _____

26. $^+31 + {}^-42 =$ _____

27. $^+54 + {}^-34 =$ _____

28. $^-300 + {}^+300 =$ _____

29. $^+250 + {}^+250 =$ _____

30. $^+300 + {}^-200 =$ _____

Solve.

31. Daniella had $150 in a savings account. She spent $75 of that amount, and wrote the expression $^+150 + {}^+75$ to represent the action. Explain why the expression is not correct. Then write the correct expression.

_____

_____

32. Sameer wrote $^-0$ as the answer for the addition $^+500 + {}^-500$. Did he write the correct answer? Explain why or why not.

_____

33. Ben recorded the temperature at 6 A.M. as $^-19°F$. By 4 P.M. the temperature had risen 15°F. Write an addition equation using integers that represents the 4 P.M. temperature.

_____

_____

34. **On the Back** Explain how you would use +/− models to add 6 and $^-8$.

E–3

Homework

Add.

1. $^-3 + {}^+4 =$ _____

2. $^+9 + {}^-5 =$ _____

3. $^-10 + {}^+2 =$ _____

4. $^+1 + {}^-7 =$ _____

5. $^-3 + {}^-5 =$ _____

6. $^+4 + {}^+6 =$ _____

7. $^+16 + {}^-9 =$ _____

8. $^-11 + {}^+2 =$ _____

9. $^-13 + {}^+9 =$ _____

10. $^+15 + {}^-11 =$ _____

11. $^-18 + {}^+8 =$ _____

12. $^+5 + {}^-22 =$ _____

13. $^-14 + {}^-16 =$ _____

14. $^-27 + {}^+19 =$ _____

15. $^-13 + {}^+29 =$ _____

16. $^+31 + {}^+19 =$ _____

17. $^+20 + {}^-41 =$ _____

18. $^+16 + {}^-16 =$ _____

Solve.

19. Luigi used the number line to add $^+2 + {}^-5$.

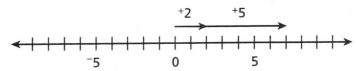

Decide if the arrows Luigi drew are correct. If the arrows are not correct, explain his error and redraw the arrows to show the correct sum.

_____

_____

_____

20. Marcia used the number line to add $^-3 + {}^+6$.

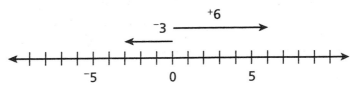

Decide if the arrows Marcia drew are correct. If the arrows are not correct, explain her error and redraw the arrows to show the correct sum.

_____

_____

21. **On the Back** At noon, the temperature was 5°F. It then decreased 14°F. What was the new temperature? Draw a number line to solve. Explain how you used the number line.

_____

_____

_____

_____

_____

_____

_____

_____

_____

_____

_____

_____

_____

_____

Homework

1. Using your ruler, draw a rectangle that has the origin (0, 0) as its center. Label the ordered pairs at each vertex of your rectangle.

2. Compare the ordered pairs and describe the patterns you find.

_____

_____

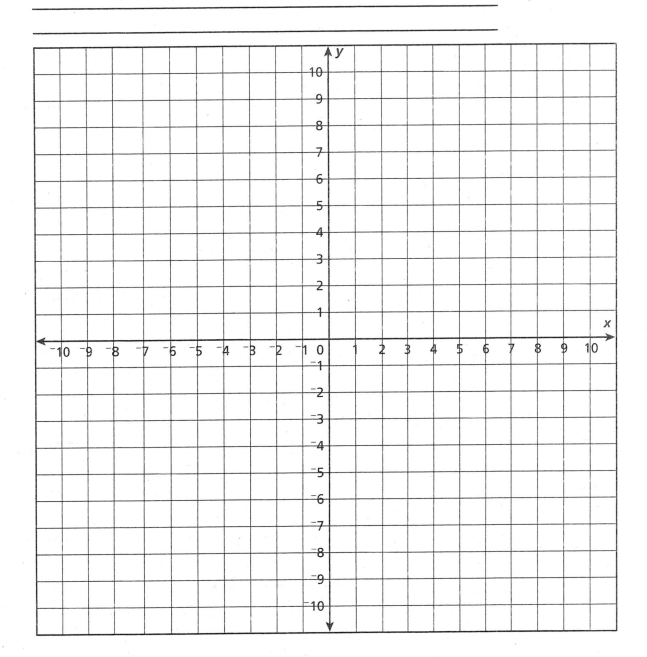

3. **On the Back** Make a table to show the coordinates of 5 points on the line $y = {}^-x - 3$. Plot the points and use your ruler to connect them with a line. Then label the line with its equation.

Name _____   Date _____

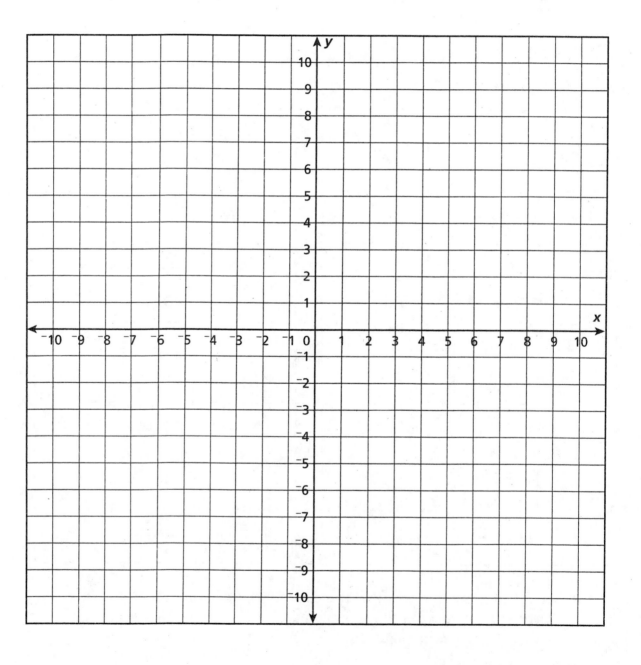

Integers and the Coordinate Plane